Hard Work

The Working Class in American History

A list of books in the series appears at the end of this book.

HARD WORK

The Making of Labor History

MELVYN DUBOFSKY

UNIVERSITY OF ILLINOIS PRESS

Urbana and Chicago

7-2-01

Library of Congress Cataloging-in-Publication Data
Dubofsky, Melvyn, 1934–
Hard work : the making of labor history / Melvyn Dubofsky.
    p.   cm. — (The working class in American history)
Includes bibliographical references and index.
ISBN 0-252-02551-2 — ISBN 0-252-06868-8 (pbk.)
1. Labor—United States—History.
2. Working class—United States—History.
3. Trade-unions—United States—History.
I. Title.
II. Series.
HD8066.D76   2000
331.88'0973'0904—dc21   99-006862

1 2 3 4 5 C P 5 4 3 2 1

CONTENTS

ACKNOWLEDGMENTS

SCHOLARSHIP being a collective enterprise in which, as the sociologist Robert Merton once put it, each new generation stands on the shoulders of the giants among its predecessors, only a foolish author assumes sole credit for what he or she has created. This is particularly true for a collection of essays that was written over the course of more than three decades in different places in the United States and Europe. In the opening essay in this volume I acknowledge in full, and sometimes in passing, the impact of scholarly ancestors, teachers, and contemporaries on my evolution and growth as a historian. Yet scores of other teachers, colleagues, and students share credit for whatever may be of value in my scholarship. To name and acknowledge separately all those who assisted my intellectual growth would be to compile a tedious list. Instead, I prefer to thank collectively those who have participated along with me over many years in a cooperative scholarly enterprise (and they will themselves certainly know who they are) and to single out only a few individuals who played a special part in helping me shape these essays.

My academic career has taken me to many institutions in the United States and overseas where I have learned from colleagues and students. Perhaps none deserve greater credit than those at Northern Illinois University who prodded and assisted me as I first taught and wrote labor history. The departmental colleagues who encouraged me when the guild was not yet a welcome place for labor historians and the graduate students in my seminars who explored the roots of western U.S. labor radicalism alongside me. From Illinois I moved to the University of Massachusetts at Amherst, where, for the first time, I enjoyed an appointment as a labor historian and where, however brief my tenure, I completed my book on the IWW, again with the encouragement and support of many generous colleagues in history and labor studies. An even shorter stay at the University of Wisconsin at Milwaukee introduced me to another cohort of stimulating colleagues and to a quite exceptional group of graduate students, several of whom have become outstanding historians. For nearly three decades now, however, I have been at Binghamton University, SUNY (formerly State University of New York at Binghamton) where numerous friends in history and other departments have made this place conducive to scholarly enterprise and excellence. Here, too, several generations of graduate students helped keep me abreast of shifting fashions in historical scholarship and, to cite a much overused cliché, tried, probably unsuccessfully, to teach an old scholar new tricks. I am particularly obligated to my many colleagues in the Fernand Braudel Center who tutored me in the complexities of world-systems analysis and widened my geographical and temporal horizons as a historian. The same must be said about the friends and acquaintances that I made while teaching at the University of Warwick in England, at the University of Tel Aviv in Israel, and at the University of Salzburg in Austria, and to those other scholars widely scattered around the globe who reminded me that the United States and its history were a small part of a larger world and story.

If colleagues and students contributed substantially to my education as a historian, little of my scholarship would have borne fruit without the aid of librarians and archivists. From my first forays into real research at the original Tamiment Library in the old Rand School of Social Science building just off Union Square in Manhattan to my most recent research efforts, others have assisted me every step of the way, whether in the National Archives, various presidential libraries, the Reuther Library at Wayne State University, the State Historical Society of Wisconsin, and state archives, historical societies, and universities scattered across the western United States. At crucial moments in my research and writing, moreover, financial support from the research foundations of the State University of New York and of Binghamton University, the National Endowment for the Humanities, the American Council of Learned Societies, and the American Philosophical Society enabled me to complete my work.

I must also acknowledge several individuals by name. What seems a lifetime ago when I was still a graduate student and just after I earned my

Ph.D. degree, I encountered two wonderful people at the old Tamiment Library who, by sharing with me their memories of service in the labor movement and their commitment to labor radicalism, made the past come alive. Words alone cannot repay the knowledge and spirit that J. B. S. Hardman (born Jacob Salutsky) and Anna Strunsky Walling shared with me. Without the road maps and constant advice provided by my fellow labor historians Herbert Gutman, David Montgomery, and David Brody, my scholarly journey likely would have terminated in a dead end. I am especially grateful to Brody for encouraging me to compile these essays and for reading the opening essay so carefully and astutely. What is of value in "True Confessions" owes much to him. The same can also be said about Robert Zieger, who equally encouraged me to bring my scattered essays together and sent me his own sharp yet constructive critique of "True Confessions." Nick Salvatore read the entire set of essays and he, too, offered especially useful criticism of the opening essay. Joseph McCartin, a former graduate student and now himself a fine historian, read and commented on my autobiographical essay with a sharp eye and subtle suggestions for its improvement. And Jose Torre, a current graduate student, ensured the accuracy of the appended list of my publications. Finally, how could I fail to acknowledge my first doctoral student and later collaborator on the biography of John L. Lewis, Warren Van Tine.

The last acknowledgment I must make remains the hardest of all. My late wife, Joan S. Klores Dubofsky, was with me every step of the way except the final stride. Particularly during my research for the book on western labor radicalism and the IWW, she spent hot summers alongside me in dusty archives in Helena (Montana), Boise (Idaho), and Denver (Colorado) and one truly steamy summer in the National Archives, reading old letters, reports, newspapers, and journals as well as taking notes in a far more neat and legible hand than mine. Then and later, she also kept the house in order and our children well behaved as I struggled to write history. Without Joan's assistance, encouragement and warmth, I doubt that I could have written any good history. The final stages of putting these essays together was especially painful. During the summer and early fall of 1997 as I worked on the final draft of "True Confessions" and the introductions to the separate sections of essays, I also nursed Joan through a fatal illness. To this day it feels strange and sad simultaneously to have given birth to a new book and to have experienced the untimely death of a loved one. The least that I can do, and it is not nearly enough, is to dedicate this book to the memory of Joan.

INTRODUCTION

A reader of this book might well ask why the author chose to publish a set of essays, many of which have appeared in print over the last thirty years (though the majority was published obscurely). I would respond that I have done so because my scholarly life has been coterminous with labor history as a recognized, legitimate subfield within the academic discipline of history and also as a part of history's accepted undergraduate and graduate curriculum. Yet, as my life in the academy approaches its end point, labor history no longer entices practitioners as an exciting new frontier in scholarship. It fails to match cultural studies, gender studies, or studies in sexual behavior in its appeal to students, younger history faculty, literati, and publishers.[1] Labor history's dwindling allure, however, may be a sign of its triumph. Today, at the end of the 1990s, few textbooks or general histories of the United States (or, for that matter, course syllabi) neglect workers, labor movements, and trade unions. I would like to think that the work of David Brody, Herbert Gutman, David Montgomery, and myself (and our younger successors as well) had something to do with the movement of labor history from the margins to the center of the study of the history of the United States. The approach of a new millennium also offers me a propitious moment to sum up a life's work in the precincts of labor history and also to describe the intellectual trajectory that carried the subject from the periphery to the core of historical study.

A reader might also inquire as to why I publish these particular essays—and why in their original, unrevised form (except for changes necessitated by the publisher's guidelines and the copy editor's desire for felicity of expression). I would respond that I did so for two reasons. First, the ten essays reprinted here (or, in several cases, published for the first time) suggest how labor history has changed over the past four decades and also how my own interests have shifted along with the field's evolution. The essays, moreover, perhaps reveal why I remain partly aloof from the trends that came to dominate academic history from the late 1980s into the 1990s; yet they also illustrate how aspects of my work from early on foreshadowed aspects of the future of the field. Second, the republication of the essays in their original form will enable readers to see more clearly the relationship between the historian in the present and the past that he/she seeks to recreate. Simultaneously, however, the occasion of republication offers me the opportunity to indicate how subsequent scholarship has affected my original interpretations and whether or not it caused me to rethink or revise the positions that I had previously taken. As is frequently the case, E. P. Thompson expressed succinctly (and in words superior to those that I might mint) the ambiguous relationship between the historian and the past that he/she recreates. "It is we, in the present," Thompson wrote, "who must always give meaning to that inert and finished past. For history is forever unresolved, it remains as a field of unfinished possibilities, it lies behind us with all its contradictions of motives and canceled intentions, and we—acting in the present reach back, refuse some possibilities and select and further others. We endorse some values of the past, we refuse others"[2]

The next question for any reader of this volume might be, Why did the author select these particular essays and organize them as he did? My opening autobiographical essay, "Starting Out in the Fifties," should need no defense or explanation. The three essays that follow illustrate that, however materialist or Marxist, and however national (U.S.) my initial approach and definition as a historian, early on, I considered culture to be thoroughly imbricated in material life, drew on anthropology to deepen my comprehension of the past, and perceived capitalism as a system that transcended regions and nation-states (i.e., before the era of Immanuel Wallerstein and his world-systems school) and that although the United States may have had its own particular historical trajectory, it was not a wholly exceptional case in the development of modern nation-states. These three essays date from the early 1960s to the end of the decade, and only the last one can be said to have been influenced by my association at the end of that period with the most commanding intellectual progenitor of the new labor history, E. P. Thompson.

The second set of three essays whose publication spanned the late 1970s to the end of the 1980s reflected my growing sense that politics and the state played a fundamental role in working-class history and that workers' relations to politics and the state proved exceptionally variable and conjunctural. Readers should readily perceive the logic that links my analysis of the relationship among workers, political parties, and the state in the United States from the turn of the twentieth century to its end. Once again, in these three essays, culture, however defined. remains at the root of the political developments described in them.

The final section and its three essays takes me back to the start and to my notion of capitalism as a global or world phenomenon; only now, my theory is enlivened through my association with Wallerstein, world-systems theory, and scholars from France and the former Soviet Union. In a sense, these essays interpret U.S. working-class history through a global lens or, in the case of the final essay, suggest how placing U.S. history in a broader international context may compel labor historians to revise their analyses and narratives of the past.

Finally, I should add a word or two concerning how these essays illustrate my conception of the historian's role and function. When I first began to publish serious studies in history during the 1960s, younger scholars made considerable noise about their obligation to write a "radical" history that would retell the story of the past from below and hence rescue the poor, the inarticulate, the oppressed, the myriad array of history's losers from, in E. P. Thompson's much-admired aphorism, "the enormous condescension of posterity." Some among them even formed radical history caucuses within the American Historical Association and the Organization of American Historians as well as autonomous organizations of their own, including the Mid-Atlantic Radical Historians Organization (MARHO), the body that gave birth to the *Radical History Review.* To this day, however, I am unsure about what it means to write radical history. From my perspective, bad history in a good cause, assuming radical ends are desirable, remains bad history; only good history has the power to save losers and the forgotten from condescension; and only good history will influence its readers and students to act better or perhaps more wisely in the present. (I remain, however, a skeptic about the past's ability to offer lessons for the present as well as a doubter about George Santayana's conclusion that those who forget the past are condemned to repeat it.) Not only am I convinced that good history can provide more service than radical history for good causes in the present, but I believe also that good history must be readable history, whether as analysis, interpretation, or narrative. Too many of today's younger historians use jargon or arcane academic language to establish their credentials as intellectuals or, if they are self-proclaimed humanists, to prove that they are as rigorous in their scholarship as natural scientists and social scientists. For me, history—whether defined as a humanity or a social science—does not need a jargon or language of its own accessible only to the cognoscenti and divorced from the comprehension of most undergraduates and common readers. For me, the function of the historian is to demystify the world, not mystify it, and to make the material worlds of the past and the present comprehensible to readers outside specialized graduate seminars and beyond the environs of the academy. I certainly hope that the ten essays in this collection, writings that are more analytical and interpretive than narrative, remain accessible to all readers and instruct them about how the past remains alive in the present.

Notes

1. For a series of essays and comments that highlight the issue of labor history's diminishing appeal, some of which bear the titles "Signs of Crisis, Fin-de-Siècle Doldrums, or Middle Age?," "Yesterday, Today, and Tomorrow: Neither Crisis Nor Stasis," "Intellectual Crisis or Paradigm Shift?," "History's Noncrisis," and "Labor History: Out of Vogue?" and involve such leading scholars as Ira Katznelson, Lizabeth Cohen, David Montgomery, Anson Rabinbach, Louise Tilly, and Sean Wilentz, to name only some, see *International Labor and Working-Class History* 46 (Fall 1994): 7–92. Few of these authorities agree as to whether there is a crisis or whether labor history is, in the words of one essay subtitle, "out of vogue."

2. E. P. Thompson, *Beyond the Frontier: The Politics of a Failed Mission—Bulgaria, 1944* (Stanford, Calif.: Stanford University Press, 1997), 100.

Starting Out in the Fifties:
True Confessions of a Labor Historian

EARLY in the 1990s, when asked to contribute to a symposium about the historian David Brody's first book, *Steelworkers in America: The Nonunion Era* (1960), I reconsidered the path that led me to define myself or, perhaps put more accurately, that led others to define me as a labor historian. With hindsight, I could see that Brody's *Steelworkers* heralded the birth of a "new" labor history; but at the time, I doubt that I, or any in my generation of historians, linked the book to such a creation. Trying to remember how it actually was that a new labor history came into existence put me in mind of what the historian Eric Hobsbawm wrote about the zone where history and memory intersect. "For all of us," he reflected, "there is a twilight zone between history and memory; between the past as a generalized record which is open to relatively dispassionate inspection and the past as a remembered part of, or background to, one's own life. . . . there is always such a no-man's land of time. It is by far the hardest part of history for historians, or for anyone else to grasp."[1] For me, at least, the terrain of memory proved as hard to grasp as Hobsbawm's twilight zone.

The origin of labor history as a subdiscipline within the larger academic field fell for me into such a twilight zone. Permitting a little hyperbole, I might say that I, among significant others (Brody, Herbert Gutman, and David Montgomery, most especially), was present at the creation in U.S. college and university history departments of the field that came to be known as labor history. Yet in recalling that moment where history and memory merge, I am not sure that any of us consciously intended to embark on a voyage to write labor history or to become labor historians. That time, not quite forty years ago, seems a distant past: so different then was the guild of academic history and its artisans. When Brody, Gutman, Montgomery, and I interviewed for our first university jobs in a world of sparse opportunities, we neither applied for positions as labor historians nor identified ourselves as such.[2] I came to teach labor history early on largely as a result of chance, finding myself in 1959 in a brand-new history department with an equally new and young chair, a scholar of Malaysian rubber workers who said to me at a party one evening: "Mel, why don't you do a course in American labor history?" And that is how I came to teach labor history, although over the next eight or nine years I rarely interviewed for a position as a labor historian, except in the case of the New York State School of Industrial and Labor Relations. Not until I went to the University of Massachusetts in 1967, where that institution's labor relations institute required its students to take a course in labor history, was I hired specifically as a labor historian. I suspect that Brody's, Gutman's, and Montgomery's careers followed comparable trajectories and that they, like me, identified themselves primarily as historians of the modern United States.[3]

I also remember that at the founding of the journal *Labor History* in 1958, except for Richard Morris, then known primarily as a historian of Colonial and Revolutionary America, the founders were not historians (although then only a graduate student, I was one of the few historians at that luncheon meeting; Gerald Grob was another). Rather than mingling with academics, I spent most of my time in the company of J. B. S. Hardman, the onetime radical, Russian-Jewish immigrant who was by then far more famous as a labor intellectual and journalist. It is probably fair to say that, at the journal's founding, labor history did not yet exist as a field of study in undergraduate or graduate history departments. I did not publish a book in labor history until 1968 (though by then I had published several articles on the subject, the most important of which appeared in *Labor History*); Herbert Gutman did not release a book-length collection of his essays on labor history until 1976, three years after the appearance of his famous article in the *American Historical Review;* and when David Montgomery's *Beyond Equality* appeared in 1967, his introduction stressed its contribution to the history of the American Civil War and Reconstruction far more than its salience as labor history.[4]

Reflecting more deeply on that zone where history and memory intersect, I now think that I became a labor historian by accident as much as by choice and that, initially, the writing and teaching of labor history were tangential to my motivation. During my first two years in graduate school, I remained committed to interests first kindled during my undergraduate studies, examining from a political perspective what was then known as the "middle period in U.S. history" (the years from Jackson through Reconstruction). Only slowly did my curiosity shift from the political to the economic and social and, ultimately, to labor history.

Brody remembers that he found his way to labor history through the writings of Walter Lippmann and Katherine Ann Porter. In my case, Richard Hofstadter, Samuel P. Hays, and John Dos Passos most proximately blazed an irregular trail. Like Brody, I, too, was intrigued with questions of power and how industrialization and urbanization affected working people. As I read Hofstadter and Hays, industrialization and urbanization (historians would soon redefine those two terms as "modernization," a concept borrowed from sociologists and political scientists but not yet in vogue among historians) lay at the heart of U.S. history between 1870 and 1920 (in the famous phrase coined by Hofstadter, the United States grew up in the country and moved to the city). Yet Hofstadter said almost nothing about working people as active subjects, and Hays accorded workers and their movements a far smaller role in the process of protest and struggle than "colonized" southerners and westerners.[5] Thus, I chose to write a dissertation about working people in New York City as a contribution to the history of modernization in the Progressive Era not as a breakthrough in the as yet unknown and unnamed subdiscipline of labor history.

That is probably why in 1959 and 1960, when Brody, Gutman, and I first began teaching, we did not define ourselves as labor historians; nor were we likely to expend undue thought and energy distinguishing ourselves from the "Wisconsin school." Our dialogue was more with other historians who had neglected workers than with John R. Commons, Selig Perlman, and Philip Taft, who had devoted their scholarship to labor but treated it in what later critics, most notably Gutman, would condemn as narrowly institutional terms.[6]

I came of age in an ethnic community in which residual forms of leftism remained alive even in their diluted New Deal version. (As a high school student, for example, I participated in the political left and campaigned for Vito Marcantonio for mayor of New York.) I also remember the impact of two high school history teachers, one of whom exemplified the "popular front" left of the World War II years; the other embodied the ethnic working-class component of the New Deal. I still recall the day my popular front history teacher held up an issue of *Time* magazine with a cover photo of Winston Churchill as its man of the first half of the twentieth century and then proceeded to inform the class that Henry Luce had mistaken his centuries. With scarcely concealed sarcasm, she told us that Churchill fit better as the man of the previous century, the age of imperialism. And I remember equally vividly the day the other history teacher reenacted for us his Jewish immigrant father's experiences as a striking clothing worker shielding himself from the fists of hired thugs and the clubs of New York City police. At home, I read Upton Sinclair's Lanny Budd novels, a perfect way to introduce an adolescent to modern world history from a reform-socialist and New Deal perspective (Sinclair probably imagined the era of the common man more creatively than Henry Wallace did), and Arthur Schlesinger's *Age of Jackson,* which reinforced my adolescent suspicions that the world was divided between business interests and the people. Charles and Mary Beard's *Rise of American Civilization* also enthralled me with its vivid prose and its portrayal of U.S. history from the colonial period to the 1920s as a form of class struggle with sectional roots. Small wonder, then, that I campaigned for Marcantonio, the last of the city's true popular fronters, joined for a time a chapter of the World Federalists, had friends whose parents remained communists, and nearly went with them to Peekskill, New York, for the celebration by leftist World War II veterans at which Paul Robeson's appearance precipitated a riot by local American Legionnaires. Buried perhaps somewhere in my subconscious also was the experience of attending an urban high school situated in the heart of Brooklyn's dark ghetto, Bedford-Stuyvesant, in which over forty percent of the students were African American. Although only a rare few African Americans sat alongside me in my regents and college preparatory courses, as a sportswriter for the school paper, I came into close daily contact with the African-American athletes who formed the core and the mass of the school's dominant basketball and track-and-field teams.

By the time I entered college, then, I had probably developed the intellectual and personal predispositions that would eventually turn me toward labor history. Once again, however, my life was shaped by chance. Accepted by Cornell University and admitted to Colby College with the prospect of a scholarship, I instead enrolled in Brooklyn College. Why? Most likely, because for a young man yet to turn seventeen and the child of second-generation immigrant parents, one of whom still spoke heavily accented English and the other of whom had not even attended secondary school, the prospect of leaving home and entering an alien environment appeared too daunting.[7] Yet I entered an academic environment that for its time and place produced an extraordinary number of graduates later to become respected historians of the United States. Let me name several who attended Brooklyn College while I was a student there: Eugene Genovese, Morton Rothstein, Samuel McSeveney, Joel Silbey, Gilbert Osofsky, and Richard Polenberg.

In retrospect, I cannot recall anything about Brooklyn College that led me toward a career studying the history of labor in the United States. Indeed, until late in my junior year and early in my senior year, I had not decided to pursue graduate studies in history. Until then, I was torn among various possibilities and pulled in conflicting directions by the teachers who had the greatest influence on me. The two faculty members who most shaped my academic growth—Samuel J. Konefsky, a political scientist, and Jesse D. Clarkson, a historian of Russia and the Soviet Union—encouraged me in the former instance to pursue a future at Harvard Law School and train to be a specialist in legal history and in the latter to enroll in the doctoral program at the Russian Institute at Columbia University. I cannot say precisely why I rejected their advice. Perhaps the experience I shared my senior year (together with Joel Silbey and a third student) as a participant in a special senior research seminar under the direction of the history department chair, Arthur Charles Cole, determined my future. Cole, a distinguished scholar of the political and social history of the American Civil War Era, had the three of us investigate the origins of antislavery politics and the Republican party in the late 1840s and early 1850s. My assignment was to explore the split in the Whig party, especially in Massachusetts, that arose from political conflicts engendered by territorial expansion and the threatened spread of slavery. The excitement and challenge of reading through crumbling old newspapers as well as the published correspondence and memoirs of mid-nineteenth-century public figures made the past come alive for me, and it also led me to pursue a graduate degree in U.S. history with a concentration on the mid-nineteenth century.

In nearly every other aspect of my undergraduate education, however, I encountered conventional ideas and expectations. Required courses formed nearly forty percent of my education, and they were exceedingly traditional, including a modern foreign language, philosophy, general social science, general science (three semesters of integrated biology, chemistry, physics, and geology), English composition, Classics (Greece and Rome), and Western history (Europe and the Americas). The key texts that we read, aside from the basic history course built on a documentary approach that stressed comparisons across time and space, emphasized American exceptionalism. David Riesman's *Lonely Crowd,* Henry Steele Commager's *American Mind,* and John Kenneth Galbraith's *American Capitalism,* each in its own way, convinced us of the singularity of the United States and perhaps even of the legitimacy of Henry Luce's "American century."

In ever so many ways, my undergraduate education was far more monochromatic than my secondary school experience. Having attended a high school in which African Americans were the largest identifiable racial-ethnic group and Jewish Americans were a minority, I moved on to a college where nonwhites were most notable by their absence (including on athletic teams) and Jewish Americans comprised the vast majority of students. Not a single course that I took examined non-Western civilizations to any considerable extent, and my one-year integrated course in contemporary social sciences made a passing bow to "multiculturalism" by having us read Ruth Benedict's *Patterns of Culture,* which was buried among an array of other required texts that covered the contemporary United States. History also failed to stretch my imagination spatially or culturally. In a relatively large department, one faculty member covered all of Asia and another handled the Western Hemisphere south of the Rio Grande (no one specialized in or taught the history of our neighbor to the north). Owing to scheduling difficulties and time conflicts, I never took a course with the Asian or Latin American historians, though I wanted to, as both instructors were among the best and most popular teachers in the department. The history courses I took were thoroughly traditional, national in focus, and structured around conventional chronological eras (every upper-division elective in U.S. history, for example, was organized by time period, with the Revolution, the Civil War, and various presidential administrations marking breaks or turning points). With rare exceptions, political history dominated the subject matter. Perhaps Jesse Clarkson influenced me so much intellectually and nearly turned me toward the study of Russian history because he was the least conventional of my teachers. In his own peculiar way, he prefigured the revisionist New Left histories and historians of the 1960s, subordinating the political to the social and economic and teaching a singular Marxian strain of class analysis in which astute ruling-class capitalists promoted reforms that subverted free-market, competitive capitalism. Clarkson's corporate capitalists—his Bismarcks, Wittes, and Lloyd Georges—played the historical role that Marx had reserved for the proletariat. From Clarkson, I now realize, I discovered the concepts and interpretations that later drew me to the writings of Joseph Schumpeter, Karl Polanyi, and John Maynard Keynes. From Clarkson, I also learned the rudiments of what later came to be characterized in the United States as "corporate liberalism" and elsewhere more broadly as "corporatism." Of all my undergraduate teachers of history, none made me challenge or rethink conventional categories and forms of knowledge more often and consistently than Jesse D. Clarkson.

Clarkson differed from the conventional flock in other, equally significant ways. My undergraduate days coincided with the depths of the cold war and the domestic Red Scare. When I entered college, the Korean War raged at fever heat, military conscription continued, and I and my closest friends enrolled in the Air Force ROTC as an alternative to military service. My first years on campus saw the Rosenberg trial, verdict, and executions (though I must admit that in my circles, the scandal and trials associated with college basketball players who had taken money from gamblers to shave points during games had more impact than the Rosenberg case) and Joe McCarthy's red-baiting capture headlines. Three of my undergraduate teachers lost their positions as a consequence of their decision to take the fifth amendment before congressional investigating committees and refuse to provide names. One was my tennis coach (a teacher of physical education); another his spouse, a biologist, and one of my general science teachers; and the third, a physicist and another of my science teachers, whose grave misfortune it was to have been associated with J. Robert Oppenheimer and his circle of "pink" acquaintances.

Such was the Red Scare on campus at its peak between 1951 and 1955. In such a milieu and at a college whose president, Harry Gideonse, exemplified the worst strains of liberal anticommunism and University of Chicago free-market economics, smart student radicals rarely surfaced or spoke their minds. The only student leftists who dared speak in public were dim bulbs whose crude and vulgar Marxism parodied the theories of their master and who were easy prey for the put-downs of more serious and knowledgeable students of Marx like Jesse Clarkson. Those naive and intellectually deficient undergraduate radicals probably did more to diminish general student respect for the left than McCarthy and his legion of red-baiters. And that was precisely what made Jesse Clarkson so special. At the same time that he denigrated the crude Marxism of our student radicals, he castigated with greater venom McCarthy's impact on society and culture, ridiculed the role of the CIA in fighting "global" communism, and urged us to understand the Soviet Union as a nation-state with security interests like any other, a twentieth-century version of Peter the Great's Russia and not an "evil empire." All this from a scion of New England settlers, rock-ribbed Republicans, and himself an Eisenhower advocate— quite shocking to a child of second-generation, Jewish-immigrant, New Deal Roosevelt Democrats.

Yet how I journeyed from a Cold War campus in Brooklyn to a career as a labor historian took several more strange twists and fortuitous turns. The one undergraduate experience that might have led me to an academic interest in workers and labor movements never happened. As an economics minor, I had always wanted to take the basic course in labor economics taught by Theresa Wolfson, who had a campus reputation as a left-liberal and a fine teacher. Her course, however, was yet another that, much to my chagrin, I could not fit into my schedule. Only later, when I began my doctoral research, did I discover how important Wolfson had been to the history of women, work, and unions during the 1920s and 1930s. She was part of that female generation that included, among others, Frances Perkins, Gertrude Barnum, Esther Peterson, Mary Van Kleeck, Rose Schneiderman, Pauline Newman, and Fania Cohn. Only later did I realize what I missed in having been unable to sit in a classroom taught by her.

Thus, when I finished my undergraduate education at Brooklyn College, a future committed to the study of workers in the United States was the farthest thing from my mind. Instead, I preferred to continue the focus I had begun in Arthur Cole's special senior seminar, and that preference shaped my choice of graduate schools, a choice affected by chance. All I remember clearly was that I wanted to leave New York City and had been discouraged from considering Columbia and Harvard by the department's undergraduate adviser. As the graduating history major with the highest overall GPA and exceptionally high GREs, I was encouraged to apply to the best graduate schools, which then included Yale, Princeton, and the University of Wisconsin at Madison (the University of California at Berkeley was a dim presence on Brooklyn's radar screen, although that would change a year or two after my graduation, when Hans Rosenberg, the department's distinguished German historian, moved to Berkeley as a visiting professor). In the mid-1950s, moreover, the federal government did not subsidize graduate education in the humanities and social sciences, and few, if any, highly ranked graduate schools offered first-year students fellowships or assistantships. In my case, finances remained a central consideration (many of my male classmates chose to enlist voluntarily in the armed services on graduation to quality for GI Bill benefits and thus finance their professional or graduate school educations; my local draft board, however, declined to offer me that opportunity). I had planned to enroll at Wisconsin, which appeared the best location to study mid-nineteenth-century U.S. history, as it would be under the direction of William Hesseltine, Merrill Jensen, Merle Curti, and Howard K. Beale. My senior year (December 1954), the American Historical Association (AHA) held its annual meeting in New York City, and I, Joel Silbey, and several other history majors served as assistants to the local arrangements committee. In that capacity, I attended a session on nineteenth-century U.S. political history at which one of the panelists, Glyndon G. Van Deusen of the University of Rochester, described the new doctoral program in history at his institution, its focus on U.S. history, the university's holdings of the papers of William Henry Seward and Thurlow Weed, and its generous four-year fellowships for select graduate students. Having more than a little familiarity with the city of Rochester because I often visited with family who lived there, and my interest piqued by Van Deusen's description of the graduate program there, I submitted an application. Before long, I was invited to Rochester for an all-expenses paid visit to the campus, where I was wined, dined, and wooed. Soon after, when graduate schools announced their decisions, I learned that I had been accepted at Yale and Princeton without financial aid; that Wisconsin accepted me with an offer of an out-of-state tuition scholarship; and that the University of Rochester offered me a four-year fellowship that included a full tuition waiver. Rochester made me an offer that I could not refuse, most especially because I still considered myself a student of mid-nineteenth-century U.S. political history and Rochester granted the opportunity to study under the direction of Van Deusen, who was an accomplished scholar in precisely that field and was then completing a major study of the Jacksonian Era for the New American Nation Series.[8]

At Rochester, my education continued in the grooves cut at Brooklyn College. During my first two years, I concentrated on the political and economic history of the United States while also reading widely in modern European and Russian history to prepare for my comprehensive examinations. My major piece of research concerned Daniel Webster and the political economy of the Whig party, an essay that some years later appeared in the *New England Quarterly* as "Daniel Webster and the Whig Theory of Economic Growth."[9] Only two minor aspects of my graduate training hinted at the new directions in which I would subsequently turn. During my second year, I agreed to prepare two lectures treating workers and labor movements from the early national era to the Civil War for Professor Van Deusen's upper-level undergraduate course on U.S. economic history. In preparing the lectures, I discovered at first that historians studying the subject focused on the relationship between workers and Jacksonianism, either stressing Jacksonian democracy's links to an emerging worker movement in the style of Arthur Schlesinger Jr. or emphasizing, in the manner of Richard Hofstadter, the gap between Jacksonian party politics and worker aspirations, portraying workers as a group on the make rather than a class in formation.[10] Secondly, to learn more about what nineteenth-century workers actually did for a living, how the development of a market economy affected their daily lives, and how workers coped with quotidian material realities, I turned to what even then were relatively dated studies written by nonhistorians, namely the first two volumes of John R. Commons's *History of Labor in the United States* and its companion documentary, *Industrial History* (both completed before World War I), and Norman Ware's *Industrial Worker,* published before the Great Depression.[11] The historians that I read drew on Commons and Ware for information, but the separate disciplinary parties to the subject scarcely conducted a dialogue, approaching labor from widely variant angles. Other than reading such literature to prepare my lectures, I gave no thought to making labor history a primary concern. The second nonconventional aspect of my graduate training derived from my contact with a junior, untenured member of the history department, Charles Vevier, who had obtained his doctorate in diplomatic history at the University of Wisconsin at Madison under the direction of Fred Harvey Harrington. (I should point out that the only historians of the United States in the department were Vevier, Van Deusen, and Richard Wade, himself only recently tenured.) Vevier brought to Rochester a combination of the traditional "Populist" approaches (Beardian and Turnerian) that had long prevailed at Madison as well as the newer and more innovative methods that were to become associated with the scholarship of William Appleman Williams, Warren Susman, and Herbert Gutman. In fact, in the spring of 1957, Williams visited Vevier in Rochester, and the latter pointedly introduced my graduate school cohort to his colleague in diplomatic history from Madison. Perhaps I should not make too much of Vevier's impact on my scholarly growth, for the subjects that I studied with him, American colonial and diplomatic history, were low on my agenda; he served neither on my comprehensive examining committee nor my dissertation committee; and in the spring of 1957, William Appleman Williams could not yet be considered a major influence on U.S. history.

Yet, in that summer of 1957, my scholarly interests began to shift. I devoted the entire summer to intensive reading in preparation for my comprehensive examination, which was scheduled for early that fall. Having every expectation that I would leap that hurdle successfully, I realized that it was time for me to choose and frame a dissertation topic. The more I concentrated on that task, the dimmer grew my interest in mid-nineteenth-century political history. Two books published the previous year, Kenneth Stampp's *Peculiar Institution* and Richard Hofstadter's *Age of Reform*, impressed me greatly, and the latter caused me to choose a dissertation topic in early twentieth-century history, which I conceived as an analysis of the relationship between workers in the nation's largest metropolis, New York, and the progressive reform movement. I planned to remedy Hofstadter's failure to treat seriously and indeed to dismiss workers as significant actors in his "age of reform."

Having chosen my subject and defined my interests, I proceeded with few scholarly road maps and little guidance. Van Deusen remained the dissertation director of record, but there was little that he could say to me or teach me about the subject of workers in early twentieth-century New York. Out of necessity, I taught myself labor history and set out to discover sources to write a new and different history. The workers that I encountered in the sources inhabited a different universe than Hofstadter's immigrant, working-class objects of middle-class, progressive reform. My workers were themselves reformers, men and women engaged in a desperate struggle to create powerful organizations; they were not declassed people battling against the fruits of organization. The struggles that I uncovered were not moral crusades to cleanse corrupt politics, nor eradicate the sins of alcoholism and prostitution, nor eliminate class as a force in society; rather, my actors struggled to implement conflicting visions of "law and order in industry" that encompassed workers, employers, and even progressives. My search to understand the world of workers in pre–World War I New York took me to the old Tamiment Library on Union Square, the lineal descendant of the People's House and the Rand School of Social Science and, for the first three decades of the century, a gathering place for workers, labor radicals, and socialists. There I met and conversed with Max Eastman, Alexander Trachtenberg, and, most importantly, J. B. S. Hardman, who offered me access to his unsurpassed knowledge about workers and worker movements. There I discovered the papers of the Socialist Party of America, New York City branch, a collection that provided me with new perspectives on the relationship among socialism, trade unionism, and progressive reform. And there, too, I made the contacts that resulted in my invitation to the 1958 meeting that announced the founding of the journal *Labor History*.

Dissertation research also introduced me to the pleasures and perils of oral history: not the transcripts that I read at the Columbia University collection, but the interviews that I conducted myself. Here I met the men and women who actually made the history about which I planned to write. Among the subjects whom I interviewed were Joseph Schlossberg, the long-time secretary treasurer of the Amalgamated Clothing Workers; Rose Schneiderman; Pauline Newman; and Frances Perkins. My interview with Perkins provided an exemplary education in the perils of oral history. Young and naive, I came to the interview eager to learn how and why Perkins had become a socialist (was it the influence of her mentor, Florence Kelley?) and why, in 1911, shortly after her appointment by Al Smith to the New York State Factory Investigating Commission, she had resigned from the Socialist Party of America (SPA). I knew that she had been a member of the SPA and that she had resigned in 1911 because when I discovered the party papers hidden at Tamiment Library and collated them, I found three letters of resignation from Walter Lippmann, W. E. B. Du Bois, and Frances Perkins clipped together. When I questioned Perkins about her relationship to Kelley and socialism, she responded by denying membership in the SPA and asking me why I assumed that she had been a party member. Innocently, I replied that I had found her letter of resignation at the Tamiment Library. The next time that I visited the library, however, and looked for Perkins's letter, it was missing. The other unsettling aspect of the Perkins interview was not apparent at the time. I thought that she might help me discover more information about Paul Wilson, an adviser to John Purroy Mitchel, the reform mayor of New York; Wilson acted as the mayor's primary adviser on labor affairs. Perkins denied any knowledge of Wilson or his role in Mitchel's administration. Two decades later, I learned that Perkins and Wilson were wife and husband and also why she claimed ignorance about her spouse.[12]

As my dissertation neared completion, and I entered the academic labor market to seek a full-time position, the farthest thing from my mind was to identify myself as a labor historian. In those days, academic jobs were not advertised publicly; the annual meetings of the AHA and the Mississippi Valley Historical Association (as the Organization of American Historians [OAH] was then named) served as slave markets in which senior historians auctioned their young disciples; and an old-boys network controlled the allocation of loaves and fishes. To say the least, the historians at the University of Rochester were not plugged into the primary circuits of the old-boys network, although Van Deusen had his own set of connections to whom he peddled me as a historian of the early twentieth-century United States with a concentration in political and economic history. The three jobs that I was offered, including one tenure-track position, were at institutions located either in large cities or areas important to labor history: Wayne State University, Ohio State University, and the University of Akron. In 1959, however, my commitment to labor history was, so to speak, weak—and for good reason. No history departments then sought labor historians, and no career tracks existed in that field. Thus, I accepted an offer from Northern Illinois University in DeKalb, a campus set amid prairie cornfields. That decision shaped my academic and intellectual formation in ways that I could never have imagined.

When I arrived in DeKalb in the late summer of 1959, I went to work at an institution that had barely emerged from its cocoon as a normal school and state teachers college. I joined a newly created history department in which, almost overnight, young hires outnumbered the older faculty and quickly transformed departmental culture. In an academic setting in which change was the one constant, it was no surprise that the new chair asked me to design a course in U.S. labor history nor that I accepted his challenge. It was also a rare experience for a young academic barely in his mid-twenties to help build a history department and program from scratch. There, on the flatland of the northern Illinois prairie, we hired historians who were less than welcome elsewhere in the universe of higher education and its white, male, Protestant departments of history (at the time of my appointment, the department included no women or nonwhites, and I was the only non-Protestant). Leftist victims of cold war conformity; individuals who led unconventional personal and sexual lives; scholars who studied subjects outside the borders of conventional history; all for a time found a home in the department of history at Northern Illinois University.[13] The historians who passed through the university during my years there (1959–67) and those who remained formed a remarkable collection of scholars. Small wonder, then, that such a history department wasted little time in creating graduate programs, including a doctoral program. More surprising, perhaps, was the department's eagerness to allow me to train graduate students in labor history, for it remained an unrecognized field in history as the discipline was then defined and taught. Even more surprising were the number and quality of the graduate students who chose to study labor history with me.

By then, I had decided to concentrate my research in the field of labor history. I had also chosen as my next research project a subject as far afield from my dissertation topic as imaginable. I now turned to the other side of the nation, where workers in the early twentieth century built a militant and radical worker movement: the Rocky Mountain and Pacific Coast West. Most of what I had read and continued to read about western workers and their movements stressed the influence of the frontier, the absence of cosmopolitan influences, and an indigenous, violent gun culture to explain their history. Such an interpretation left me unsatisfied.

In the summer of 1961, I traveled west to begin my own explorations in the history of western workers. The journey took me to research collections in Helena, Montana; Boise, Idaho; Seattle, Washington; and Berkeley, California, among other sites. There I discovered a history that told a different story than the one I had grown familiar with from the writings of Selig Perlman, Philip Taft, Stewart Holbrook, Wallace Stegner, and others.[14] And there I collected reels of microfilm and other sources that I brought back to DeKalb. The materials I returned with provided the foundation for a graduate research seminar on the history of labor militancy and radicalism in the U.S. West. The students in that seminar assisted me to no end in rewriting the history of the subject. Two of them wrote superb master's theses that originated in the seminar, one of which later appeared in part in a refereed scholarly journal. Warren Van Tine, a member of that seminar, subsequently followed me to the University of Massachusetts, where he completed a doctoral dissertation in U.S. labor history and went on to a fine career as a historian at Ohio State University. And, collectively, the members of the seminar provided the stimulus and part of the research for the second essay in this collection, "The Origins of Western Working-Class Radicalism," which was originally presented as a paper at the 1964 meeting of the Mississippi Valley Historical Association.

Initially, during my explorations of the history of workers in the U.S. West, I decided that the creation of the Industrial Workers of the World (IWW) would end a book on the subject. Back in DeKalb, I found myself unable to locate materials I needed in the campus library. Once or twice a week, I would travel with departmental colleagues to the Newberry Library in Chicago, where one day I bumped into the historian Harold Hyman. Hyman, known best as a constitutional and legal historian of the American Civil War and Reconstruction, had just written a riveting study of the labor conflicts that roiled the woods of the Pacific Northwest during World War I, *Soldiers and Spruce*.[15] In his research for the book, Hyman found little good historical scholarship about the IWW. During a lengthy conversation between the two of us about our respective scholarly interests and current research projects, Hyman looked at me and said: "Mel, why not write a history of the IWW. We certainly need one that meets current standards of historical scholarship." Once again, a chance meeting, a fortuitous circumstance, altered my plans and career. I accepted Hyman's challenge. I also learned that several publishers shared Hyman's belief that the time was ripe for a new history of the IWW. So what was to have been a book-length study of the origins and development of western working-class radicalism from the 1880s to 1905 became instead the first chapter in a history of the IWW.

My decision to write a history of the IWW coincided with other significant changes in my scholarly and academic life. In the mid- to late 1960s, labor history remained marginal to the guild of history as practiced in the United States and to most departments of history. Journal editors frequently returned to me articles that I had submitted with the comment that they published history, not ideology, and that such categories as capital, capitalism, capitalists or workers, labor, class were unacceptable. I found it equally difficult to find a press willing to publish my revised dissertation. Still, I went ahead working on the IWW book while I spun off articles about labor in the West and published them in such journals as *Pacific Northwest Quarterly* and *Mid-America*.[16] I found myself growing stale at Northern Illinois, increasingly eager to leave, when the University of Massachusetts advertised for a historian of American labor to be appointed in the department of history. I applied for the position, visited the campus, enjoyed a successful interview, and found myself with an attractive job offer that included, among other benefits, the prospect that my revised dissertation manuscript would be published by the University of Massachusetts Press. The only drawback in moving to Massachusetts was that I relinquished the tenure and promotion to associate professor that I had earned at Northern Illinois. In 1967, however, I was young, optimistic, and sure of myself.

My short tenure at Massachusetts, only two years, consisted of highs and lows. The University of Massachusetts Press did publish my book on New York workers in the Progressive Era under the title *When Workers Organize* (1968). I finished my history of the IWW at the end of my first summer in Amherst and saw it into production during my second and last year there. I worked closely with the director of the Labor Relations Program, Ben Seligman, a great autodidact, veteran of the New Deal left, and participant in the labor wars of the 1930s. From him, I learned much about workers, unions, and the labor movement that I never obtained from research in the archives or reading the published literature. I made friendships in the history department, several that have been of long standing, especially one with the distinguished historian of American culture and thought Paul Boyer. In the spring of 1968, I accepted an invitation to appear on a panel at the Socialist Scholars Conference held at Rutgers University to comment on a paper by Herbert Gutman that subsequently turned into his famous *American Historical Review* essay "Work, Society, and Culture in Industrializing America." It was the first time that Gutman had presented the paper formally to a public audience, and I, despite my relatively junior status, subjected the paper to a withering critique, certainly gentler yet much in the manner of Nick Salvatore's more recent inquiry into the deficiencies of Gutman's scholarship.[17]

The lows were more deflating. The history department at Massachusetts was riven by jealousies and rivalries between and among junior and senior faculty. Between 1967 and 1969, it was not the happiest of places. I grew to despise the dean, who had rejected the department's recommendation to promote me to associate professor with tenure, a part of my original letter of appointment. Rejected for promotion and tenure, I grew angry and discontented. I began to seek other positions, even considering a return to Northern Illinois. At perhaps my lowest point, a letter arrived from Edward P. Thompson, inviting me to come to the Centre for the Study of Social History at the University of Warwick, England, to serve as the Visiting Senior Lecturer in American Labour History. Thompson asked me to succeed David Montgomery, who had finished two years at Warwick during which he and Thompson had created an M.A. Program in Comparative Anglo-American Labor History. It is hard to imagine how much pleasure that invitation brought me. Thompson was then at the peak of his acclaim as the leading practitioner of a new labor history and a new Marxism that deemed culture as significant as economy, the celebrated author of *The Making of the English Working Class* and "The Moral Economy of the Crowd" and an ally of the rising New Left.[18] It was an invitation that I never considered rejecting, although the University of Massachusetts did little to encourage my acceptance. Just then, the University of Wisconsin at Milwaukee, invited me to consider a position as a senior historian for a new doctoral program in urban and labor history. Not only did Wisconsin offer me an associate professorship with immediate tenure and a substantial increase in salary; they also promised a year's leave of absence to enable me to accept

Thompson's generous invitation plus a substantial research fellowship during my year in England; and they assured me that I would be promoted to professor on the publication of my history of the IWW, an event scheduled to occur well before I would return to Milwaukee.

For a labor historian, especially one about to publish a book on the Wobblies, it was the best of times in the best of worlds. The young campus radicals of the 1960s, whether involved in the civil rights movement or the antiwar protest, whether American, British, French or Czech (only a year had passed since the Paris May Revolt and the Prague Spring of 1968), recalled the Wobblies, who had practiced direct action, mass protest, the transvaluation of values, and gleefully sung the anthem of revolution, "The Internationale," bellowing: "We have been nought; We shall be all!" Current events—that is, contemporary history—created a public and a market for my book. And the New Left, by demanding that the neglected, the oppressed, and the outcast deserved a place in the university curriculum, created a demand for a new labor history that Gutman, Montgomery, Brody, and I were more than glad to satisfy. Graduate programs in history that integrated labor and social history began to flourish at the University of Pittsburgh with Montgomery, the State University of New York at Buffalo (and, later, the University of Rochester) with Gutman, and Brody at the University of California at Davis. History departments even began to advertise positions for labor historians. Clearly, then, to write about past radicals seemed synonymous with doing "radical" history and also in harmony with the spirit of the times. It was easy to believe, as I probably did in the mid- and late 1960s, that historians could do as much as civil rights and antiwar protesters to create a better, freer, and more egalitarian society. The introduction to the original edition of *We Shall Be All*, my history of the IWW, shows clearly how I linked the history of the Wobblies and their cause to that of the 1930s generation of young radicals associated with the New Left. And, best of all, I was on my way to England to work with the scholar who was the acknowledged master of the new labor history and an inspiration to the New Left, E. P. Thompson, and to meet the equally distinguished English practitioner of labor history, Eric Hobsbawm.

The year in England had a profound impact on me. It also was one of the more peculiar years in my academic life. While I was literally at sea on an ocean liner in the middle of the Atlantic, my publisher cabled me with the news of the publication of *We Shall Be All*. Soon after I had settled in the English Midlands, I began to receive copies of the favorable—some glowing—early reviews of the book. Working with Thompson at the Centre for Social History, jointly teaching the seminar in comparative Anglo-American labor history, and participating as a regular member of the Centre's fortnightly seminar on eighteenth-century social history (a seminar that resulted in the publication of two major books in English history: *Whigs and Hunters* and *Albion's Fatal Tree*)[19] was an intellectual experience that I will never forget. It taught me to understand labor history in its proper context, as a small part of the broader discipline of history that sought to comprehend the human experience in all its variety. If Thompson and I jointly taught a graduate course in labor history, he concentrated his undergraduate teaching on the English Romantic poets and the literary and cultural history of England in the age of revolutions, an interest that would produce Thompson's final book, his life of William Blake. From Thompson, I learned, as if I did not already know, that history "from the bottom up," a people's history, only created good scholarship if the historian treated with equal gravity the rulers and their intermediaries as well as the ruled (or, as some might say today, the subaltern); that the serious scholar must distinguish between history as a scholarly enterprise and politics as a public cause. I still remember the sarcasm with which Thompson responded to those young U.S. scholars who identified themselves as "radical" historians and solicited his support in their efforts to assume control of the AHA and OAH: Some way to start a revolution, said Thompson, by seizing power in a scholarly society. (Only in the United States!)

As it happened, however, we had our own little revolution at the University of Warwick, in which Thompson played a leading role. My first term in what was then the traditional British three-term academic calendar proceeded uneventfully. For the second term, Thompson had scheduled a five-part public lecture series for me, the first lecture of which proceeded as scheduled. But that was to be the last one that I delivered in the series, for on the evening of my second scheduled lecture, the students in our graduate seminar occupied the university administration building and shut down the campus. I remember clearly our students asking Thompson and me to hold the comparative history seminar in the occupied building, and Thompson responding that the students had to make a choice: act either as scholars or revolutionaries, for politics was as much a full-time enterprise as scholarship. Our graduate students' seizure of the administration building precipitated a wider protest among undergraduates and sympathetic faculty that effectively closed the university until after the long spring break and the commencement of a third term devoted primarily to examinations.

In retrospect, it is not easy to remember the precise factors that precipitated the occupation of the administration building, especially since the
evidence most damaging to the university vice chancellor was discovered
only after the occupiers searched the office's filing cabinets. Generally,
Warwick's student rebels, much like their counterparts in the United States
and Paris the previous year and earlier, evinced unhappiness with the
university's links to corporate enterprise and culture, especially Barclay's
Bank, Pressed-Steel Fisher, Courtauld's, and Rootes Motors (then linked
with Chrysler), all of which subsidized chairs and programs in the economics and industrial relations departments. More specifically, rumors circulated that agents of Rootes-Chrysler had sought to arrange the deportation
of my predecessor, Montgomery, as an undesirable alien because of his
contacts with the local Labour party. The purloined files indeed provided
evidence that Rootes had spied on Montgomery and sought his deportation as well as proof that the vice chancellor had rejected an undergraduate applicant for political reasons. (Those who want to learn more about
the causes and circumstances of the strike at Warwick can turn to the
Penguin Special that Thompson edited under the title *Warwick Limited*.)[20]

The student revolutionaries were quite a group, including undergraduates (exchange students from the United States) as well as graduates,
Americans and Canadians as well as British nationals. A number of them
also went on to become fine historians. Among the graduate students,
Douglas Hay and Peter Linebaugh have written superb studies of crime,
criminals, and justice in seventeenth- and eighteenth-century England;
Calvin Winslow and Barbara Winslow have published in labor and
women's history, respectively, and hold academic position in different units
of the City University of New York. Among the undergraduate exchange
students from the United States, Ronald Schatz has become a respected
labor historian and a senior faculty member at Wesleyan University, and
Peter Gottlieb has achieved success both as a scholar, the author of a book
on African-American worker migration to Pittsburgh, and as an archivist
in charge of labor history collections at Penn State University and at the
State Historical Society of Wisconsin. From them collectively, I probably
learned as much as I taught about how to do history.

How the protest and occupation affected the participants can well be
contested. It effectively ended their academic education for the term and
sabotaged the completion of the M.A. Program in Comparative Anglo-
American Labour History for those enrolled in it. It also terminated academic learning for far larger numbers of undergraduates and graduate stu-

dents uninvolved in the cause. Neither in the short run nor the long run, moreover, did the occupation succeed in altering Warwick University's relations with its corporate sponsors, transforming the university's educational programs, or causing the vice chancellor to resign. Hence, it is hard to say what political lessons the student radicals took away from their little rebellion. Did they take to heart Thompson's homily about the distinction between politics and scholarship as separate enterprises? In a manner of speaking, Thompson himself did so by resigning his position at Warwick, declining other academic offers, and devoting by far the larger part of his remaining life to the politics of antinuclear weapons movement and anti-cold war activities, though he continued to do research and write history (as well as science fiction) and occasionally to take a short-term visiting academic appointment in the United States. Obviously, I did not make Thompson's choice, having remained primarily an academician. I did conclude that, however much one's personal politics and deepest beliefs shape scholarship, a firm boundary must demarcate a life devoted to politics from one committed to academics. One may be an intellectual and a political activist simultaneously or an intellectual and a scholar but not both equally. I also wondered about the value of shutting down campuses and learning as a form of political action, departing Warwick with the notion that more was lost than gained in the process. Might not student radicals have accomplished more to promote their goals by allowing Thompson to continue teaching, letting me complete my public lecture series, and permitting the comparative labor history program to move forward? Is not education a permanent teach-in? To choose a life in the academy instead of one in the political arena is not to discard one's beliefs but rather to put them to work in a different setting. And to write good history rather than "radical" or "party" history does far more to promote human betterment, as Thompson proved when he revised his original party-line biography of William Morris into a more believable and sounder form of scholarship in a revised second edition.

While my year abroad caused me to ponder the relationships between politics and scholarship, between campus protest and higher education, labor history came of age in the United States. At that year's meeting (spring 1970) of the OAH, David Brody presented a paper that described and evaluated the transformation of labor history into a serious and respected field. In that paper, subsequently published in *Labor History* as "The New and the Old Labor History," Brody cited Irving Bernstein's book on the New Deal years, *Turbulent Years,* and my history of the IWW as the best evidence that labor history had matured as an academic field.[21] Several major university history departments sought to recruit me to teach labor history. I was effectively committed and contractually obligated to teach at Wisconsin (Milwaukee), a prospect rendered more enticing by a decision that I had recently made to write a biography of John L. Lewis in collaboration with my former student, Warren Van Tine. Milwaukee placed me close to the resources of the State Historical Society of Wisconsin, which included the papers of the American Federation of Labor (AFL), John L. Lewis, Adolph Germer, and many other central actors in twentieth-century labor history. What better place to begin research on a life of John L. Lewis.

In most respects, Milwaukee proved a delightful experience. I enjoyed the city and especially the opportunity to walk regularly from my home in a pre–World War II, near north suburb along Lake Shore Drive to campus. Large numbers of undergraduates, most from working-class families, enrolled in my one-year course in U.S. labor history. I was even more pleased by the large number of excellent M.A. students who chose to study labor history with me. Several of them later followed me to Binghamton; and another who eventually completed a Ph.D. at Pittsburgh with David Montgomery, Shelton Stromquist, has become an outstanding labor historian and chair of the history department at the University of Iowa. And it was true joy for this onetime Brooklyn playground basketball player to reside in Milwaukee in the year that Kareem Abdul-Jabbar and Oscar Roberston led the Bucks to the National Basketball Association championship and to attend games in which Abdul-Jabbar and Robertson competed against Willis Reed and Walt Frazier of the New York Knicks and Wilt Chamberlain and Jerry West of the Los Angeles Lakers. Milwaukee pleased me in all respects save one: the Wisconsin system had decided not to allow the Milwaukee campus to offer doctoral training in history. Even that did not persuade me to seek academic employment elsewhere.

As happened more often than I would prefer to remember, chance once again intruded. In 1970–71, the State University of New York (SUNY) system was in the midst of the expansion generated by Governor Nelson A. Rockefeller's desire to transform it into one of the leading public university systems in the nation. Its campus in Binghamton had just hired a new history chair, the medievalist Norman Cantor, with ambitious plans to build a doctoral program of the first rank. Having sought and failed to recruit David Donald for a chair as Distinguished Professor, Cantor resorted to an alternate strategy, in which I played a role. Labor history may have matured as a field within the larger discipline, and *We Shall Be All* may have made my scholarly reputation, but Cantor could not sell the administration at Binghamton on the recruitment of a labor historian. Instead, he recruited and promoted me as an urban historian (after all, my first book was on New York City), an easier sell during the days of the "urban crisis," the Kerner Commission report, and the model cities program. That was a sell the administration bought, and Binghamton made me a substantial offer that included a salary increase, research support, and a prominent role in the doctoral program.

What a strange two years it had been since I left Massachusetts for England. I departed the United States as an untenured, junior faculty member. I arrived in Binghamton as a tenured professor with a salary that had more than doubled. Truly an academic success story and an even odder commentary on the character of the academic labor market in the United States and its version of free agency.

My arrival in Binghamton coincided with the flowering of labor history as a respected field within departments of history. During my first several years there, the size of my graduate colloquium in labor and social history as well as the number of students studying under my supervision steadily increased. Panels on labor and working-class history became common at annual OAH and AHA meetings; Columbia University added a seminar on labor and working-class history to its traditional program of university seminars; the journal *International Labor and Working-Class History* (*ILWCH*) had its beginnings in the spring of 1972 at a social gathering of a small group of younger historians of U.S. and European labor during a conference in Madison, Wisconsin, that I attended; in 1975, Alan Dawley won the Bancroft Prize in history for his book on the shoemakers of Lynn, Massachusetts; state and regional labor history and labor studies societies sprouted like the proverbial Green Bay Tree; and the New York State School of Industrial and Labor Relations, in conjunction with the family of Philip Taft, created the Taft Prize to be awarded annually to the best book published in the field of U.S. labor history. An especially excellent illustration of how the field had matured occurred in the spring semester of 1974, when I traveled with members of my seminar in labor history to Pittsburgh to meet jointly with the students in David Montgomery's seminar. Among the members of that joint seminar meeting who later established themselves as labor historians of the first rank were Bryan Palmer, Peter Friedlander, Ronald Schatz, Shelton Stromquist, Peter Rachleff, and Peter Gottlieb. (Montgomery's appointment later in the decade as Farnham Professor of History at Yale University certified that labor history had arrived even at the most elite universities.)

If labor history had come of age by the mid-1970s, its practitioners began to change in subtle but perceptible ways. Fifteen years earlier, in 1962, Carl Bridenbaugh had complained about the new historians who were transforming the guild of history from his kind of old-boys club of WASPish gentlemen into a nest of aliens incapable of understanding the "American experience."[22] True, many (but certainly not all) of the new labor historians came from distinctly working-class or lower-middle-class origins and eastern and southern European families. But we were a new-*boys* club, almost totally male in membership. By the middle of the 1970s, however, half or more of the graduate students in my seminars and studying with me were female. In September 1974, the history department at Binghamton convened perhaps the first major national scholarly conference in the new women's history, coordinated by Mary Ryan under the rubric "Class and Ethnicity in Women's History." Among the panelists were such notable historians as Edward Shorter, Maris Vinovskis, Judith Walkowitz, Alice Kessler Harris, Tamara Hareven, Mari Jo Buhle, and Herbert Gutman. Aside from attracting a large audience of scholars from around the Northeast, the papers and discussions at the conference presaged the shift in scholarly focus from women's history to the history of gender (this could be seen in panels that numbered nearly as many male as female historians). The shifting gender balance among labor historians, combined with an emphasis on gender, not only altered how its practitioners approached their subject; it also slowly eroded labor history's primacy of place among many young scholars. That could be seen in fall of 1984 at the conference sponsored by the history department at Northern Illinois University and funded by the National Endowment for the Humanities (NEH) on the theme of the need for "synthesis" in labor history specifically and in U.S. history generally. Meeting in a literal and figurative fog, the invited participants talked past each other. Older and younger scholars appeared to inhabit different intellectual worlds, as did male and female historians. Eric Hobsbawm, who sat next to me through most of the conference, muttered persistently about the ahistorical consciousness of the women theorists of patriarchy and female identity.[23] The sensibility struggling to express itself among several participants at the conference led directly to postmodernism, identity scholarship, and the "linguistic turn." Joan Scott, who began her scholarly career in the mid-1970s as a labor historian, became, by the end of the 1980s, a leading advocate of the linguistic turn and postmodern historical scholarship.[24]

As labor history's arc began to descend rather than rise, my interests also shifted. I became deeply involved in creating the Fernand Braudel Center as a site for organized research at SUNY at Binghamton. With the appointment in 1975 of Immanuel Wallerstein as Distinguished Professor of Sociology and director of a new research center without a formal name, the largest part of my responsibility for creating what became the Braudel Center ended. Still, I found myself busy as a member of the center's executive board, as an editorial board member for its journal, *Review,* as a participant in several of its research working groups, and, on several occasions, as acting director during Wallerstein's absences in Paris. My involvement with the Braudel Center entangled me in the universe of world-systems analysis, causing me to learn a new scholarly language and to engage more seriously with theoretical issues. As first director and then codirector of a research working group on world-scale worker movements, I faced the challenge that I had issued at the close of my essay on the origins of Western working-class radicalism, a demand that worker response to capitalism be examined on a global scale. To be sure, that proved no easy task as our research group functioned for more than a decade without producing much of substance, other than panels we organized at several major scholarly meetings. We were denied research grants either because our proposals were insufficiently theoretical and scientific—the National Science Foundation (NSF)—or too scientific and ideological—the NEH. But the project did bring several rewards, including an officially sanctioned bilateral exchange with a research institute in the Soviet Academy of Sciences. The exchange included three joint meetings in Binghamton and three in the former Soviet Union, where we had the opportunity to witness firsthand the impact of Gorbachev on the Soviet Union. A second reward consisted of two joint meetings held with a group of French economic historians, where I enjoyed intellectual exchanges with the French pioneers of the "regulation school," whose theoretical edifice provided the foundation on which David Gordon, Richard Edwards, and Michael Reisch constructed their *Segmented Work, Divided Workers.*[25] Not until the winter of 1995, however, did our research group publish our findings—and then in a special issue of the Braudel Center's journal, *Review* (vol. 18). The final section of essays in this collection reflects on the impact of the Center and of world-systems analysis on my scholarship.

My experience in learning a new academic language, mastering recondite theory, and meeting and working with a variety of different scholars, mostly nonhistorians, probably best explains why nearly two decades passed between the publication of my biography of John L. Lewis and my next "real" book, *The State and Labor in Modern America*. Between 1977 and 1994, labor history itself seemed to pass from the prime of life to a senescence in which younger, newer, and more vigorous subfields of history overtook it. How many advertisements for positions in labor history did one see by the end of the 1990s? How competitive were labor historians with scholars who proclaimed the primacy of gender and sexuality, or identity and diversity, or carnival and transgression? In the fall 1994, *International Labor and Working-Class History* even printed a series of essays and comments under the title "*ILWCH* Roundtable: What Next for Labor and Working-Class History?" The scholars contributing to the roundtable, including some quite distinguished historians, disagreed as to whether there was in fact a crisis or whether labor history was, in the words of one essay title, "out of vogue."

Yet the timing and circumstance of the publication of the "*ILWCH* Roundtable" raised the question of whether labor history in the United States was following the trajectory of the nation's labor movement with a lag of twenty-five years, falling from its heights and a state of grace to diminishing appeal and never-ending crisis. Or, perhaps, do labor historians have better reasons to proclaim the triumph of their cause than did George Meany and his successor Lane Kirkland, who repeatedly lauded the record of the AFL-CIO even as it lost members and influence? Perhaps our dwindling presence on the academic landscape derives from how well the history of working people has been integrated into the broader narrative of U.S. history. Neither political, social, cultural, nor even intellectual and diplomatic history can be written and taught today without considering the impact of working people, their institutions and movements. The books nominated for 1998's Taft Prize compare well with any that I have read in my nearly twenty years on the committee, and they illustrate the extent to which newer emphases on gender, identity, and language have enriched labor history. Labor history remains alive and well to the extent that its practitioners are able simultaneously to incorporate new approaches to the past, whatever their source, into their writing and teaching and to integrate the history of working people into the larger epic of U.S. and world history. To the extent that is true, labor history's vital signs remain positive.

Looking back, however, it seems hard to believe that labor history as an indispensable aspect of U.S. history and as an essential course of study in history curricula has existed for barely more than one-quarter of a century. It is also difficult to fathom that Herbert Gutman died in 1985, that David Brody and David Montgomery retired in 1993 and 1997, respectively, and that my own days as an active teaching historian may end with the new millennium. Yet, today in mid-1998, there are more labor historians at work than in the 1960s, and those historians are attempting to build a new national labor history society to achieve what the stillborn society of the years 1967–69 failed to accomplish. Labor history also manages to support two successful scholarly journals and an Internet discussion group, H-Labor.[26] For the foreseeable future, at least, the founding generation of labor historians in the United States need not fear for their scholarly construction the fate of Ozymandias. If, temporarily, labor history exists in the shadows cast by cultural studies, gay and lesbian studies, gender history, identity scholarship, and many other vogues, it survives in a healthier form than at its somewhat uncertain birth between 1959 and 1968.

Notes

A shorter version of this essay appeared in *Labor History* 34 (Fall 1993): 473–78.

1. Eric Hobsbawm, *The Age of Empire, 1875–1914* (New York: Pantheon, 1987), 3.

2. While still ABD, Montgomery, for example, took a temporary summer session teaching position at Northern Illinois University in the early 1960s, teaching general U.S. history; he was not associated with the field of labor history as such.

3. I still remember in 1964, during a meeting of the Organization of American Historians, being interviewed simultaneously with Brody for a position in history at the University of Maryland; both of us were probed about our teaching and research in twentieth-century U.S. history but not about our work in labor history.

4. At the end of the 1950s, Gutman had begun publishing articles in several state historical society journals about a series of strikes during the depression of the 1870s. His book *Work, Culture, and Society in Industrializing America* (New York: Knopf, 1976) included some of the best of those articles. David Montgomery, *Beyond Equality: Labor and the Radical Republicans, 1862–1872* (New York: Knopf, 1967). While recently reviewing old files, I discovered an issue of the newsletter of the Labor Historians, a national organization founded in 1967 that vanished by the end of 1969. So ephemeral was the organization's existence that, until coming across the file by chance, I had forgotten that I served on its executive board. The third and final newsletter of the Labor Historians reported in response to a survey concerning courses offered in labor history that, as of 1968, such courses were offered in only four departments of history: University of Massachusetts at Amherst, taught by me; University of Pittsburgh, Montgomery; University of Toledo, Lorin Lee Cary; and Northern Illinois University, J. Carroll Moody—my re-

placement). Gutman reported that at the University of Rochester he offered a graduate seminar on riots but made no mention of undergraduate courses in labor history. A larger number of courses in labor and/or union history were reported offered in economics departments, business programs, and industrial and labor relations schools.

5. Richard Hofstadter, *The Age of Reform* (New York: Knopf, 1955); Samuel P. Hays, *The Response to Industrialism, 1885–1914* (Chicago: University of Chicago Press, 1957).

6. Gutman, *Work, Culture, and Society,* 3–11.

7. Unlike Alfred F. Young, a former colleague of mine at Northern Illinois, I do not recall that the factor of anti-Semitism shaped my decision about which college to attend. Growing up in World War II as the son of a father who worked in the most heavily German-American of the city's still-ethnic neighborhoods on the border of Brooklyn and Queens (Ridgewood), I heard more than my share of anti-Semitic barbs and asides. Columbia University may have rejected my application (it still maintained a quota on the admission of Jewish-American students), but several of my classmates who were in many ways more evidently Jewish were admitted. And I was accepted at Cornell University, no less Ivy League than Columbia, and had the prospect of a scholarship at Colby College, far more WASP-ish than Columbia or Cornell. See Alfred F. Young, "An Outsider and the Progress of a Career in History," *William and Mary Quarterly* 52 (July 1995): 500–501.

8. Glyndon G. Van Deusen, *The Jacksonian Era, 1828–1848* (New York: Harper, 1959).

9. Melvyn Dubofsky, "Daniel Webster and the Whig Theory of Economic Growth, 1828–1848," *New England Quarterly* 42 (Dec. 1969): 551–72.

10. Arthur Schlesinger Jr., *The Age of Jackson* (Boston: Little, Brown, 1945); Richard Hofstadter, *The American Political Tradition* (New York: Knopf, 1948). Cf. Edward Pessen, "Did Labor Support Jackson?: The Boston Story," *Political Science Quarterly* 64 (June 1949): 262–74; idem, "The Workingmen's Movement of the Jacksonian Era," *Mississippi Valley Historical Review* 63 (Dec. 1956): 428–43; William A. Sullivan, "Did Labor Support Andrew Jackson?," *Political Science Quarterly* 62 (Dec. 1947): 569–80.

11. John R. Commons et al., *History of Labour in the United States,* 2 vols. (New York: Macmillan, 1918); idem, *A Documentary History of American Industrial Society,* 11 vols. (Cleveland: A. H. Clark, 1910–11); Norman Ware, *The Industrial Worker, 1840–1860* (Boston: D. C. Heath, 1924). The first volume of Philip Foner's *History of Labor in the United States* (New York: International Publishers, 1947), which replicated the coverage of Commons et al., *History of Labor,* was not available in the university library. Moreover, I doubt that reading Foner's book would have altered my preparation of the lectures. See Melvyn Dubofsky, "Give Us That Old-Time Labor History: Philip Foner and the American Worker," *Labor History* 26 (Winter 1985): 118–37.

12. George Martin, *Madame Secretary, Frances Perkins* (Boston: Houghton Mifflin, 1976), 122–26 and passim.

13. See Young, "Outsider," for comparable insight about the department and the graduate program at Northern Illinois.

14. Selig Perlman and Philip Taft, *History of Labor in the United States, 1896–1932* (New York: Macmillan, 1935); Stewart Holbrook, *The Rocky Mountain Revolution* (New York: Henry Holt, 1956); Wallace Stegner, *Joe Hill: A Biographical Novel* (New York: Penguin, 1990), originally published as *The Preacher and the Slave* (Garden City, N.Y.: Doubleday, 1950).

15. Harold Hyman, *Soldiers and Spruce: Origins of the Loyal Legion of Loggers and Lumbermen* (Los Angeles: University of California Industrial Relations Series, 1963).

16. Melvyn Dubofsky, "James H. Hawley and the Origins of the Haywood Case, 1892–1899," *Pacific Northwest Quarterly* 26 (1965): 118–37; idem, "The Leadville Strike of 1896–1897: A Re-Appraisal," *Mid-America* 48 (Apr. 1966): 99–118.

17. Nick Salvatore, "Whose History, Whose Footnotes? Herbert Gutman's Narrative of the American Working Class," paper read at the Newberry Library Seminar in U.S. Social History, January 1997, and at the State University of New York at Binghamton, Graduate Student Colloquium, April 1997.

18. Edward P. Thompson, *The Making of the English Working Class* (New York: Pantheon, 1964); idem, "Time, Work-Discipline, and Industrial Capitalism," *Past and Present* 38 (1967): 56–97; idem, "The Moral Economy of the English Crowd in the Eighteenth Century," *Past and Present* 50 (1971): 76–136.

19. Douglas Hay, Peter Linebaugh, John G. Rule, E. P. Thompson, and Cal Winslow, *Albion's Fatal Tree: Crime and Society in Eighteenth-Century England* (New York: Pantheon, 1975); Edward P. Thompson, *Whigs and Hunters: Origins of the Black Act* (New York: Pantheon, 1975).

20. E. P. Thompson, ed., *Warwick University Ltd: Industry, Management and the Universities* (Middlesex, Eng.: Penguin, 1970).

21. David Brody, "The Old Labor History and the New: In Search of an American Working Class," *Labor History* 20 (Winter 1979): 111–26.

22. Carl Bridenbaugh, "The Great Mutation," *American Historical Review* 68 (Jan. 1963): 315–31.

23. For some of the papers presented at the conference, see J. Carroll Moody and Alice Kessler Harris, eds., *Perspectives on American Labor History: The Problems of Synthesis* (DeKalb: Northern Illinois University Press, 1989). See also my review essay on that volume, "Lost in a Fog: Labor Historians' Unrequited Search for a Synthesis," *Labor History* 32 (Spring 1991): 295–300.

24. For Joan Scott's style of labor history, see *The Glassmakers of Carmaux: French Craftsmen and Political Action in a Nineteenth-Century City* (Cambridge, Mass.: Harvard University Press, 1974); for her "linguistic turn," see *Gender and the Politics of History* (New York: Columbia University Press, 1988), *Feminists Theorize the Political* (New York: Routledge, 1992), and *Feminism and History* (New York: Oxford University Press, 1996). Ironically, one of my former doctoral students published the most vehement critique of Scott's linguistic turn and the triumph of postmodernist discourse in history. See Bryan D. Palmer, *Descent into Discourse: The Reification of Language and the Writing of Social History* (Philadelphia: Temple University Press, 1990).

25. Michel Aglietta, *A Theory of Capitalist Regulation* (London: New Left Books, 1979); Alain Lipietz, *Mirages and Miracles: The Crisis of Global Fordism* (London:

Verso, 1987); Robert Boyer, *Capitalismes Fin de Siècle* (Paris: Presses Universitaries de France, 1986); idem, *The Search for Labour Market Flexibility: The European Economies in Transition* (New York: Oxford University Press, 1988); David Gordon, Richard Edwards, and Michael Reich, *Segmented Labor, Divided Workers: The Historical Transformation of Work in the United States* (New York: Cambridge University Press, 1982).

26. The International Institute for Social History in Amsterdam, the Netherlands, has helped form an international association of labor historians that incorporates members from national and regional labor history societies spread around the globe. It also coordinates an Internet labor history listserve discussion group with a worldwide membership and publishes an excellent scholarly journal, *International Review of Social History,* that has included a number of special issues on U.S. labor history to which such notable American labor historians as David Montgomery, Shelton Stromquist, Eric Arnesen, Bruce Nelson, David Roediger, and Judith Stein have contributed.

PART 1

Labor Radicalism, Culture, and Comparative History

THE three essays in this section—each in its own way, however—reflect the political and intellectual ferment of the 1960s. This should be most evident in the second essay, "The IWW and the Culture of Poverty," which I wrote in the midst of the upheavals of the 1960s, when the United States, in the words of William O'Neill's book title, seemed to be *Coming Apart.* The opening essay was written during the days of "Camelot on the Potomac," and the closing essay was composed after the fires of rebellion had largely dampened. Also, each was originally presented in a different form as a paper at an annual meeting of a major national historical association ("The Origins of Western Working-Class Radicalism" in 1964, at the Mississippi Valley Historical Association [MVHA]; "The IWW and the Culture of Poverty" in 1968, when the MVHA had become the Organization of American Historians [OAH]; "Bill Haywood and Tom Mann" at the American Historical Association [AHA] in 1970). They are linked by my beliefs that capitalism, as a system, has had comparable effects on all nation-states or societies and that the interaction between economic change, on the one hand, and culture and society, on the other, has produced variable outcomes that follow no general law of historical development.

Since I initially wrote, presented, or published these essays, a veritable explosion of new scholarship has enriched our knowledge of the subjects I first assayed in the 1960s. Had the fruits of that scholarship then been at hand, I am sure that all three essays would have taken a slightly different form and reached partly different conclusions. Yet nothing that has been added to scholarly knowledge since the 1960s would cause me to alter my interpretations significantly.

Take, for example, "The Origins of Western Working-Class Radicalism," which I wrote when there was not yet a new "western" history. Over the last three decades, we have been the beneficiaries not only of a new western history but also of a revised and enriched history of workers in the Mountain West. As I read the new western history and its labor dimension, its practitioners have built on rather than razed the edifice that I constructed between 1964 and 1966. Richard White's much admired general history of the West, *"It's Your Misfortune and None of My Own": A History of the American West,* narrates labor and working-class history in a manner that resonates with mine;[1] White even draws some of his language quite generously from my essay and the first chapter of my book on the IWW.[2] And, like me, White perceives the economic development of the American West as part of the larger story of the growth of capitalism in a world economy.[3] The same can be said about the essays written by Donald Worster, Michael P. Malone, and especially William G. Robbins in the collection edited by Patricia Limerick, *Trails: Toward a New Western History,* in which all three historians link western U.S. history to the development of capitalism and the incorporation of the region into a world-system.[4] (A similar historical consciousness manifests itself in the essays brought together by William Cronon under the title *Under an Open Sky: Rethinking America's Western Past,* especially Cronon's own contribution, "Kennecott Journey: The Path Out of Town."[5])

I should, however, clarify one aspect of my essay that merits separate comment. In it, I aimed to explain the sources of radicalism among western wage workers, not the history, politics, culture, and ideology of the entire western working class. The fine scholarship of David M. Emmons and Mark Wyman explores with sensitivity and sophistication the western workers who preferred moderate to radical politics, who chose responsible rather than militant unionism, and, in Emmons's case, those who cherished the ties of ethnicity as much as those of class.[6] To be sure, some of the new scholarship continues to mine the vein of radicalism that I originally tapped: conventionally, in the case of David Brundage's study of the sources of radicalism among Denver's workers in the late nineteenth century; and imaginatively, in Alan Derickson's treatment of how militancy among members of the Western Federation of Miners (WFM) produced creative forms of worker-financed and worker-administered health care for union members.[7]

What I then concluded about the origins of western working-class radicalism as a response to capitalist transformation of the American West fueled by the culture that workers brought with them to the contest with their employers has been further legitimated by the research of Richard White, Donald Worster, and William G. Robbins, among others. And it seems clearer even in 1998 than it was in 1966 that the United States and its western "frontier" were incorporated parts of a capitalist world-system.

The interpretation that I broached in "The IWW and the Culture of Poverty" remains part of an academic and public controversy that has reverberated down the decades since its first appearance, from Michael Harrington's rediscovery of poverty and the "other America" at the end of the 1950s to the 1990s version of the "war on poverty," in which welfare has been defined as the enemy. A quick run through any computer-generated subject search on the topic "poverty/culture of poverty" or a glance at the relevant section in James Patterson's *America's War against Poverty* shows the extensive scholarly and public debate that has raged on the topic. The culture of poverty remains a concept that has had and still has its advocates and critics.[8] I would rather not entangle myself once again in that heated debate.

Instead, I prefer to explain how I came to write the essay, why I framed it as I did, and why I chose not to revise it. I never lifted the concept of "culture (or subculture) of poverty" from cultural anthropology and grafted it on to the IWW's philosophy; nor did I take it undiluted from the crude environmentalism of Carleton Parker or the subtler version offered by Rexford Tugwell. The words, terms, tropes, metaphors later to be associated with the culture of poverty flashed before my eyes for more than five years as I read the official publications, public testimony, and private correspondence of IWW leaders and spokespersons. The images and behavioral patterns that Oscar Lewis ascribed to the culture of poverty had sixty years earlier been associated by IWW leaders with the workers that they hoped to lift out of Big Bill Haywood's metaphorical gutter. I was in the midst of writing the paper for the OAH meeting when I attended a lecture by Oscar Lewis at Smith College in the late winter of 1968. As Lewis spoke about the culture of poverty and how to eliminate it, I heard words and formed images that would have been familiar to a Wobbly. The next day, I began to read Lewis's writings about the poor in Mexico, Cuba, Puerto Rico, and the barrio in New York. When I finished, I concluded that the IWW had constructed its own cultural anthropology to describe marginal workers in the early twentieth-century United States.

Like Lewis, the Wobblies did not "blame the victims" for their disarray and misery. Rather, they saw the poor and marginal as victims of capitalist exploitation in a state and society that preferred economic growth and rising profits to human betterment. The issue, then, for Lewis and the Wobblies was to teach the victims of capitalism how to turn the tables on their exploiters, how to obtain and use power to rise out of the gutter and its culture of poverty. That, I thought, was the theme of my original essay: the notion that the creation of power through organization would liberate the oppressed from their cultural restraints and create instead a society of free and equal men and women. And it should be obvious to readers knowledgeable about the history of the 1960s how the ferment precipitated by that decade's advocates of "black power," "student power," and "people power" is manifested in the essay.

"Bill Haywood and Tom Mann" was my manifesto of sorts to reject the conventional wisdom of "American exceptionalism." At the time I wrote it, most U.S. historians stressed the uniqueness of the American experience, often in words similar to those I cited from David Shannon's essay in C. Vann Woodward's collection *The Comparative Approach to American History*. Comparing the lives of two of the most famous English-speaking labor radicals of the early twentieth century enabled me to show how capitalism and the wage relationship produced career trajectories that followed almost identical parabolas. The similarities between the lives and careers of Haywood and Mann seemed almost too eerie to be true. Now, nearly thirty years later, having been enriched by the scholarship of Eric Foner, Sean Wilentz, Jeffrey Haydu, Ira Katznelson, and Aristide Zolberg, which challenges the validity of American or any other sort of exceptionalism, I have less reason to doubt the validity of my dual portrait of labor radicals. There is only one point in the original essay that I might change. Had Haywood lived into the period when the United States and the Soviet Union became allies in World War II against Hitler's Germany, as Mann did in Britain, Haywood, too, might have been restored temporarily to official legitimacy as part of a popular front. Overall, however, this essay confirms the conclusion that Zolberg draws in his essay "Many Exceptionalisms": although no two capitalist societies are precisely alike, they share as much as they diverge.[9] Or, put another way, the debate about American exceptionalism is quite beyond the point. What matters are the historical experiences and cultural reference points that historical personages and subsequent scholars choose to emphasize, whether they prefer to focus on what is different and singular about the American experience— of which much was—or to examine aspects of broad structural change and everyday life that the United States shared with comparable states and societies that experienced the potent innovative impact of capitalism.[10] My reading of the twin lives of Mann and Haywood suggests that capitalism had a comparable impact on the two radical labor leaders; others, however, might prefer to stress how the "peculiarities" (to use a Thompsonian word) of British and American cultures created two quite different life stories.

Notes

1. Richard White, *"It's Your Misfortune and None of My Own": A History of the American West* (Norman: University of Oklahoma Press, 1991).

2. Ibid., 277–96, 346–51.

3. Ibid., chap. 10, esp. 236–69.

4. Patricia Limerick, ed., *Trails: Toward a New Western History* (Lawrence: University Press of Kansas, 1991).

5. William Cronon, "Kennecott Journey: The Path Out of Town," in *Under an*

Open Sky: Rethinking America's Western Past, ed. William Cronon (New York: W. W. Norton, 1992), 110–31.

6. David Emmons, *The Butte Irish: Class and Ethnicity in an American Mining Town, 1875–1925* (Urbana: University of Illinois Press, 1989); Mark Wyman, *Hard Rock Epic: Western Miners and the Industrial Revolution, 1860–1910* (Berkeley: University of California Press, 1979).

7. David Brundage, *The Making of Western Labor Radicalism: Denver's Organized Workers, 1870–1905* (Urbana: University of Illinois Press, 1994); Alan Derickson, *Workers' Health, Workers' Democracy: The Western Miners' Struggle, 1891–1925* (Ithaca, N.Y.: Cornell University Press, 1988). See also Jerry W. Calvert, *The Gibraltar: Socialism and Labor in Butte, Montana, 1895–1920* (Helena: Montana Historical Society Press, 1988), for a story much like Brundage's and Richard E. Lingenfelter, *The Hardrock Miners: A History of the Mining Labor Movement in the American West, 1863–1893* (Berkeley: University of California Press, 1974), for a more conventional narrative.

8. For examples of how lively and heated that debate remains more than twenty-five years after the cultural anthropology of Oscar Lewis and the public policy prescriptions of Daniel Patrick Moynihan precipitated it, see most especially the following additions to the debate: *Radical History Review* 69 (Fall 1997), a special issue on "Culture and Poverty," esp. 1–5; Michael B. Katz, *The Undeserving Poor: From the War on Poverty to the War on Welfare* (New York: Pantheon Books, 1989); Michael B. Katz, ed., *The "Underclass" Debate: Views from History* (Princeton, N.J.: Princeton University Press, 1993); Linda Gordon, *Pitied but Not Entitled: Single Mothers and the History of Welfare, 1890–1935* (New York: Free Press, 1994); Linda Gordon, ed., *Women, the State, and Welfare* (Madison: University of Wisconsin Press, 1990); James Patterson, *America's War against Poverty* (Cambridge, Mass.: Harvard University Press, 1996).

9. Aristide Zolberg, "How Many Exceptionalisms?," in *Working-Class Formation,* ed. Ira Katznelson and Aristide Zolberg (Princeton, N.J.: Princeton University Press, 1986), 397–455.

10. See the exchange between Sean Wilentz and Nick Salvatore in "Against Exceptionalism," *International Labor and Working Class History* 26 (Fall 1984): 1–24, and Wilentz's response in ibid. 28 (Fall 1985): 46–55. For thoughtful treatments on the subject, see Jeffrey Haydu, *Between Craft and Class: Skilled Workers and Factory Politics in the United States and Britain, 1890–1922* (Berkeley: University of California Press, 1988); idem, *Making American Industry Safe for Democracy: Comparative Perspectives on the State and Employee Representation in the Era of World War I* (Urbana: University of Illinois Press, 1997). For a comparison between U.S. and German historical experiences in the industrial era, see the essays in Katznelson and Zolberg, *Working-Class Formation,* especially those by the editors, and Alan Dawley, *Struggles for Social Justice: Social Responsibility and the Liberal State* (Cambridge, Mass.: Harvard University Press, 1991). For a scholar who still insists on the salience of American exceptionalism in explaining the historical trajectory and contemporary choices made in U.S. social policy, see Seymour Martin Lipset, *American Exceptionalism: A Double-Edged Sword* (New York: W. W. Norton, 1996); idem, *Continental Divide: The Values and Institutions of the United States and Canada* (New York: Routledge, 1990).

· 2 ·

The Origins of Western Working-Class Radicalism, 1890–1905

FIFTY years ago, the labor economist and historian Louis Levine (Lorwin) explained the origins of the radical unionism and syndicalism that the Lawrence, Massachusetts, textile strike of 1912 had brought to the American nation's attention. Rather than viewing American syndicalism as the product of a few inspired individuals or as a sudden decision to imitate French ideas and methods, Levine insisted that working-class radicalism could only be understood by a proper examination of U.S. economic and political developments. He wrote: "The forces which drove American toilers to blaze new paths, to forge new weapons and to reinterpret the meaning of life in new terms were the struggles and compromises, the adversities and successes, the exultation and despair *born of conditions of life in America.*"[1] Unfortunately, in the half-century since Levine's seminal article, too few historians have chosen to investigate his hypothesis. The field has been left to labor economists more concerned with the nature of industrial relations and the internal history of individual trade unions than with the dynamics of historical change.[2] This paper will apply the historical method and research into unused or seldom used documents to analyze the forces that impelled the working class in a part of the American West to adopt socialism and syndicalism.

At the outset, several concepts require clarification. By the American West, I mean the metals-mining area stretching from the northern Rockies to the Mexican border and particularly the states of Colorado, Idaho, and Montana. By radicalism, I do not mean murder or mayhem[3] but a concept of social change and a program for altering the foundations of American society and government, which was proscripted ultimately from the Marxian indictment of capitalism. This paper makes no pretense, however, of offering an exegesis on the theoretical foundations of western working-class radicalism or of its decline and fall; instead, it simply seeks to comprehend why, within a particular historical, social, and economic context, a group of American workers found radicalism relevant.

During the Populist and Progressive Eras (1890–1917), when radicalism took root among western workers, reform crusades—middle class and lower class, urban and rural, moderate and militant, conservative and revolutionary—challenged the classic capitalist order. This order, described fifty years earlier by Marx and Engels, was dying throughout the industrial world, the United States included; and social groups struggled to control or shape the economic order to come. None were sure of the future, but all wanted it to accord with their concept of a just and good society. In America, many options appeared to exist, for in 1890 and 1900, the triumph of the modern corporation and the corporate state was still in the future. And western workers were among those Americans who opted for an alternative to the capitalist order.

At this time, the American Federation of Labor (AFL), with its conservatism and "pure and simple" policies, dominated organized labor. Its original competitor, the Knights of Labor, had declined and died; Populism had failed to cement a farmer-labor alliance; and in the East, the immigrant needle-trades workers had not yet built stable, semi-industrial, socialist organizations offering an alternative to the AFL craft unions. Western workers, however, presented a direct and radical challenge to AFL hegemony. Around the Western Federation of Miners (WFM) rallied America's radical dissidents, those dissatisfied with things as they were—with McKinley, Roosevelt, Bryan, and the political parties they represented; with Samuel Gompers and craft unionism; and especially with corporate capitalism.

Nowhere was the economic and social change that produced American radicalism in the late nineteenth century so rapid and so unsettling as in the mining West. There, in a short time, full-blown industrial cities replaced frontier boom-camps, and substantially capitalized corporations displaced grub-staking prospectors. The profitable mining of refractory ores (silver and gold) and base metals (lead, zinc, and copper) required railroads, advanced technology, large milling and smelting facilities, and intensive capitalization. "The result," in the words of Rodman Paul, "was that [by 1880] many mining settlements were carried well beyond any stage of society that could reasonably be called the frontier. They became, instead, industrial islands in the midst of forest, desert, or mountain."[4] During the 1890s and 1900s, with continuing economic growth, mining communities moved still further beyond the frontier stage. Corporations such as William Rockefeller's Amalgamated Copper Company and the Phelps-Dodge Company consolidated the copper industry; other large corporations exploited the lead and silver mines; and the American Smelting and Refining Company and the United States Reduction and Refining Company apparently monopolized the refining and smelting of ores.[5]

As early as 1876, Colorado, though still sparsely settled and far removed from the nation's primary industrial centers, had been colonized by corporations and company towns. In Leadville, for example, the population increased from 200 in 1877 to 14,820 in 1880, by which time Leadville was a primary smelting center. Cripple Creek, the famous Colorado gold camp, surpassed Leadville. Beginning in 1892, when it was hidden in the wilderness, the Cripple Creek region changed overnight into an industrial fortress. By 1900, Cripple Creek advertised its 10,000 inhabitants, three railroads connecting the region to the outer world, and trolleys and electric lights serving the district's own needs. Domestic and foreign capital rushed to exploit Colorado's opportunities. Between 1893 and 1897, 3,057 new mining corporations were organized, each of which was capitalized at over $1 million. By 1895, all Colorado's larger cities boasted mining exchanges, and the Colorado Springs Mining Exchange handled over 230 million mining shares valued at over $34 million in 1899.[6]

Montana followed the Colorado pattern. Its production of ores, valued at $41 million in 1889, made it the nation's leading mining state. Butte, the copper capital by that time, had a population of 30,000, three banks with deposits in excess of $3 million, an adequate public school system, four hospitals, two fire companies, newspapers, and water, gas, and electric companies. Its wealthier classes lived in elegant homes and worked in handsome business residences; its miners and mill workers received more than a half million dollars monthly in wages, and over a hundred smoke stacks poured out their residue night and day in what was hardly a frontier environment.[7] Idaho, on a lesser scale, repeated Montana's and Colorado's development.[8]

In their mill and smelter towns, their shoddy company houses and stores, their saloons, and their working-class populations, the cities of the Mountain West bore a distinct resemblance to their eastern industrial counterparts.[9] The speed of the transition from a primitive to a more mature economy, from the village to the city, combined with the great instability of a mining economy, had important social consequences.[10] Rapid economic growth, instead of bringing prosperity and contentment, brought unrest, conflict, violence, and radicalism.

Those workers who filled the young industrial cities of the West shared a tradition of union organization, a common language, and a certain amount of ethnic similarity. Miners had organized unions by the 1860s on the Comstock Lode in Virginia City, Nevada. When that area's mines played out, its miners moved on to new lodes in Idaho, Colorado, and Montana, carrying the union idea with them.[11] While in some mining districts the foreign-born outnumbered the native Americans, no great ethnic division separated foreigners from natives. In most communities, the dominant foreign nationalities were of Irish, British (mostly Cornishmen), and Canadian extraction.[12] The foreign-born, particularly the Cornishmen (better known as "Cousin Jacks") and the Irishmen, were professional miners, and many of their American-born counterparts had forsaken prospecting and striking it rich for the steadier returns of wage labor.[13] Furthermore, the western mining centers shared with other mining communities throughout the world the group solidarity derived from relative physical isolation and dangerous, underground work.

At first, owing largely to the ethnic composition of western mining communities and to the reliance of local merchants and professionals on the patronage of miners, workers and local businessmen were not split into hostile camps. Local businessmen and farmers often supported the miners in their struggles for union recognition and higher wages. In Idaho's mineral-rich Coeur d'Alene area, the local inhabitants—farmer and merchant, journalist and physician, public official and skilled worker—sympathized with striking miners. A leading Idaho attorney and Democratic politician, Boise's James H. Hawley, from 1892 to 1894 defended indicted strikers, referred to them as friends and allies, and importuned President Cleveland to provide several with patronage positions.[14] East of the Continental Divide in Montana, mine and smelter owners, battling among themselves, wooed their labor forces with promises of union recognition, higher wages, the eight-hour day, and improved working conditions.[15] And even Bill Haywood admitted that in Colorado's Cripple Creek district prior to the 1903–4 "civil war," miners and businessmen associated with each other, belonged to the same fraternal societies, and were bound together by ethnic ties.[16]

Into these urban communities, the modern corporation intruded to disrupt the local peace and to drive a wedge between the workers and their non-working-class allies. The 1890s was an uneasy decade for American businesses, and for none more so than mining, milling, and smelting enterprises. The falling price of silver, the Depression of 1893, the repeal of the Sherman Silver Purchase Act, and the inherent instabilities of extractive industries made mine owners and smelter operators anxious to reduce production costs and, consequently, less tolerant of labor's demands. Mining corporations formed associations to pressure railroads by threatening to close down mining properties and cease shipments until rates declined. But capitalists found it easier to make the necessary savings by substituting capital for labor.[17]

Technological innovations increased productivity; but in so doing, they diluted labor skills and disrupted traditional patterns of work. While technological change did not as a rule decrease total earnings, it tended to lower piece rates and to reduce some formerly skilled workers to unskilled laborers (and thus lowered their earnings).[18] Since the mining enterprises competed in a common market, all the western mining areas experienced similar pressures on piece rates and established skills.[19] In Bill Haywood's hyperbolic words: "There was no means of escaping from the gigantic force that was relentlessly crushing all of them beneath its cruel heel. The people of these dreadful mining camps were in a fever of revolt. There was no method of appeal; strike was their only weapon."[20]

Thus, in 1892, Coeur d'Alene miners revolted against technological change, corporate concentration, and a recently organized Mine Owners' Association. Supported by local citizens, the community's newspapers, and local officials, miners appeared on the verge of success when their capitalist opponents, aided by state and federal authorities, outflanked them. Federal troops crushed the labor revolt, imprisoning union leaders and prominent nonunion local residents alike. Strike leaders, while awaiting trial in prison, brooded about their recent experiences and the future of western mining communities. Then and there, in an Idaho prison, they decided to create a new labor organization, joining together the separate miners' unions in Idaho, Montana, Colorado, California, Nevada, and the southwestern territories. On their release from prison, they called a convention, which met in Butte in 1893 and established the Western Federation of Miners (WFM).[21]

By 1893, the mining West, as shown above, had passed well beyond the frontier stage, and the working class's emerging radicalism was hardly the response of pioneer individualists to frontier conditions. The WFM did not consist mostly of men who had been prospectors and frontiersmen; it was not "permeated with the independent and often lawless spirit of the frontier"; nor did its radicalism result from a lack of respect for the social distinctions of a settled community, a disregard by labor for the "elementary amenities of civilized life," or the absence of farmers, a neutral middle class, and others who might keep matters within bounds.[22] Perlman, Taft, and their disciples had in fact reversed the dynamics of social change in the Mountain West. The violent conflicts that they so fully described came not on an undeveloped western frontier but in a citadel of American industrialism and financial capitalism. Perlman and Taft's "class war without a class ideology" resulted from a process of social polarization, not from an absence of middle groups, and consequently brought Marxian class consciousness. After 1910, farmers and others did not suddenly settle the area to blur sharp class distinctions and end the class war. The Ludlow Massacre occurred in 1914, Butte erupted into violent industrial warfare from 1914–17, and the bitter Colorado coal wars developed still later in the 1920s.

Violent conflict came not from the "general characteristics of the frontier" or "quick on the trigger" employers and employees but from the general nature of early industrialism.[23] Western working-class history is the story not of the collapse of social polarization but of its creation. Prior to the triumph of corporate capitalism, western workers retained numerous allies among local merchants, professionals, farmers, and party politicians. The interesting historical feature is the manner in which corporate executives separated labor from its quondam allies and polarized society and politics to the disadvantage of the worker. The remainder of this paper will demonstrate that class war in the West created a class ideology and that this ideology was Marxist because, from 1890 to 1905, the Mountain West followed the classic Marxian pattern of development.

The westerners' radicalism derived quite directly and naturally from the forces that had successfully refashioned American society. Together with other individuals and groups forced by corporate capitalism to the bottom of the economic and social ladder, miners asserted their claim to a more decent treatment and a better place in the American system. They joined the Knights of Labor, crusaded with the Populists, and eventually united with eastern socialists. Western workers wedded to the utopianism of the Knights, allured by the promise of Populism, and victimized by the corporation could not rest content with the "pure and simple" unionism of Samuel Gompers.

The local miners' unions that coalesced to form the WFM in many cases had simply dropped their Knights of Labor affiliation without shedding the Knights' essential spirit and carried with them the fundamental idea of the Knights: "the unity of all workers." Although many miners may have joined the Knights of Labor simply to gain better conditions or job security, many certainly became imbued with that organization's spirit of solidarity and its antipathy to capitalism. While the Knights vanished in the East, their organization had a marked rebirth in the Mountain West. Montana labor papers reported in 1894 that their state's Knights of Labor were advancing at a rate not attained in years and were ready to lead laborers into the Populist crusade.[24] On the other side of the Bitterroot Range in Idaho, the former Grand Master Workman, J. R. Sovereign, the editor and publisher of the Wallace *Tribune*—the Coeur d'Alene miners' official union publication—was amalgamating the Knights, Populism, and the WFM.[25] As late as 1903, a WFM member from Slocan, British Columbia, wrote to the *Miner's Magazine:* "Now there are thousands of old-line K. of L.s in the W.F. of M. and the unsavory acts of the A.F. of L. officials have not been all together forgotten."[26]

WFM members learned their political lessons in Populist schools. Unlike other areas of the nation, where Populism was primarily an agrarian protest and labor, organized and unorganized, declined overtures from farm organizations for a political alliance, Populism in the Mountain West was a working-class movement, and labor organizations courted farmers.[27] Thus, politics and Populism intruded at the early conventions of the WFM. The 1893 founding convention, meeting before panic and depression swept the West, considered the necessity of united political action. The 1895 convention, convened during the depths of depression, gave its endorsement and "undivided support to the party [Populist] advocating the principles contained in the Omaha platform."[28] Mining districts across the Mountain West elected miners' candidates to local office on labor or Populist tickets. And, on occasion, working-class Populists held the balance of power in statewide elections. Western miners, like farmers elsewhere, learned that politics paid.[29]

⌐

Although free silver was obviously an important Populist attraction in the Mountain West, miners, unlike their employers, demanded sweeping political and economic reforms. If free silver had been the only manifestation of western working-class political radicalism, it could have found an outlet in the Republican or Democratic parties as well as the People's party.[30] The western workers instead supported a radical Populism—sometimes cranky, sometimes funny—that was the industrial counterpart of C. Vann Woodward's Southern Alliancemen and Norman Pollack's midwestern agrarians.[31] Consequently, after the failure of the Populist coalition with Silver Democrats and the defeat of Bryan, WFM president Ed Boyce, speaking at the union's 1897 convention, denounced the free silver fraud and informed his audience: "The silver barons of the west are as bitter enemies of organized labor as the gold bug Shylock in his gilded den on Wall Street." Boyce then called for more intelligent and effective political action, a call that could lead in only one direction: toward the Socialist party. As the AFL turned away from socialism and political action to the narrower path of "pure and simple" trade unionism,[32] the Western Federation moved toward socialism, political action, and the broad road of radical unionism.

Initially, however, the WFM, except for its unusual concern with Populism and politics, appeared much like any other trade union. It waged strikes to protect wages, reduce hours, or gain union recognition, not for the cooperative commonwealth. So famous an American radical as "Big Bill" Haywood, during his early years as an officer of the Silver City, Idaho local, concerned himself not with the coming revolution but with enrolling all working miners in the union. Nowhere do the minute books of Haywood's local, which he kept, hint of a future revolutionist.[33] Ed Boyce, the union leader most responsible for transforming the WFM into the cynosure of left-wing socialists, initially bore no taint of radicalism. During its first four years (1893–96), the WFM seemed a rather ordinary trade union waging a losing battle against corporations and depression; in 1896, the organization was weaker and numbered fewer members than at its birth in 1893. Then the WFM revived.[34] And with apparent success came not conservatism or self-satisfaction but radicalism and revolutionary ardor.

The WFM's radicalism was buried deep in the organization's conscious and unconscious past. The Knights of Labor had contained an obvious utopian tinge; Populism, while less utopian, nevertheless proposed for the America of the 1890s a meaningful radical alternative. Many miners remained at heart Knights and Populists. Given the proper circumstances and the necessary motivation, both strains came alive in the WFM. The Western Federation of Miners transformed the naive idealism of the Knights and the native radicalism of the Populists into a brand of radicalism shared by socialist workers throughout the industrial world.

The Western Federation began as an open, inclusive union and became more so. "Open our portals to every workingman whether engineer, blacksmith, smelterman, or millman," President Boyce advised the union convention in 1897. "The mantle of fraternity is sufficient for all." Three years later, Boyce expanded his concept of fraternity: "We will at all times and under all conditions espouse the cause of the producing masses, regardless of religion, nationality or race, with the object of arousing them from the lethargy into which they have sunk, and which makes them willing to live in squalor."[35] With Boyce and the WFM, commitment to solidarity and fraternity became more than platform oratory; the western organization epitomized in philosophy and practice the spirit of industrial unionism.

Boyce's presidency also established economic and political radicalism as union policy. In his presidential inaugural speech, he directly challenged Samuel Gompers's approach to industrial relations and working-class organization. Speaking of his experience at the 1896 AFL convention, Boyce remarked: "surely it is time for workingmen to see that trades unionism is a failure."[36]

One might well ask, as Gompers himself wondered, what prompted the leader of a growing labor union to declare trade unionism a failure. And the answer might be that Boyce arrived at his conclusion not on theoretical or philosophical grounds but on the basis of the miners' unions' actual experiences in dealing with corporations. Even before the WFM appeared, miners had discovered the weakness of ordinary trade unions facing employers allied with state and federal authorities. And after the WFM's founding in 1893, events in Idaho and Colorado illustrated further the weaknesses inherent in a pure and simple trade union. Weakness drove the western miners toward radicalism, and radicalism apparently resulted in strength and success.

Twice in the Coeur d'Alenes, in 1892 and 1899, miners' unions were impotent against concentrated capital and hostile state and federal forces. Although miners at first elicited sympathy and support from the local middle class, controlled municipal and county offices, and published the community's leading newspapers, their local power proved insufficient. Mine owners, organized in an employers' association, influenced the governor, maintained their own newspaper just across the state line in Spokane, and kept their own judge in the Idaho federal district court to hand down sweeping injunctions. When injunctions failed to end strikes and state militia proved inadequate and unwilling to repress strikers, Idaho's chief executives, responding to mine owners' pleas, requested federal troops.[37] The reaction of mine owners and state officials was frightening in its implications. Idaho's attorney-general, for example, demanded of his state's congressional delegation: "The mob must be crushed by overwhelming force"; and to implement his objective, he suggested the use of Gatling guns and howitzers.[38] The governor and other state officials, counseled by the Mine Owners' Association, demanded the permanent presence of federal troops in northern Idaho to prevent future troubles and protect citizens against guerrilla warfare.[39]

Idaho's mine owners and state officials did not desist until they had crushed the miners' unions. In 1899, again abetted by federal troops, they incarcerated workers and strike sympathizers in the infamous bullpen and denied employment to union miners. Some of those who had defended the self-same miners in 1892 now turned against them. James H. Hawley, together with his junior associate, William Borah, prosecuted the union leaders he had defended in court seven years earlier. His onetime, warm political friends had become dangerous criminals. Hawley also engaged in the extracurricular practice of organizing a company union. "No matter how it [the court case] goes," he wrote to his law partner, "we will win our fight by breaking the power of the Union."[40] The corporations had finally succeeded in polarizing Idaho politics and society.[41] Against this type of activity, the WFM—and particularly President Boyce, a former Coeur d'Alene miner—found strict trade-union tactics unavailing. The WFM learned the same bitter lesson in Colorado. With the aid of a Populist governor, "Bloody Bridles" Waite, they had defeated a mine owners' private army in 1894. But two years later, with a Republican in the state house, mine owners obtained the state militia to break a strike in Leadville.[42] After the unsuccessful Leadville strike of 1896, the WFM made the crucial shift to the left in politics and practice.

As the union moved further left, Colorado's Mine Owners' Association prepared to turn to its own advantage American fear of radicalism and socialism. In 1902, mine owners formed a state-wide organization to combat unions with money, propaganda, and Pinkerton detectives. Simultaneously, they enlisted the aid of local businessmen and professionals previously allied with the miners. Again, the process of social polarization came relatively late and was consummated on the initiative of the larger corporate interests. By February 24, 1903, Boyce's successor as president of the WFM, Charles Moyer, informed union members: "We are being attacked on all sides at this time by the Mill Trust and Mine Owners' Association."[43]

WFM officials, although on the defensive, tried to negotiate with Colorado employers. During a dispute with Colorado City mill and smelter operators, Moyer emphasized that the purpose of the WFM was to build, not destroy—to avoid by all honorable means a war between employer and employee. But Haywood, at the same time, probably described the WFM's position more accurately: "We are not opposed to employers, and it is our purpose and aim to work harmoniously and jointly with the employers as best we can under this system, and we intend to change the system if we get sufficiently organized and well enough educated to do so."[44] In brief, union leaders separated long-term from immediate goals: in the short run, they barely differed from the AFL, but the America they desired for the future was vastly different from and hardly acceptable to the AFL or to the American business community.

Corporate interests in Colorado, like corporations elsewhere in America, would have no compromise with labor for the short run or the long run. Company attorneys callously viewed labor as another commodity to be bought and sold in the marketplace; and company managers denied to unions, the state, and the public the right to intervene in company affairs.[45] Between management's deepest commitments and WFM objectives, compromise was impossible; thus, a delicately balanced modus vivendi collapsed, and a miniature civil war erupted in Colorado's Cripple Creek district in 1903–4.

The WFM's now-clear desire to abolish the prevailing economic system turned previously moderate employers against the union. Employers might tolerate and bargain with a labor organization prepared to accept the status quo, but not one dedicated to the abolition of capitalism. Nationwide corporations, local businessmen, and state and national officials united to rid the West of working-class radicalism. Martial law gripped Colorado's mining districts. Military officers made, administered, and executed the law, flaunting with impunity established courts.[46] The WFM's executive board declared a state of open war in Colorado in December 1903 but still maintained its willingness to compromise: "The W.F. of M. has at all times been ready and willing to go more than half way in meeting the Mine Operators of the State, and use every honorable means to bring a close to this conflict, that has left scars upon the welfare and prosperity of every citizen of the State."[47] Though the WFM preferred negotiation, employers, aware of their unity and strength, crushed the union in Colorado.

Industrial conflicts in the Coeur d'Alenes, Leadville, and Cripple Creek convinced WFM leaders of the need to convert their organization from an industrial union concerned with wages and jobs into an advocate of revolutionary change and socialism. The WFM had been formed after the first Coeur d'Alene conflict. After the 1896 Leadville debacle, Boyce castigated Gompers and the AFL, called on union miners to join rifle clubs, and demanded a more radical brand of politics.[48] Then, as both Democrats and Republicans turned against labor and allied with corporate interests while middle-class friends deserted it, the WFM became more radical—as well as more politically conscious. The organization's adoption of Marxian Socialism (1900–1903) finally completed the process of social polarization in the urban industrial centers of the Mountain West as the WFM lost the remainder of its local middle-class allies. Simultaneously, for the same reasons, the western labor organizations came into overt conflict with Gompers and the AFL.

Western hostility to Gompers was of long standing, as he had not been forgiven for destroying the Knights of Labor and neglecting the Populists. As early as 1894, when John McBride defeated Gompers for the AFL presidency, the Western Federation's official paper exulted: "good riddance of bad rubbish," and later it accused Gompers of belonging "to that class of leaders which is fast being relegated to the rear—a narrow-minded, self-seeking, and trouble breeding element."[49] During the 1896 Leadville conflict, when AFL assistance to striking miners proved negligible, Boyce and Gompers debated the deficiencies of the AFL and the advantages of radical unionism. Gompers warned Boyce against breaking with the AFL and bringing grief to the house of labor, while Boyce informed the AFL leader that western workers were one hundred years ahead of their eastern comrades. Thus, at its 1897 convention, the WFM withdrew from the AFL, to which it had belonged for only one year, and established a rival regional labor organization.[50]

In 1898, the WFM's executive board, following similar attempts by Montana's State Trades and Labor Council, invited all western unions to attend a meeting in Salt Lake City to organize the Western Labor Union (WLU).[51] A loyal AFL man described the new western labor organization to Gompers as "only the Western Federation of Miners under another name. . . . Boyce dominated everything. . . . Boyce's influence with the miners is unquestionably strong. The majority believe him sincerely, and all of them fear to oppose him."[52]

During the Salt Lake meeting, western workers stressed their desire to escape conservative unionism and demanded an industrial, educational, and political organization, uncompromising in policy and "broad enough in principle and sufficiently humane in character to embrace every class of toil, from the farmer to the skilled mechanic, in one great brotherhood."[53] The new Western Labor Union insisted that industrial technology had made trade-union methods obsolete and left the working class but one recourse: "to take up the arms of a modern revolutionary period . . . the free and intelligent use of the ballot." Thus, in 1900, the WLU's newspaper endorsed the socialist ticket, and its 1901 convention adopted a preamble and platform denouncing American government, "the very foundations of which is crumbling to decay, through the corruption and infamy of the self-constituted governing class." The WLU professed to be ready to spill every drop of its blood at the point of a bayonet rather than submit to further capitalistic aggressions.[54] If the WLU intended to frighten conservative America, it succeeded.

The differences between the AFL and western labor grew. Even those WFM members who favored union with the AFL did so as western missionaries and not as true believers in Gompersism; they insisted that in the face of united capital, labor must do likewise or fail. "We must try to teach our benighted brothers in the 'jungles of New York' and [in] the East what we have learned here in the progressive, enterprising West."[55] This attitude, which represented the more conservative elements of the WFM, could lead only to conflict. Suddenly, AFL organizers appeared in the previously neglected mountain states to compete with their WLU counterparts.[56] In Denver, AFL organizers tried to destroy WLU locals. Insisting that it had only attempted to organize the unorganized within its territory, the WLU, through its executive board, informed the AFL that it was too busy battling corporations to seek a fight with another labor organization. "If the officers and members of organized labor will do their duty, the Western Federation of Miners, the Western Labor Union included, there is a broad field for all while ninety per cent of those who toil remain unorganized."[57]

Instead of submitting to the AFL's demands,[58] western workers became more aggressive. They carefully cataloged the indignities that the WFM had borne with extreme patience but warned: "there comes a time in the history of all such imposition when patience ceases to be a virtue, and this juncture for the Western Federation of Miners has now arrived."[59] In the spring of 1902, when the AFL sent two delegates to the WFM convention urging reaffiliation with the federation, the WFM's journal commented: "The Western Federation of Miners and the Western Labor Union are ready to join forces with any labor organization that offers a remedy, but they don't propose to be led like sheep into a slaughter pen to await the butcher's knife without a struggle." Thus, the WFM, instead of dissolving the WLU and returning to Gompers's waiting arms, transformed the WLU into the American Labor Union (ALU) and more firmly embraced socialism.[60]

The American Labor Union, considered by Paul Brissenden to be the climactic development in the evolution of industrial unionism of the political-socialist type,[61] appeared too radical and too revolutionary for some socialists. While party leaders welcomed the ALU's endorsement, they deprecated its war on the AFL, compared the ALU to DeLeon's infamous Socialist Trades and Labor Alliance, and refused to acknowledge its existence as a recognized national labor organization.[62] The socialist left, however, immediately rose to defend the westerners. Debs characterized western labor as militant, progressive, liberal in spirit, with a class-conscious political program. "The class-conscious movement of the West," he wrote, "is historic in origin and development and every Socialist should recognize its mission and encourage its growth. It is here that the tide of social revolution will reach its flood and thence roll into other sections, giving impetus where needed and hastening the glorious day of triumph."[63]

Clearly, little room for compromise existed between western radicals and eastern labor leaders. The AFL could not allow its western competitor to enter national organizing territory without suffering potential losses. By the same token, the ALU, a declared enemy of capitalism, could not inch closer to the AFL, whose leader it accused of being controlled absolutely by capitalism.[64] Instead, the western radicals defied Gompers, continued to organize the unorganized of the West, and made threatening gestures east of the Mississippi and even beyond the Hudson. "We believe that the time has arrived when our organization should say in no uncertain language to this band of disruptionists [AFL leaders], 'hands off'," the WFM's executive board announced at the end of 1902. "We have no desire to interfere with their organization and demand that they discontinue their efforts to create disruption in our ranks."[65]

The more radical the WFM became, the more it grew, and the more popular its president became among western workers. By 1900, the WFM had won the warm backing of Debs, who became more enthusiastic as the western organization heightened its political consciousness and radicalism. In January 1902, Debs, accepting an invitation to address the coming convention, responded: "I have always felt that your organization is the most radical and progressive national body in the country, and I have it in my mind that it is to take a commanding part, if it does not lead, in the social revolution that will insure final emancipation to the struggling masses." The 1902 convention made Debs still happier by formally endorsing socialism, founding the American Labor Union, and proclaiming, in Boyce's farewell address: "Trade unions have had a fair trial, and it has been clearly demonstrated that they are unable to protect their members."[66]

While union leaders were most responsible for converting the WFM into a socialist organization, the rank and file exhibited no strong reservations about such radicalism, for in a labor organization more democratic than most, ideologically equivocal officials would have been removed. When Boyce retired, his successor, Charles Moyer, was equally committed to socialism. Moyer immediately reaffirmed the WFM's commitment to independent political action in "a determined effort to bring about such a change in our social and economic conditions as will result in a complete revolution of the present system of industrial slavery." He found politics and socialism no bar to union growth and in fact claimed that radicalism was responsible for the growth in the number of locals and members.[67] Correspondence to the WFM's journal from rank and filers also showed a heavy preponderance in favor of independent political action and socialism.[68] While the political views of the majority of WFM members are unclear, a significant, literate, and articulate union group certainly evinced an abiding concern for a radical transformation of American society.

Politics and socialism, however, did not by themselves bring the new dawn. Local battles were won, but the employers, allied with the older parties controlling state and national governments, seemed to be winning the war. "Pure and simple" trade unionism may have failed; but, seemingly, so had socialism. Consequently, just as Populism gave way to socialism and the WLU to the ALU, socialism was to give way to syndicalism; and the ALU would be succeeded by the IWW.

In 1904, the WFM, admitting the failure of its two previous attempts at dual unionism, tried for a third time with the Industrial Workers of the World (IWW). Much in the same way that the WLU and the ALU had been the Western Federation in disguise, the IWW for two years was simply the Western Federation plus a smattering of fellow travelers.[69] Though the WFM and the IWW broke sharply in 1907, the Western Federation could not fully deny its progeny. To an earlier generation of less sophisticated, more provincial Americans, Wobblies appeared the greatest threat to the established order—in short, "a clear and present danger."

The foundation of the Industrial Workers of the World seemed to confirm a prophecy made by Friedrich Engels in 1893. "In America, at least," he wrote, "I am strongly inclined to believe that the fatal hour of capitalism will have struck as soon as a native American working class will have replaced a working class composed in its majority by foreign immigrants."[70] The men who created the IWW were by and large native Americans, or the most Americanized immigrants, committed to interring capitalism in America.[71] In a sense, as Engels prophesied, the most radical working-class movement in American history, the one most feared by capitalists and government officials, came not from alien radicals but from native revolutionaries. And today it remains well worth asking why.

Though no simple and complete answers are at hand, some facts are apparent. The American West, through a unique conjunction of circumstances, produced the conditions most conducive to radical unionism. This region's industrialism altered social and economic arrangements more rapidly and drastically than elsewhere in America. Modern technology and corporate capitalism advanced too quickly for smooth adjustment—the rapid pace of economic growth resulted in individual failures and frustrations, social breakdowns, and mob violence. Seeking to stabilize competition, rationalize work processes, and reduce costs, western corporations encountered a labor force less tractable than the uprooted and ethnically divided immigrants of the East. The American West, like early industrial England, produced militant and destructive working-class demonstrations. Mining corporations and smelting companies could only control and discipline their workers with assistance from state and federal authorities. The alliance between corporate capitalism and government, which succeeded in polarizing western society, convinced western workers that the American nation suffered from grave political and social disorders that could be cured only through revolutionary action. Their past, their experiences, and their hopes for the future shaped western miners into radicals and revolutionaries.

In a larger sense, however, the development of radical unionism and the emergence of syndicalism in the American West was hardly unique. Simultaneously, thousands of miles removed geographically and farther away socially and spiritually, Italian and French labor organizations declared for syndicalism.[72] The origins of radical unionism in America, France, or Italy thus must be sought in the process of capitalist growth and the larger trends transforming the industrial world. Today, we need fewer vague generalizations about the uniqueness or significance of the American frontier and more intensive studies of social and economic structures in the capitalist, industrial, and urban American West. We also need comparative studies placing American labor history in the broader context of worldwide economic history, where all workers, regardless of nationality, tasted the fruits, both bitter and sweet, of the capitalist order.

Notes

This essay first appeared (in slightly different form) in *Labor History* 7 (Spring 1966): 131–54. An earlier version, entitled "The Role of Environment: The American West and Labor Radicalism," was read at a session on American Labor History sponsored by the Labor Historians' Association at the Mississippi Valley Historical Association Convention in April 1964. The present version has benefited from the trenchant critiques of session commentators Mark Perlman and Gerd Korman. I am also indebted to two of my former graduate students, Michael L. Johnson and Clyde Tyson, for research assistance and suggestions and to two of my colleagues at Northern Illinois University, Charles Freedeman and Kenneth N. Owens, for their helpful comments on the original version.

1. Louis Levine, "The Development of Syndicalism in America," *Political Science Quarterly* 28 (Sept. 1913): 451–79, quote on 452 (emphasis added).

2. Even among labor economists, there have been few substantial works dealing with western working-class developments. Vernon Jensen's *Heritage of Conflict: Labor Relations in the Nonferrous Metals Industry up to 1930* (Ithaca, N.Y.: Cornell University Press, 1950) is by far the best of such books and is indispensable to any student of the subject, particularly for its insights into the process of industrial relations and the evolution of the WFM. But it suffers from a lack of historical perspective and the failure to use the papers of public officials in the West and of other individuals involved in the area's labor conflicts. Equally indispensable to students of the subject is Selig Perlman and Philip Taft's *History of Labor in the United States, 1896–1932* (New York: Macmillan, 1935), 169–281. Here, again, historical perspective is limited to Turner's insights about the frontier, and local newspapers and trade union journals provide the bulk of the sources. Of less use is Benjamin M. Rastall's "Labor History of the Cripple Creek District," *Bulletin of the University of Wisconsin, No. 198,* Economic and Political Science Series, vol. 3, no. 1 (Madison, Wis., 1908), which, while providing solid information about the labor war in Cripple Creek, is strongly biased against radical labor organizations and thus accepts at face value many of the employers' charges against the WFM. A similar but superior work by a historian is Robert W. Smith's *Coeur d'Alene Mining War of 1892: A Case Study of an Industrial Dispute* (Corvallis: Oregon State University Press, 1961), an unrevised 1935 doctoral dissertation that refers to Perlman and Taft's work of the same year as the most recent and authoritative interpretation of labor developments in the Mountain West and thus also falls into the Turnerian trap. The two best treatments of the IWW, Paul Brissenden's *I.W.W.: A Study of American Syndicalism* (New York: Russell and Russell, 1957) and John G. Brooks's *American Syndicalism: The I.W.W.* (New York: Macmillan, 1913) are both dated and contain only the briefest treatments of the western origins of working-class radicalism. Robert F. Tyler's "I.W.W. and the West," *American Quarterly* 12 (Summer 1960): 175–87, is more concerned with investigating the views of the IWW held by eastern literary figures and dilettantes than with the actual western origins of syndicalism, which he tends to devaluate.

3. During industrial conflicts, the American West produced more than its share of murder and mayhem. Harry Orchard, the siege at Bull Hill, and the Everett

Massacre cannot be ignored. John Dos Passos can excite the reader with wild tales of Wobblies acting in the American pioneer spirit (*U.S.A.* [New York: Modern Library, 1937] and *Midcentury* [Cambridge, Mass.: Houghton Mifflin, 1961]), and Stewart Holbrook can fabricate a "Rocky Mountain Revolution" (*The Rocky Mountain Revolution* [New York: Henry Holt, 1956]). But of greater importance to the historian is an understanding of the sources of western working-class radical economic, social, and political doctrine.

4. Rodman W. Paul's *Mining Frontiers of the Far West, 1848–1880* (New York: Holt, Rinehart and Winston, 1963), 9–10, 136–38 (quote on 136), 195–96, is by far the best scholarly account of the urban-industrial transformation of the Mountain West and proves decisively the irrelevance of old Turnerian terminology.

5. The changing nature of mining and smelting processes and their increasing corporate concentration can best be followed in *Report of the Industrial Commission on the Relations and Conditions of Capital and Labor Employed in the Mining Industry,* vol. 12 (Washington, D.C., 1911), 191–618 passim (hereafter *Capital and Labor in Mining*).

6. Percy S. Fritz, *Colorado: The Centennial State* (New York: Prentice Hall, 1941), 304, 311–12, 367; Robert G. Athearn, *High Country Empire: The High Plains and Rockies* (New York: McGraw-Hill, 1960), 267–68.

7. Hubert Howe Bancroft, *The Works of Hubert Howe Bancroft,* vol. 31: *History of Washington, Idaho, and Montana, 1845–1889* (San Francisco: History Co., 1890), 752n, 755n, 763–64, 769; Joseph K. Howard, *Montana: High, Wide, and Handsome* (New Haven, Conn.: Yale University Press, 1943), 83–84.

8. Bancroft, *Works of Bancroft,* 31:572; Merrill D. Beale and Merle W. Wells, *History of Idaho* (New York: Lewis Historical Publishing Co., 1959), 1.

9. Most historians of the region agree on its achievement of an urban and industrial character by the 1890s. As Athearn writes in *High Country Empire:* "The very concentration of miners' cabins, crowded together in an area of highly concentrated wealth automatically provided an urban type of living" (77). See also Bancroft, *Works of Bancroft,* 31:752n, 755n, 759; Fritz, *Colorado,* 367; Paul, *Mining Frontiers,* 68–69.

10. The same authorities agree on the speed of change, which can be charted in the federal census returns from 1890 to 1910 for the mining counties and smelter cities of the Mountain West. See U.S. Census Office, *Compendium of the Eleventh Census: 1890,* pt. 1: *Population* (Washington, D.C., 1892), 478, 481, 496, 541, 599; idem, *Twelfth Census of the United States Taken in the Year 1900,* pt. 1: *Population* (Washington, D.C., 1901), 495–96, 499, 511, 648, 664, 739–41, 744, 768; U.S. Bureau of the Census, *Thirteenth Census of the United States Taken in the Year 1910,* pt. 2: *Population* (Washington, D.C., 1914), 216–27, 228, 430, 432, 1156, 1158–59. For the rapidity of the social and economic change in Montana, see Howard, *Montana,* 4–5. On the destabilizing effects of rapid economic growth, see Mancure Olson Jr., "Rapid Growth as a Destabilizing Force," *Journal of Economic History* 23 (Dec. 1963): 529–52, and Carter Goodrich's comments in ibid., 553–58.

11. For the early origins of miners' unions in California and Nevada, see Paul, *Mining Frontiers,* 69–70, 94–95; Jensen, *Heritage,* 10–18.

12. The census figures cited above reveal the ethnic characteristics of the mountain states' mining and smelting centers. Every district in Colorado, Idaho, and

Montana had, unlike other American industrial cities, a native-born majority. Furthermore, the foreign-born came predominantly from the British Isles (including Ireland) and Scandinavia and were hardly representative of the more recent waves of immigration altering the U.S. ethnic complexion. An unusually large number of foreign-born were also naturalized citizens. Paul found that by the 1870s Cornishmen and Irishmen predominated among the foreign-born miners (*Mining Frontiers*, 122, 182). Emma F. Langdon, a union sympathizer and a participant in the 1903–4 Cripple Creek civil war, saw the local miners, who were mostly native-born plus German, Swedish, and Irish immigrants, as more difficult to subdue than the Italians and Hungarians employed in eastern coal mines (*The Cripple Creek Strike* [New York: Arno Press, 1969], 34). In the Coeur d'Alenes in 1899, 132 of 528 imprisoned miners were native-born, the remainder being of greatly varying nationalities; and 208 of the foreign-born were naturalized citizens. See U.S. Congress, *Coeur D'Alene Mining Troubles*, 56th Cong., 1st sess., S. Doc. 24, 13. For other estimates of the ethnic complexion of western mining communities, see the testimony of union officials and mine and smelter managers in *Capital and Labor in Mining*, 313, 377, 485, 572, 588, 595. The overwhelmingly Anglo-Saxon origins of the WFM's local and national leadership becomes obvious when one looks at the names listed in the monthly union directory published in the *Miners' Magazine*.

13. Paul points out that as mining became more complex and costly, Irish and Cornish professionals replaced American amateurs (*Mining Frontiers*, 69–70, 94–95, 122, 182). John Calderwood, the first union leader in Cripple Creek, had entered coal mines at the age of nine and later attended mining school. Holbrook notes that Ed Boyce, the WFM president from 1897 to 1903, worked as a professional miner from 1884 until his election to the presidency in 1896 and that his successor, Charles Moyer, had been a skilled worker in the Lead, South Dakota, smelter complex (*Rocky Mountain Revolution*, 74). WFM, *Proceedings of the Eleventh Convention* (1903), 17; May A. Hutton, *The Coeur d'Alenes; or, A Tale of the Modern Inquisition in Idaho* (Denver: by the author, 1900), 53–54. Furthermore, there is every reason to believe that mine and smelter operators preferred skilled, professional workmen to "pioneers" or "frontiersmen" and that wage differentials would attract European and eastern miners to the American West.

14. The testimony of Coeur d'Alene residents in *Capital and Labor in Mining*, 389–546 passim, reveals the community support won by striking miners. See James H. Hawley to H. F. Brinton, Esq., Nov. 1, 1892; Hawley to George A. Pettibone, Nov. 15, 1892; Hawley to Pettibone, Jan. 3, 1893; Hawley to Patrick F. Reddy, Mar. 20, 1893; Hawley to J. F. Poynton, Apr. 29, 1893; Hawley to Pettibone, May 4, 1893; Hawley to Poynton, Oct. 17, 1893; Hawley to Reddy, Feb. 5, 1894, all in James H. Hawley Letter Books, Idaho State Historical Society, Moscow; Smith, *Coeur d'Alene Mining War of 1892*, 38–40; Hutton, *Coeur d'Alenes*.

15. F. Augustus Heinze to Michael McCormack, President, Butte Miners' Union, June 12, 1900, in *Miners' Magazine* 1 (July 1900): 47, 49; ibid., 2 (Jan. 1901): 12–13; Butte *Reveille*, May 23, 1904, 8, and June 6, 1904, 5. The *Reveille*, which was the Butte Miners' Union's official paper, was owned at various times by the union, by Heinze, and by the Amalgamated Copper Company. It is one of the better printed sources from which to follow the tangled Butte story. Cf. Jensen, *Heritage*, 298.

16. "Stenographic Report of the Advisory Board Appointed by Governor James H. Peabody to Investigate and Report upon Labor Difficulties in the State of Colorado and More Particularly Colorado City," in James H. Hawley Papers, Idaho State Historical Society, Moscow, best describes the anxiety of Cripple Creek businessmen and mine owners to settle labor disputes equitably with their workers and the friendlier attitude of local business and capital as compared with national interests in Colorado City symbolized by the United States Smelting and Reduction Company. Cf. *Capital and Labor in Mining*, 389–564 passim; William D. Haywood, *Bill Haywood's Book: The Autobiography of William D. Haywood* (New York: International Publishers, 1958), 117–28.

17. B. Goldsmith to Simeon G. Reed, June 6, 1887; Reed to Victor M. Clement, Mar. 29, 1889; Clement to Reed, Nov. 23 and Dec. 2, 1889, all in Simeon G. Reed Papers, microfilm, Idaho State Historical Society, Moscow; Job Harriman, "The Class War in Idaho," *Miners' Magazine* 5 (Oct. 8, 1903): 8; Haywood, *Bill Haywood's Book*, 80–81; Smith, *Coeur d'Alene Mining War of 1892*, 24–35.

18. The sources cited above describe fully the impact of technological change.

19. The testimony of mine owners and mill and smelter managers in *Capital and Labor in Mining*, passim, covers the pressures common to all such enterprises in labor and product markets.

20. Haywood, *Bill Haywood's Book*, 80–81.

21. Smith's *Coeur d'Alene Mining War of 1892* is the fullest account of the conflict and its relation to the founding of the WFM. Cf. J. Harriman, "The Class War," *Miners' Magazine* 5 (Oct. 22, 1903): 9–12, and (Nov. 5, 1903): 13; Jensen, *Heritage*, 25–37.

22. The quotations come from Foster Rhea Dulles, *Labor in America* (New York: T. Y. Crowell, 1949), 209; Louis Lorwin, *The American Federation of Labor* (Washington, D.C.: AFL, 1933), 84–85; Charles A. Madison, *American Labor Leaders* (New York: Harper, 1950), 264; Selig Perlman, *A History of Trade Unionism in the United States* (New York: Macmillan, 1922), 213; idem, *A Theory of the Labor Movement* (New York: Macmillan, 1949), 227; Perlman and Taft, *History of Labor*, 169, 178, 189; Fred Thompson, *The I.W.W.: Its First Fifty Years* (Chicago: IWW, 1955), 9.

23. It seems strange to seek to explain violent conflict in the Mountain West in Turnerian terms when at the very same time in the "settled, civilized" East, open warfare prevailed at Homestead, in Chicago during the Pullman strike, and even later in Lawrence, Massachusetts, and Paterson, New Jersey. It seems equally foolish to account for the creation in the Mountain West of private armies in frontier terms when eastern employers and workers did likewise. The coal and iron police appeared in Pennsylvania, not Montana; Colorado employers and workers may have utilized western "desperadoes" and gunmen, but employers and workers in New York's garment industry made ample use of similar services provided by the metropolis' gunslingers and club wielders. Such violence and conflict, wherever it erupted, seems more a characteristic of the early stages of industrialism than of any peculiar geographical environment.

24. Butte *Bystander,* Jan. 20, 1894, 2; Jan. 27, 1894, 1; Apr. 21, 1894, 2; May 5, 1894, 2; Sept. 1, 1894, 2; *Populist (Butte) Tribune,* Jan. 20, 1894, 6; *Montana Silverite,* Apr. 20, 1894, 4.

25. *Capital and Labor in Mining*, 389–90, 531–32, 537; Butte *Bystander*, Apr. 21, 1894, 3; Hutton, *Coeur d'Alenes*, 70.

26. Anonymous, Slocan, British Columbia, Miners' Union, to Editor, *Miners' Magazine* 3 (Apr. 1902): 30–31; ibid., 1 (Feb. 1900): 28; Haywood, *Bill Haywood's Book*, 30–31; Fritz, *Colorado*, 368. For the principles of the Knights of Labor, which must have influenced some western members, see Brissenden, *I.W.W.*, 32; Gerald Grob, *Workers and Utopia* (Evanston, Ill.: Northwestern University Press, 1961), 34–137 passim; Norman Ware, *The Labor Movement in the United States, 1860–1895* (New York: D. Appleton, 1929).

27. In Montana, the major Populist newspapers were labor journals; reading them makes clear the working-class nature of Montana populism. State labor conferences and Populist conventions often met at the same time in the same city and passed resolutions supporting and complimenting each other. See Butte *Bystander*, Jan. 20, 1894, 2, and Feb. 24, 1894, 1. The Silver Bow (Butte) Trades and Labor Assembly called for all lower-class groups to unite at the polls: "The farmer must join hands with the wage earners of all classes. . . . The people's party is organized by those from the humble walks of life to destroy monopoly and give equal and exact justice to all" (*Bystander*, Oct. 1, 1894, 1). The Populist State Committee chairman was an official of the American Railway Union, and party candidates in Silver Bow County were mostly union members (*Bystander*, Oct. 3, 1894, 2, and Oct. 8, 1894, 2). In 1895, the separate labor parties in Montana amalgamated to obtain more effective political action and issued a call to the state's farmers: "We . . . appeal to the farmers of Montana to organize into some form of union . . . and send delegates to the States Trades and Labor Council, in order that we may mutually aid and assist each other in the great struggle to emancipate labor from . . . industrial slavery" (*Bystander*, Nov. 26, 1895, 2–3, and Dec. 3, 1895, 2). In Anaconda, the local Populist paper, the *Populist Courier*, was edited by a member of the WFM and the Knights of Labor; the Missoula paper, the *Montana Silverite*, was the official journal of the local AFL unions and always emphasized labor reforms before free silver. See *Montana Silverite*, June 22, 1894, 1; Aug. 3, 1894, 7; Aug. 31, 1894, 1; Feb. 1, 1895, 1; Nov. 29, 1895, 1. The *Populist (Butte) Tribune* also was primarily a labor paper (Jan. 20, 1894, 1; Apr. 21, 1894, 1; May 5, 1894, 4; June 30, 1894, 8; June 16, 1894, 5; Feb. 20, 1895, 5). In Idaho's Coeur d'Alenes, local labor groups were indistinguishable from the Populists, and Ed Boyce, the WFM president, was a power in the party and a Populist representative in the state assembly. See the testimony of J. R. Sovereign and Sheriff James D. Young in *Capital and Labor in Mining*, 405, 437, 531–32, 537. The *Pueblo Courier*, the official WFM organ in Colorado, was also a Populist political sheet.

28. Butte *Bystander*, June 2, 1894, 1, and May 21, 1895, 3; *Montana (Missoula) Silverite*, May 24, 1895, 1.

29. The James H. Hawley Papers show clearly the dependence of the Democratic party in Idaho on the support of working-class Populists in the Coeur d'Alenes; for example, the Populist governor "Bloody Bridles" Waite of Colorado was elected largely through the efforts of working-class supporters and always promptly paid his debts. The full strength of working-class Populism is revealed in the election statistics for the mining counties in W. Dean Burnham, *Presidential Ballots, 1836–*

1892 (Baltimore, Md.: Johns Hopkins University Press, 1955), 306–17, 366–67, 600–601; Edgar E. Robinson, *The Presidential Vote, 1896–1932* (Stanford, Calif.: Stanford University Press, 1934), 150–54, 174–77, 256–60.

30. All political parties in the Mountain West were officially for free silver, but this similarity tends to cloak important qualitative differences. For example, mine owners were not as committed to free silver as popular legend implies. Weldon B. Heyburn, attorney for the Coeur d'Alene Mine Owners' Association (and himself a mining speculator), led the Gold Republicans in Idaho. See Claudius O. Johnson, "The Story of Silver Politics in Idaho, 1892–1896," *Pacific Northwest Quarterly* 33 (July 1942): 283–96. Elmer Ellis, in his study of Henry Moore Teller, the Colorado Silver Republican, discovered the same tendencies. He found free silver sentiment waning among mine owners by 1894 as they recognized the hard economic facts of life; and he emphasizes that Fred Dubois, leader of Idaho's Silver Republicans, would not consider a coalition with Populism because simple silverites differed with Populism on all issues except free silver. Most wealthy mine owners had drifted into the more conservative Republican party by 1899: "It seems almost impossible in this State (Colorado) for any man with an independent fortune to refrain from allying with the Republican party" (Governor Charles S. Thomas to William Jennings Bryan, Dec. 22, 1899, quoted in Elmer Ellis, *Henry Moore Teller: Defender of the West* [Caldwell, Idaho: Caxton Printers, 1941], 237, 248, 325).

31. The mountain states' Populists endorsed all the usual planks (including free silver; nationalization of telephones, telegraphs, railroads, and mines) as well as specific labor reforms (the eight-hour day; sanitary inspections of workshop, mill, and home; employers' liability; the abolition of the contract system on public works; and the abolition of the sweating system). See *Montana (Missoula) Silverite,* Nov. 29, 1895, 1; Butte *Bystander,* Feb. 24, 1894, 1, and May 14, 1895, 2. On the radical content of midwestern and southern Populism, see Norman Pollack, *The Populist Response to Industrial America* (Cambridge, Mass.: Harvard University Press, 1962); C. Vann Woodward, "The Populist Heritage and the Intellectual," *American Scholar* 29 (Winter 1959–60): 55–72; idem, *Tom Watson: Agrarian Rebel* (New York: Macmillan, 1938).

32. The movement of the AFL toward less radical political action can best be followed in *The American Federationist* 1–3 (1894–96) and in convention debates for 1893–96 contained in *Proceedings of the American Federation of Labor, 1893– 1896* (Bloomington, Ill.: AFL, 1906).

33. Minute Books, Silver City, Idaho, Miners' Union, Local 62, Bancroft Library, University of California at Berkeley.

34. The growth of the union can be followed in correspondence and reports in the *Miners' Magazine,* especially the regularly published union directory, which grew much longer between 1900 and 1903. See particularly 2 (June 1901): 2024 and 4 (July 1903): 28, in which the executive board reported that, since the 1902 convention, which endorsed independent political action and progressive unionism, WFM membership increased by one-third to reach its peak.

35. Butte *Bystander,* May 15, 1897, 4; *Miners' Magazine* 1 (Jan. 1900): 16–18 and 5 (Oct. 22, 1903): 5; Haywood, *Bill Haywood's Book,* 71; Jensen, *Heritage,* 70–71.

36. Butte *Bystander,* May 15, 1897, 1; cf. *Proceedings of the American Federation of Labor* (1896), 59.

37. Governor Norman Willey to Senator George Shoup, July 5, 1892; Willey to President Benjamin Harrison, June 24, 1892, both in Governor's Letter Books and Correspondence, microfilm, Idaho State Historical Society, Moscow.

38. Attorney-General George H. Roberts to Senators Fred Dubois and George Shoup, July 12, 1892; Roberts to Dubois, July 13 14, 1892, all in ibid.

39. Willey to Charles W. O'Neil, July 15, 1892; A. J. Pinkham to Senators Dubois and Shoup, July 18, 1892; Willey to President Harrison, July 27, 1892, all in ibid.

40. Between 1894 and 1899, the WFM had rebuilt its strength in the Coeur d'Alenes and fully organized most of the area's mines, with the exception of the most important, the Bunker Hill and Sullivan mines. The Bunker Hill's intransigent management made labor conflict inevitable, setting the stage for the 1899 debacle and the eradication of the WFM from the Coeur d'Alenes. James H. Hawley's letters to his law partner Will Puckett (June 19, 21, 27, 29, 1899, and July 2, 13, 1899, Hawley Papers) reveal the Boise attorney's newfound detestation of the WFM and his flirtation with the Mine Owners' Association, which was paying the cost of the prosecution. Cf. Pinkerton Reports to Governor Frank Steunenberg, June 24–25 and July 2–3, 1899, Steunenberg Papers, microfilm, Idaho Historical Society, Moscow; James H. Hawley, *History of Idaho*, vol. 1 (Chicago: S. J. Clarke, 1920), 250–55.

41. After 1899, the Mine Owners' Association successfully organized a company union (thus denying employment to WFM members), exerted political coercion on their workers, and attempted to employ Borah as their political manager. See M. A. Folsom to William A. Borah, May 7, 1902, Borah Papers, microfilm, Idaho State Historical Society, Moscow; Pinkerton Report to Governor Frank Steunenberg, July 6, 1899, Steunenberg Papers; Testimony of Joseph MacDonald, Manager, Helena-Frisco Mine, *Capital and Labor in Mining*, 484; Hutton, *Coeur d'Alenes*, 133–34.

42. U.S. Congress, *A Report on Labor Disturbances in the State of Colorado from 1880 to 1904*, 58th Cong., 3d sess., S. Doc. 122, 75–85, 87–101; Butte *Bystander*, Sept. 24, Nov. 26, 1896, Feb. 7, 1897; Rastall, "Labor History of the Cripple Creek District," 37–43; Jensen, *Heritage*, 41–53, 57–59.

43. *Miners' Magazine* 3 (Jan. 1902): 22–23, 3 (May 1902): 15–18, 4 (Feb. 1903): 1–3; WFM, *Convention Proceedings*, 1902, 17; *American Labor Union Journal*, Mar. 5, 1903, 1; Jensen, *Heritage*, 88–95.

44. Testimony of Moyer and Haywood, "Stenographic Report of the Advisory Board Appointed by Governor James H. Peabody," 80, 81, 84, 109, 118.

45. Ibid., 170, 158–95.

46. U.S. Congress, *A Report on Labor Disturbances in the State of Colorado*, 115–282; *Miners' Magazine* 4–5 (1904–5) contains full coverage on the Colorado conflict as seen by the WFM; Jensen, *Heritage*, 127–55.

47. *Miners' Magazine* 5 (Dec. 10, 1903): 6.

48. Butte *Bystander*, May 15, 1897, 4; *Miners' Magazine* 1 (June 1900): 41.

49. Butte *Bystander*, Dec. 22, 1894, 2, and May 7, 1895, 2.

50. Ed Boyce to Samuel Gompers, Mar. 16, 1897, Gompers to Boyce, Mar. 26, 1897, Boyce to Gompers, Apr. 7, 1897, Gompers's Statement, May 1, 1897, all printed in U.S. Congress, *Labor Troubles in Idaho*, 56th Cong., 1st sess., S. Doc. 42, 8–13. For an uncritical defense of the AFL position, see Philip Taft, *The A. F. of L. in the Time of Gompers* (New York: Harper, 1957), 150–52.

51. The Salt Lake City meeting was the culmination of a labor conference called in Chicago on September 27, 1897, by Eugene Debs to rally all radical labor unionists and believers in solidarity and industrial unionism. See Butte *Bystander,* Oct. 16, 1897, 1; Nov. 20, 1897, 2; Nov. 27, 1897, 1; *Miners' Magazine* 1 (Jan. 1900): 24–26.

52. Walter MacArthur to Gompers, May 20, 1898, quoted in Taft, *A. F. of L. in the Time of Gompers,* 153. MacArthur's impressions about the miners' sincere belief in Boyce's radicalism contradicts John McMullen's (leader of the WFM conservatives) assertion that the majority of WFM members were neither radicals nor socialists. See Jensen, *Heritage,* 189.

53. Butte *Reveille,* May 14, 1901, 1; Butte *People,* Nov. 9, 1901, 1; *Miners' Magazine* 1 (Feb. 1901): 31–33.

54. Butte *Reveille,* Sept. 4, 1900, 3; Sept. 18, 1900, 6; Apr. 9, 1901, 4; Apr. 23, 1901, 4; June 11, 1901, 2.

55. Press Committee, Local 89, Gilman, Colorado, to Editor, Dec. 27, 1901, *Miners' Magazine* 3 (Feb. 1902): 42–43. Another rank and filer seeking a rapprochement with eastern labor criticized pure and simple unionism and called on both the AFL and the WLU to give way before a new national organization based on solidarity and free transfer between crafts. He concluded: "If we ever unite with the East on these broad lines the West must give way first. If we don't they will continue to place the burden on us and the Western Labor Union." See M. F. Coll to Editor, *Miners' Magazine* 3 (Apr. 1902): 25–26. Of course, I must agree with Perlman and Taft (*History of Labor,* 214–15, 217) that local conditions had something to do with western dualism; but to concentrate on geographical peculiarities is to overlook what were real ideological differences. Western workers, as shown above, had radical backgrounds. They had engaged in partisan political activity and would continue to do so, and they supported industrial unionism of a strong social reformist nature. While western short-run objectives—higher wages, reduced hours, and so forth—did not differ basically from those of AFL unions, their long-run aims and avowed opposition to time contracts flaunted basic AFL principles.

56. In the past, the AFL had made no attempts to organize western workers, thinking it an unpromising possibility. See John B. Lennon to Frank Morrison, Aug. 8, 1898, AFL Papers, State Historical Society of Wisconsin, Madison. By 1901, however, AFL organizers were busy in Denver and other mountain-state cities. See Butte *People,* Nov. 16, 1901, 1, and Nov. 30, 1901, 1.

57. Butte *People,* Dec. 21, 1901, 7; *Miners' Magazine* 2 (Dec. 1901): 4–8 and 3 (Jan. 1902): 10–11.

58. These demands included disbanding all "dual" unions in Denver, the abolition of the WLU, and the WFM's reaffiliation with the AFL.

59. *Miners' Magazine* 3 (Mar. 1902): 38–42 and 3 (Apr. 1902): 2–5; Butte *People,* Feb. 12, 1902, 5, and Mar. 17, 1902, 1.

60. *Miners' Magazine* 3 (June 1902): 4, 14–16; *Labor World,* May 19, 1902, 5; June 2, 1902, 1–2; June 9, 1902, 1, 5; *American Labor Union Journal,* Nov. 20, 1902, 1, 4.

61. Brissenden, *I.W.W.,* 45–46.

62. G. A. Hoehn, "The American Labor Movement," *International Socialist Review* 3 (Jan. 1903): 410–11; *Labor World,* Aug. 8, 1902, 3; *Miners' Magazine* 3 (Dec.

1902): 33–42; Ira Kipnis, *The American Socialist Movement, 1897–1912* (New York: Columbia University Press, 1952), 144–45; Nathan Fine, *Farmer and Labor Parties in the United States, 1828–1928* (New York: Russell and Russell, 1928), 277–78.

63. Eugene V. Debs, "The Western Labor Movement," *International Socialist Review* 3 (Nov. 1902): 257–65.

64. *American Labor Union Journal*, Oct. 23, 1902, 2.

65. Ibid., Nov. 6, 1902, 1, and Jan. 1, 1903, 4; *Labor World*, July 11, 1902, 3; June 5, 1903, 2; July 3, 1903, 1; *Miners' Magazine* 3 (Nov. 1902): 23–34 and 4 (Jan. 1903): 40–41.

66. WFM, *Convention Proceedings*, 1902, 8–10; *Miners' Magazine* 3 (July 1902): 23–33; Debs's quotations are in ibid. 3 (Jan 1902): 16 and 4 (Feb. 1903): 37–39.

67. WFM, *Convention Proceedings*, 1904, 202–3; *Miners' Magazine* 4 (July 1903): 4–5.

68. While there is apparently no way to quantify the political sentiments of WFM members—resulting in dispute as to the extent of radicalism and socialism in the union—the available evidence suggests strong socialist leanings. The mining-smelter areas, especially Butte and Denver, were the strongest socialist regions in the Mountain West and among the strongest in the nation. The letters-to-the-editor column of the *Miners' Magazine* was open to a variety of opinions, even those opposed to official WFM policy, but the bulk of the letters from rank and filers and local unions endorsed either socialism or other forms of independent political action. The testimony of labor leaders and rank-and-file hard-rock miners before a government commission showed overt hostility to capitalism and explicit endorsement of public ownership of the basic means of production. See *Capital and Labor in Mining*, 213–14, 246, 255, 362–63. As late as 1906, WFM rank and filers refused to cooperate with the AFL's political program because it was based on employer-employee harmony. See William H. Pierce, Secretary, Randsburg, California, Miners' Union, to Frank Morrison, July 30, 1906; R. D. Mitchell, John McClunes, David M. Speare, Phoenix, British Columbia, Miners' Union Committee, to Samuel Gompers, Aug. 4, 1906, both in AFL Papers. Emma Langdon, an observer of the Cripple Creek labor war and a WFM sympathizer, pointed out the anticapitalist bias of the local miners in *Cripple Creek Strike*, 283.

69. Brissenden, *I.W.W.*, 57–228 passim; Jensen, *Heritage*, 160–96.

70. Quoted in Pollack, *Populist Response*, 84.

71. See p. 44 for the WFM's ethnic characteristics. An examination of the trial transcript (*United States v. W. D. Haywood, et al.*) of the 1918 Chicago Wobbly trials shows that of the IWW leaders who testified about their nationality and citizenship, more than half were citizens, one-third of whom were native-born, and nearly a majority of the aliens came from Great Britain, Ireland, and Canada.

72. Val R. Lorwin, *The French Labor Movement* (Cambridge, Mass.: Harvard University Press, 1954), 29–40; Maurice F. Neufeld, *Italy: School for Awakening Countries* (Ithaca, N.Y.: Cornell University Press, 1961), 336–38, 352–54.

· 3 ·

The IWW, the Culture of Poverty,
and the Concept of Power

IN June 1905, over one hundred individuals reflecting every nuance of American radicalism met in Chicago to declare total war on American capitalism. Resolving that "the working class and the employing class have nothing in common," they founded the IWW to carry on their struggle against the established order. Created in the same year that revolution shocked czarist Russia, the IWW was born in a flood of optimism, only to drown thirteen years later (1917–18) beneath a wave of federal repression.

Between its birth and its repression, the IWW existed perilously. Internal dissension—not unlike the sectarian warfare common to other left-wing organizations—at times paralyzed it; secessionist movements took away its largest affiliates and the bulk of its membership; and violent opposition by private employers, combined with governmental hostility, recurrently threatened its total destruction. Yet, somehow or other, the IWW maintained a precarious life. Even after the federal government imprisoned its most prominent leaders in 1918, and various states made IWW membership a crime, it survived. Unable to maintain a vital role in American radicalism after 1918, however, the IWW disappeared into what journalist Dan Wakefield characterized as "haunted halls," from which its ghostly spirit emerged occasionally to trouble America's conscience. In this essay, I would like to analyze the nature of the IWW's radicalism; its relationship to the "Other America" of the Progressive Era; and, by implication, at least, its relationship (if there was any) to radical social movements in the contemporary United States.

The Wobblies were as much an uneasy but vital presence in Progressive America as the black militants and middle-class white radicals are in today's "Great Society." Yesterday's undisciplined radicals—and they were certainly that—shed unwanted light on dark spots in an otherwise bright social and economic landscape. The IWW, like contemporary black and white militants, despised the "power structure" and confronted established authority with nonviolent, direct action. Wobblies also preached power and promised revolution, beliefs that sometimes involved the organization in riots and violence. Moreover, Wobblies, like many contemporary critics of American society, practiced an antiorganizational, semiutopian, almost anarchistic radicalism. Today's emergent radicalism leads one to inquire again into the character of the IWW's protest, and, by suggesting different questions about the Wobblies' history, it also opens up new modes of historical analysis.[1]

A good place to start any analysis of the IWW is with the work of three scholarly pathfinders on that radical frontier: Carleton Parker, Louis Levine, and John Graham Brooks.[2] All three saw the IWW for what it indeed was: a distinctive American response to a singular concatenation of circumstances peculiar to the period 1890–1917. Writing long before the "consensus school" of American historiography came into existence and living in an age when class conflict ruptured American society,[3] Parker, Levine, and Brooks did not look to Europe for the ideological taproots of Wobbly radicalism; nor did they dismiss IWW ideology as unrelated to the realities of American society. Instead, they located its origin and the sources of its radical ideology directly within the national tradition; in fact, they found it in the most American of environments: the Wild West.

However brilliant Levine's insights into the origins of American syndicalism, he did not carry his analysis far enough to explain or to assess the IWW's unique role in the history of American radicalism. However enlightening Parker's description of the Wobbly ideal-type as a finished product of Progressive America's antisocial environment, his attempt to apply social psychology to labor economics placed too great a burden on the relatively young disciplines of psychology and psychiatry.[4]

Just as Parker fifty years ago expanded knowledge of the IWW's essence by using the then novel concepts of social psychology in his investigation of the organization's members, we today can broaden our comprehension of the Wobblies by examining IWW history and theory in the light of certain precepts borrowed from cultural anthropology. Particularly relevant in this context, I think, is the concept of the "culture of poverty"—more precisely, the "subculture of poverty"—as elaborated by Oscar Lewis.[5]

Lewis's studies demonstrate that the subculture of poverty emerges from a society that contains the following dominant characteristics: (1) a cash economy, wage labor, and production for profit; (2) a persistently high rate of unemployment and underemployment for unskilled labor; (3) low wages; (4) a paucity of social, political, and economic organization, whether on a voluntary basis or by government imposition, for the low-income population; and (5) pervading the whole society, a set of values imposed by the dominant class, which stress the accumulation of wealth and property and the possibility of upward mobility through thrift and explain low economic status as the result of personal inadequacy or inferiority.[6]

Although Lewis's loosely defined characteristics might apply to almost any society in the process of early industrialization, they are particularly relevant to the America of 1877–1917. Unencumbered by a feudal-aristocratic tradition and the paternalistic anticapitalism associated with it, America's dominant business class could impose its values on society with a vengeance. This was singularly true in the American West, where, in less than a generation, industrialization and urbanization tamed a wilderness. There, where social structure was fluid, government was weak, trade unionism remained relatively ineffective, and the spirit of rugged individualism reigned supreme, the strong prevailed. Those who failed to rise were pushed off into society's backwaters to endure as best they could the ills associated with failure in a competitive industrial society.[7]

The men who dominated the IWW—Vincent St. John, William D. Haywood, Ben H. Williams, Frank Little, and Joseph J. Ettor, among others—formed their images and ideas of American society within just such a competitive environment.[8] They saw a society that had no place for workers whose skills had been rendered obsolete by technological innovation; African Americans emancipated by law but denied the social and economic freedom to make their emancipation meaningful; European immigrants drawn to the land of promise, only to dwell in urban slums and work in dark mills; farmers' sons forced off the land to search for work wherever it could be had. All of these groups came from, or were pushed into, the fringes of America's subcultures of poverty. There, they absorbed the characteristic life experiences associated with poverty as defined by Lewis: "family disruption, violence, brutality, cheapness of life, lack of love, and lack of education." Moreover, existing within the subculture of poverty, they lacked the intermediate social and economic institutions necessary to shield them from the worst shocks involved in the process of industrialization.[9]

The men and women—mostly men—who associated with the IWW in its heyday were largely first-generation citizens of an industrial society. In the case of immigrants from the south and east of Europe, this was obvious: Italians, Jews, Poles, Slovaks, Hungarians, and others first experienced urban-industrial life on their arrival in the New World. But dispossessed, native-born Americans were equally newcomers to industrial society; like E. J. Hobsbawm's first-generation English industrial workers, such native Americans could be considered internal immigrants who journeyed from a preindustrial to an industrial society.[10] Caught between two systems and two modes of existence, these immigrants—internal and external—were indeed uprooted. Torn from an old, ordered, and comprehensible way of life, they had not yet been able to replace it with an integrated and meaningful mode of existence. So they remained the human flotsam and jetsam abandoned during early industrial capitalism's frequent shipwrecks.

Contemporary students of the IWW perceived as much. The IWW "has thrived on the discontent of overworked and underpaid foreign laborers," commented a reporter. Rexford Tugwell aptly characterized the timber beast that was attracted to the IWW. "He is wracked with strange diseases and tortured by unrealized dreams that haunt his soul. . . . The blanket-stiff is a man without a home. . . . the void of his atrophied affections is filled with a resentful despair and bitterness against the society that self-righteously cast him out." Carleton Parker, after a careful study based on personal interviews with many West Coast Wobblies, concluded that they were floaters, men without homes, wives, women, and normal sex. The men who appear in his case studies shared lives of brutality, degradation, and violence, "starting with the long hours and dreary winters of the farms they ran away from, or the sour-smelling bunkhouse in a coal village through their character-debasing experience with the drifting 'hire and fire' life . . . on to the vicious social and economic life of the winter unemployed."[11]

European immigrants, although more likely to experience normal family lives, also dwelled closer to the subculture of poverty than they did to the mainstream of American society. In this country but not of it, as Oscar Handlin has perceptively noted, they too lacked the intermediate institutions necessary to insulate them from the ravages of the industrial order.[12] If they were fortunate enough—like most Jewish and Italian immigrants—to find a minimal measure of security within the warm family circle, they met more than their share of brutality, violence, degradation, and exploitation out on the job or, sometimes, on the picket line. And if they came from ethnic groups lacking the traditional family links cherished by Jews and Italians, they also might lead lives without homes, wives, women, and normal sex.[13] When Big Bill Haywood came east to organize for the IWW, he saw the possibilities for mass recruiting among the new immigrants, telling an inquisitive reporter: "Here were millions and millions of people working desperately and barely able to exist. All I needed was to stir these millions into a sense of their wrongs."[14]

The nature of the two primary groups—native-born American itinerants and new immigrants—among which the IWW recruited explains the organization's ability to achieve the abiding loyalty of one group and not the other. Fortunate immigrant groups, like the eastern European Jews, already had a completely developed institutional life of their own built on a centuries-old tradition of communal existence outside the confines of the dominant society.[15] Less fortunate ethnic groups also began to develop intermediate social organizations—mostly ethnic in nature—to make urban-industrial life bearable, if not pleasurable. The IWW consequently had to compete with other socioeconomic institutions to win the allegiance of immigrants; too often, it had less to offer immigrants than did the latter's families and ethnic societies.[16] But among native-born American migratories, the IWW had no competition. To them it promised, in Carleton Parker's words, "the only social break in the harsh search for work they have ever had; its headquarters the only competitor of the saloon in which they are welcome." To them it offered, according to Tugwell, "a ready made dream of a new world where there is a new touch with sweetness and light and where for a while they can escape the torture of forever being indecently kicked about."[17] And they repaid the IWW's attentiveness with loyalty.

So, almost from the outset, the IWW tailored its ideology and its tactics to fit the needs and status of its followers. I say *almost* from the outset because, at first, the IWW's founders had different dreams. They had anticipated a day when AFL affiliates would desert the house that sheltered them to seek more spacious rooms in the IWW's mansion. They expected skilled workers to unite with the unskilled in a common labor front based on an industrial unionism that would bring American capitalism to its knees. But these original dreams died within three years. No AFL affiliates flocked to the IWW; no skilled workers evinced interest in a united labor front; indeed, the only IWW affiliate that resembled an industrial union and included skilled workers—the WFM—seceded in 1907, taking with it the bulk of the IWW's membership. Unable to appeal to the craft unions or to organize the skilled, the IWW of necessity sought different recruits, which it then discovered among American migratories and immigrant industrial workers.

Let me emphasize, however, that at no time in the IWW's history were its leaders or its theoreticians themselves products of the subculture of poverty. The organization's leadership consisted of two types: skilled workers and formerly successful trade-union officials such as Haywood, St. John, Ettor, and Little; or resident intellectuals such as *Solidarity*'s editor, Ben Williams, who put himself through a small Iowa college and considered himself something of an expert on Marx, Darwin, and Spencer. There were also Justus Ebert and John Sandgren, who used the IWW press to enlighten Wobblies about the ideological foundations of revolution and the IWW's similarity to Europe's revolutionary syndicalist organizations.[18] The trade unionists and the intellectuals were united by a shared desire to effect a nonpolitical revolution in America and by a common alienation from the AFL and reformist American socialists.

Although not in or of the culture of poverty, these leaders became aware of it when the IWW failed to marshal skilled workers into a revolutionary vanguard. Even at the first IWW convention in 1905, Haywood had demanded "an uplifting of the fellow in the gutter," a sentiment shared by other founders, who opened the IWW's doors to all workers, regardless of skill, nationality, sex, age, or race. And after 1908, the IWW focused its primary attention on Haywood's figurative gutter dwellers.[19]

Eager to make a revolution that would destroy the existing system root and branch, the IWW turned to those most alienated from the American Dream, locating them amidst the lower strata of a rapidly changing society. Feeling marginal, dependent, and inferior, Wobbly recruits harbored deep-seated resentments against the essential institutions of the ruling class—police, government, and clergy. In their alienation from and despair with America's dominant institutions, IWW followers, like Lewis's Latin Americans living in a culture of poverty, exhibited high potential for unrest and for utilization in a radical movement aimed at destroying that order.[20]

The IWW shaped its doctrine and its tactics to attract recruits from the gutter. It belittled trade-union welfare systems as "coffin benefits," business unionism as pork-chop unionism, and union leaders as the labor lieutenants of capitalism, for IWW members simply could not afford the initiation fees and dues required to sustain business unionism. Also, men in the gutter needed self-discipline and self-leadership more than they required the counsel of professional, bureaucratic officials. Only by following policies designed to keep its treasury bare and its bureaucracy immobilized could the IWW win the followers it sought. To that degree, the IWW's critique of business unionism as an obstacle to the creation of a revolutionary working-class consciousness should be understood as much as a rationalization of what was—and not necessarily as a hardcore belief in what should be.

More important than offering its supporters low dues and open membership books, the IWW promised them a way out of their respective subcultures of poverty. "Any movement which organizes and gives hope to the poor and effectively promotes solidarity and a sense of identification with larger groups, destroys the psychological and social core of the culture of poverty," writes Lewis. The IWW taught its members class consciousness, organization, and solidarity; it gave them the same element that Lewis found Fidel Castro had offered Cuba's peasants: "a new sense of power and importance. They were armed and given a doctrine which glorified the lower class as the hope of humanity."[21]

One word—power—distilled what IWW ideology and rhetoric were all about. In *The Iron Heel*, a novel well known to Wobblies, Jack London expressed better than any IWW pamphlet the organization's notions about power. Ernest Everhardt, London's fictional Haywood,[22] responds to a capitalist adversary who had just given him a lesson in realpolitik: "Power. It is what we of the working class preach. We know and well we know by bitter experience, that no appeal for the right, for justice, for humanity, can ever touch you. . . . So we have preached power." "Power will be the arbiter," Everhardt proceeds, "as it has always been the arbiter. . . . we of the labor hosts have conned that word over till our minds are all a-tingle with it. Power. It is a kingly word."[23] Whoever held power ruled society, the IWW agreed. And it proposed to transfer power from the capitalists, who used it antisocially, to the proletariat, who would exercise it for the benefit of humanity.

The IWW's emphasis on power made a great deal of sense to men who existed in the social jungle and saw naked force—by employers, police, and courts—used against them constantly. When an IWW pamphlet proclaimed, "it is the law of nature that the strong rule and the weak are enslaved," Wobblies saw reality writ large. George Speed, a famous old Wobbly, expressed their emotions tersely: "Power," he said, "is the thing that determines everything today. . . . it stands to reason that the fellow that has got the big club swings it over the balance. That is life as it exists today." So when Speed asserted that neither socialism, nor politics, nor legislation could aid the Wobblies, and that they would suffer until they learned to exert power themselves, he made sense to those he represented.[24]

The IWW's antipathy toward political action made equally as much sense to its members. Migratory workers moved too often to establish legal voting residences. Millions of immigrants lacked the franchise, as did the African Americans, women, and children to whom the IWW appealed. Even immigrants and natives who had the right to vote nourished a deep suspicion of government. To them, the policeman's club and the magistrate's edict symbolized the state's alliance with entrenched privilege. Who knew the injustices of the state better than an IWW member imprisoned for exercising his right of free speech, or one clubbed by a cop while picketing peacefully for higher wages. Daily experience demonstrated the truth of Elizabeth Gurley Flynn's comment that the state was simply the slugging agency of the capitalists. So, Wobblies simply refused to believe that stuffing pieces of paper—even socialist ones—into a box would transform a basically repressive institution—the state—into one that was humane.[25]

Representing workers who could not conceive of political power as a means to alter the rules of the game as played in America, Wobblies had to offer an alternative, which they discovered in economic power. Naively believing themselves better Marxists than their socialist critics, Wobblies insisted that political power was but a reflex of economic power and that, without economic organization behind it, labor politics was "like a house without a foundation or a dream without substance." IWW leaders taught their followers how to obtain economic power. To quote some of their favorite aphorisms: "Get it through industrial organization; organize the workers to control the use of their labor power; the secret of power is organization; the only force that can break tyrannical rule . . . is the one big union all the workers."[26]

Through working-class economic organization, the IWW hoped to exert direct action as the essential means for bringing its new society into existence. Direct action included any step taken by workers at the point of production that improved wages, reduced hours, and bettered conditions. It included ordinary strikes, intermittent strikes, silent strikes, passive resistance, sabotage, and the ultimate measure of direct action—the social general strike—which would displace the capitalists from power and place the means of production in working-class hands.[27]

Emphasis on direct action in preference to parliamentary politics or socialist dialectics represented a profound insight by IWW leaders into the minds of industrial workers and inhabitants of the culture of poverty. Abstract doctrine meant nothing to the disinherited; specific grievances meant everything. Justus Ebert expressed this idea for the IWW:[28] "Workingmen on the job don't care a whoop in hell for free love. . . . they are not interested in why Bakunin was fired out of the International by Marx . . .

nor do they care about the cooperative commonwealth; they want practical organization first, all else after. They want to know how they can win out against the trusts and the bosses. . . . Give us specific shop methods. We plead for them."

It was "the obscure Bill Jones [the prototypical Wobbly] on the firing line, with stink in his clothes, rebellion in his brain, hope in his heart, determination in his eye, and direct action in his gnarled fist"[29] alongside whom the IWW fought from 1908 to 1918. In cities such as Spokane, Fresno, and Missoula, Wobblies showed numerous Bill Joneses how authority could be challenged through direct action and passive resistance. By fighting for free speech, taking to the streets in defense of civil liberties, courting arrest, and paralyzing courtrooms, Wobblies compelled civic authorities to succumb to massive passive resistance. More important than gaining free speech for its members, it also achieved reforms in private employment agencies and won improved conditions in farms and forests, specific job issues that stirred migratories to action more readily than civil liberties crusades.[30]

In eastern industrial centers, the IWW instructed mass-production workers in the possibilities of industrial unionism; as solidarity prevailed over traditional craft distinctions, Wobbly recruits learned industrial warfare and direct action in the manner prescribed by Marxian theorists and John Dewey: by doing. The IWW organized, agitated, and advised the immigrant industrial workers; but the immigrants themselves led the industrial struggles and decided their outcome. When authorities queried IWW strikers about their leaders, they could indeed respond with one voice: "We are all leaders."[31]

Bill Haywood expressed exceedingly well the IWW's major contribution during the Progressive years. "It has," he said, "developed among the lowest strata of wage slaves in America a sense of their importance and capabilities such as never before existed. Assuming control and responsibility of their own affairs, the unorganized and unfortunate have been brought together, and have conducted some of the of the most unique strikes, fights for free speech and battles for constitutional rights."[32] This was just what Oscar Lewis would write fifty years later about Castro's impact on the Cuban peasantry, who were lifting themselves out of the culture of poverty while Puerto Ricans remained mired within it.[33]

Although the IWW succeeded in training America's dispossessed in the uses of direct action and instilled in them a new sense of their own self-respect, it failed to transform them into a revolutionary vanguard. That, it seems to me, was almost inevitable, given the internal inadequacies of Wobbly doctrine, the aspirations of individuals existing within the culture of poverty, and the dynamics of American capitalism.

First, a few words about internal weaknesses. Wobbly doctrine certainly taught workers how to gain short-range goals indistinguishable from those sought by ordinary trade unions. In other words, while able to rally exploited workers behind crusades to abolish specific grievances, the IWW failed to transform its followers' concrete grievances into a higher consciousness of class, ultimate purpose, and necessary revolution. Aside from vague allusions to the social general strike and to "building the new society within the shell of the old," it never explained how it would achieve its new society, or how it would govern that new society once in existence. All that Wobblies could agree on was that the state, as most Americans knew it, would be nonexistent. Somehow, in Wobbly utopia, each industrial union would possess and manage its own industry. At their best, Wobbly ideologues offered only warmed-over versions of St. Simon's technocratic society, with borrowings from Bellamy's *Looking Backward,* hardly a prescription for effective working-class revolution in the modern world.[34]

Even had the Wobblies possessed a more palatable prescription for revolution, it is far from likely that their followers would have taken it. IWW members, in fact, had limited revolutionary potential. Haywood dreamed of lifting impoverished Americans up from the gutter. But those lying in the gutters could think only of rising to the sidewalk and, once there, of entering a house. Only then could they entertain notions of rising to heaven, be it on earth or in the sky. In other words, individuals lying in the gutter, or in the subculture of poverty, have narrow perspectives on life and society. Struggling just to maintain body—they lacked the time or comfort to worry about the soul—they could think only of the moment, not the future; only of a better job or more food, not of a distant utopian society.[35]

This placed the IWW on the horns of an impossible dilemma. On the one hand, it was committed to ultimate revolution; on the other, it sought immediate improvements for its followers. And Wobblies, like all who really care about humanity—all who feel in the concrete as well as think in the abstract—always accepted betterment for their members today at the expense of achieving utopia tomorrow. This was true at Lawrence, McKees Rocks, and Paterson, among other places, where the IWW allowed workers to fight for immediate improvements that, if achieved, diminished the discontent of those workers. Even at Paterson, where the IWW strikers failed to win concessions, some Wobblies perceived the dilemma of their organization—the leaders' desire for revolution coming up against the members' desire for more now.[36]

The American environment compounded the IWW's dilemma. Unlike revolutionary Mexico or pre-Castro Cuba, where Lewis's radicals contended with an established order that proved unresponsive to lower-class discontent and impervious to change from within, Wobblies struggled against flexible and sophisticated adversaries. The years of IWW growth and success coincided with the era in which welfare capitalism was born in America, all levels of government showed solicitude for the worker, and reform ramified through all aspects of American society. This process became even more pronounced during the First World War, when the federal government utilized its vast power and influence to hasten the spread of welfare capitalism and conservative unionism. While IWW leaders experienced federal repression, their followers enjoyed eight-hour days, grievance boards, and company unions. Just after the war ended, Rex Tugwell wrote an epitaph for the prewar Wobblies: "No world re-generating philosophy comes out of them and they are not going to inherit the earth. When we are a bit more orderly they will disappear . . . at the first breath of capitalistic industrial sanity."[37] Which is almost what happened, although the true believers—few in number and limited in influence after 1919—retreated into their haunted halls.

It might be well for today's advocates of black power and romantic anarchism to recall Tugwell's remark and to heed the Wobblies' experience. By their commitment to ultimate revolution and through their use of militant, direct-action tactics to achieve immediate improvements in living conditions, radicals such as the Wobblies stimulated the emergence of powerful industrial unions and midwifed the birth of the welfare state. But their successes only produced a working class attracted by the promises of a consumer society and willing to trade in working-class consciousness for a middle-class style of life. The ultimate tragedy, then, for most radicals has been that the brighter they have helped make life for the masses, the dimmer has grown the prospects for the revolution to which they dedicated, sometimes even sacrificed, their lives. Yet pessimistic as this historical lesson may seem to contemporary black and white radicals, they might take comfort from these words written in 1917 by an imprisoned Wobbly: "The end in view is well worth striving for, but in the struggle itself lies the happiness of the fighter."

Notes

1. For the standard historical treatments and analyses of the IWW, see Paul F. Brissenden, *The I.W.W.: A Study of American Syndicalism* (New York: Columbia University Press, 1919); John S. Gambs, *The Decline of the I.W.W.* (New York: Columbia University Press, 1932); Patrick Renshaw, *The Wobblies* (New York: Doubleday, 1967); Robert L. Tyler, "Rebels of the Woods and Fields: A Study of the I.W.W. in the Pacific Northwest" (Ph.D. diss., University of Oregon, 1953); idem, "The I.W.W. and the West," *American Quarterly* 12 (Summer 1960): 175–87; idem, "The Rise and Fall of an American Radicalism," *Historian* 19 (Nov. 1956): 48–65; Donald M. Barnes, "The Ideology of the Industrial Workers of the World, 1905–1921" (Ph.D. diss., Washington State University, 1962); Selig Perlman and Philip Taft, *History of Labor in the United States, 1896–1932* (New York: Macmillan, 1934), 230–47, 262–81; Charles Madison, *American Labor Leaders* (New York: Harper, 1950), chap. 10; Thomas Brooks, *Toil and Trouble* (New York: Delacorte Press, 1964), chap. 9. Joseph Rayback, *A History of American Labor* (New York: Macmillan, 1956), chap. 16; Foster Rhea Dulles, *Labor in America* (New York: T. Y. Crowell, 1966), chap. 12.

Expecting to find untapped riches of radical doctrine in IWW mines, only to discover ideological fool's gold, has led many scholars to conclude, in the words of Tyler, that the IWW was an organization that offered "merely an oversimplified, antipolitical Marxism" and so "quietly withered on the radical vine without leaving many tangible fruits" ("The I.W.W. and the West," 175).

Those who have found some sweet fruits (usually industrial unionism and labor solidarity) on the Wobbly vine have tasted the wrong variety. Although the IWW advocated industrial unionism and appealed to immigrants and African Americans, it broke no ground on those two frontiers that had not already been pioneered by AFL affiliates, particularly the United Mine Workers and the needle-trades unions.

Left-wing interpretations have been equally unrewarding. Philip Foner, in his recent history of the IWW (*History of Labor in the United States*, vol. 4: *The Industrial Workers of the World, 1905–1917* [New York: International Publishers, 1964]), and others of similar persuasion view the IWW as an infantile disorder inflicted on the more mature and realistic American Left. See my review of Foner's volume in *Industrial and Labor Relations Review* 21 (Oct. 1967): 129–30. Cf. William Z. Foster, *From Bryan to Stalin* (New York: International Publishers, 1937), 48–58; Elizabeth Gurley Flynn, *I Speak My Piece* (New York: Masses and Mainstream, 1955), 225–26; Ray Ginger, *The Bending Cross* (New Brunswick, N.J.: Rutgers University Press, 1949), 256–57.

2. Carleton Parker, *The Casual Laborer and Other Essays* (New York: Harcourt, Brace, and Howe, 1920), 61–124; idem, "The I.W.W.," *Atlantic Monthly* 120 (Nov. 1917): 651–62; Louis Levine, "The Development of Syndicalism in America," *Political Science Quarterly* 28 (Sept. 1913): 451–79; John Graham Brooks, *American Syndicalism: The I.W.W.* (New York: Macmillan, 1913).

3. On the existence and theme of class conflict in the progressive era, see Gra-

ham Adams Jr., *Age of Industrial Violence, 1910–1915* (New York: Columbia University Press, 1966).

4. Parker's behaviorism led him to condemn more than to understand the existence of the migratories about whose lives his research revealed so many new facets. His psychology interpreted the IWW as a destructive, antisocial agency, and he saw many of its members—if not leaders—as mental defectives. A similar but less fully substantiated psychological analysis of the IWW has been offered by Marc Karson, *American Labor Unions and Politics, 1900–1918* (Carbondale: Southern Illinois University Press, 1958), 151, 210.

In this context—that is, charges that Wobblies misread objective social reality as a result of their neuroticism—it is well to bear in mind what the Italian communist Antonio Gramsci said that revolutionaries should take as their slogan: "Pessimism of the Intelligence, Optimism of the Will."

5. Oscar Lewis, *La Vida* (New York: Random House, 1966); cf. Lewis's *Five Families* (New York: Basic Books, 1959), *The Children of Sanchez* (New York: Random House, 1961), *Pedro Martinez* (New York: Random House, 1964), and his similar studies.

6. Lewis, *La Vida,* xliii.

7. Melvyn Dubofsky, "The Origins of Western Working-Class Radicalism, 1890–1905," *Labor History* 7 (Spring 1966): 133–38; Rodman Paul, *Mining Frontiers of the Far West, 1848–1880* (New York: Holt, Rinehart, and Winston, 1963). On changing socioeconomic conditions, see *Report of the Industrial Commission on the Relations and Conditions of Capital and Labor Employed in the Mining Industry,* vol. 12 (Washington, D.C., 1911), 191–618.

8. Dubofsky, "Origins of Western Working-Class Radicalism," 131–55; William D. Haywood, *Bill Haywood's Book: The Autobiography of William D. Haywood* (New York: International Publishers, 1929); Ralph Chaplin, *Wobbly* (Chicago: University of Chicago Press, 1949); Warren R. Van Tine, "Ben Williams, Wobbly Editor" (Master's thesis, Northern Illinois University, 1967).

9. Lewis, *La Vida,* xlv.

10. E. J. Hobsbawm, *Primitive Rebels* (New York: Praeger, 1963), 108 and passim.

11. Arno Dosch, "What the I.W.W. Is," *World's Work* 26 (Aug. 1913): 17; Rexford G. Tugwell, "The Casual of the Woods," *Survey* 44 (July 3, 1920): 472; Parker, "I.W.W.," 651–62.

12. Oscar Handlin, *The Uprooted* (Boston: Little, Brown, 1951), 4–6.

13. On Italian and Jewish immigrant traditions, see Nathan Glazer and Daniel P. Moynihan, *Beyond the Melting Pot* (Cambridge, Mass.: MIT Press, 1963), 143–218.

14. Dosch, "What the I.W.W. Is," 417.

15. Glazer and Moynihan, *Beyond the Melting Pot,* 143–85; Moses Rischin, *The Promised City: New York's Jews, 1870–1914* (Cambridge, Mass.: Harvard University Press, 1962), 34–47.

16. On this point, see Donald Cole, *Immigrant City: Lawrence, Massachusetts, 1845–1921* (Chapel Hill: University of North Carolina Press, 1963), chaps. 6–9; Stephan Thernstrom, *Poverty and Progress: Social Mobility in a Nineteenth-Century City* (Cambridge, Mass.: Harvard University Press, 1964), 166–91.

17. Parker, "I.W.W.," 656; R. Tugwell to Editor, *Survey* 44 (Aug. 16, 1920): 641–42.

18. Haywood had been a hard-rock miner at the age of fifteen, a successful local union official at twenty-seven, and a respected international officer by thirty. The best source for Haywood's life is not his unreliable autobiography but his testimony in the transcript of *The State of Idaho v. Haywood,* June 4–July 30, 1907, microfilm, Idaho State Historical Society, Boise; *Final Report and Testimony of the United States Commission on Industrial Relations,* 12 vols. (Washington, D.C., 1915), 11:10,569–73; *Evidence and Cross Examination in the Case of the United States of America v. W. D. Haywood, et al.,* n.p. St. John was also a successful and respected local union official in the WFM; see *Final Report and Testimony,* 2:11,455ff.; Ettor was born in Brooklyn, raised in Chicago, and lived in San Francisco as a skilled building-trades worker and union member. See *Industrial Worker,* May 23, 1912, 1–4. Little, like Haywood and St. John, was a hard-rock miner, WFM member, and successful union organizer. Williams, the editor of *Solidarity* from 1909 to 1917, educated himself at Tabor College, Iowa, and was a skilled printer; see Van Tine, "Ben Williams." Sandgren was a Swedish immigrant who wrote learned exegeses on Marxism and syndicalism for the IWW press and also translated Scandinavian articles into English. Ebert, a German immigrant, did the same for articles in German and the other languages of Central Europe. All these men at one time had played prominent roles in the Socialist party or Socialist Labor party.

19. *Proceedings of the First Annual Convention of the Industrial Workers of the World* (New York: Labor News Co., 1905), 28, 153–57; Brissenden, *I.W.W.,* 96–103.

20. Lewis, *La Vida,* xlv–xlvi.

21. Ibid., xlviii–xlvi.

22. Although some literary critics believe that Eugene V. Debs was the real-life counterpart to Everhardt, my own inclination is otherwise. Given London's empathy for the IWW, Everhardt's physical and temperamental resemblance to Haywood, and the brutal class war in Colorado that involved Haywood and the WFM just prior to *The Iron Heel*'s publication, I am convinced that Everhardt was patterned after Haywood.

23. Jack London, *The Iron Heel* (New York: Grosset and Dunlap, 1907), 96–99.

24. *The Lumber Industry and Its Workers* (Chicago: n.p., n.d.), 59; *Final Report and Testimony,* 5:4940, 4946–47.

25. *Final Report and Testimony,* 5:4942, 11:10,574; *Solidarity,* July 9, 1910, 3.

26. The above quotations come from *Solidarity,* July 9, 1910, 3; Vincent St. John, "Political Parties Not Endorsed by Us," *Industrial Worker* Aug. 12, 1909, 3; idem, *The I.W.W.: Its History, Structure, and Methods* (Chicago: IWW, 1917), 40–45; *Final Report and Testimony,* 2:1449, 11:10,575; *Lumber Industry and Its Workers,* 99.

27. *Lumber Industry and Its Workers,* 73; *Industrial Worker,* June 6, 1912, 2; *The Silent Defense* (Chicago: n.p., n.d.); *Final Report and Testimony,* 11:10,578.

28. *Solidarity,* Feb. 14, 1914, 2.

29. *Industrial Worker,* May 3, 1913, 3.

30. The free-speech fights are adequately covered in the standard histories of the IWW cited above. There is also fresh information on them in the unpublished re-

ports prepared for the Commission on Industrial Relations and now in the General Records of the Department of Labor, Record Group 174, National Archives.

31. These events are also fully treated in standard IWW histories, especially in Foner's volume.

32. Haywood as quoted by Dosch, "What the I.W.W. Is," 417.

33. Lewis, *La Vida,* xlix–li.

34. *Industrial Worker,* Jan. 9, 1913, 2; John Sandgren, "The Syndicalist Movement in Norway," *Solidarity,* Feb. 14, 1914, 3; Robert Rives LaMonte, "Industrial Unionism and Syndicalism," *New Review* 1 (May 1913): 527; *Final Report and Testimony,* 11:10,583.

35. On this point, see Lewis, *La Vida,* 1, and Seymour Martin Lipset, *Political Man: The Social Bases of Politics* (New York: Doubleday, 1960), 115–22.

36. Elizabeth Gurley Flynn, "The Truth about Paterson," typecopy of speech, Tamiment Institute Library, New York.

37. Rexford G. Tugwell to Editor, *Survey* 44 (Aug. 16, 1920): 641–42.

· 4 ·

Tom Mann and William D. Haywood:
Culture, Personality, and Comparative History

IN a 1966 essay analyzing the origins of working-class radicalism in the American West, I concluded: "today we need fewer vague generalizations about the uniqueness or significance of the frontier. . . . We . . . need comparative studies placing American labor history in the broader context of worldwide . . . history where all workers, regardless of nationality, tasted the fruits, both bitter and sweet, of the capitalist order."[1] Frankly, since then, I have barely explored the treacherous terrain of comparative history. Like most historians, I have a fondness for the unique and the particular, a suspicion of the abstract; and, thus far, most comparative historical studies have been based either on sweeping abstractions or on loose generalizations. Nevertheless, it can be argued that a firm historical basis exists for comparing the experience of Britain and the United States, especially for the years from roughly 1880 to 1919.

In this essay, similarities and differences in Anglo-American history will be explored through an analysis of the lives, thoughts, and beliefs of Tom Mann and William D. Haywood, who were among the most eminent and active labor radicals in their respective societies. In the course of their lives and careers, both men followed a trajectory that carried them from working-class obscurity to radical notoriety. Mann, the son of an English Midlands miner, and Haywood, a child of the American West, both participated prominently in the most significant trade-union and radical political developments of the period 1890–1920. They rose to prominence initially within traditional trade unions, later became advocates of working-class politics and socialism, grew more radical and revolutionary with time, and ultimately linked themselves to the Bolshevik Revolution and Soviet communism. No two labor leaders in pre– and post–World War I Britain and the United States were more indelibly associated in the popular mind with working-class radicalism, massive industrial conflicts, and labor violence. An examination of their lives thus promises to shed new light on the role of radicals in British and American society.

Before analyzing the careers of Mann and Haywood in greater detail, however, one might fairly ask: Are the English and the American experiences at all comparable? A quick and easy answer would be, No. For those scholars who have most often compared English and American history— such as Seymour Martin Lipset, Louis Hartz, and Daniel Boorstin—assure us that the American experience has been exceptional; if not at all points, then certainly at those most vital in the shaping of national character and consciousness.[2]

What precisely are the attributes or conditions of American exceptionalism? First, there is the inescapable fact that the United States came into being without a distinct feudal tradition in the European sense and without a hereditary, conservative social class. Lacking an ancien régime, America produced no radicals committed to overthrowing it and no reactionaries dedicated to restoring a lost golden age of aristocratic virtues. Instead, as Louis Hartz sees it, all American citizens functioned within an agreed, Lockean, postfeudal consensus. Indeed, Lipset has asserted that, from its birth, America has been a nondeferential, nonascriptive society, which produced the second basic attribute of American exceptionalism: the extent of social mobility and the fluidity of class lines.[3]

Talk about the "promise of American life"—men who rose from log cabins to the White House and from steerage passage to business imperium— has been among the commonplaces of the national mythology. In a society in which men rose and fell solely on the basis of their abilities and in which there was always room at the top, no place existed for radical theories of social change or for radical economic and political organizations to effect such changes. There was simply no point in challenging Hartz's Lockean consensus; as Werner Sombart once commented, American socialism was shipwrecked on reefs of roast beef and shoals of apple pie.[4]

This brings us to the third attribute of American exceptionalism: the lack of a substantial socialist tradition. For the reasons cited above (and others too numerous to mention here), historians such as David Shannon have concluded that the rhetoric, the mystique, and the symbols of American labor politics are different, that "it is natural to expect the Chicago workingman of, say, 1900, to have political ideals and loyalties different from those of his counterpart in Lyon, the Baltimore truck driver to think differently politically from the Newcastle shipyard worker."[5] And these different traditions of class and thought doomed socialism in America.

Finally, all these exceptional characteristics combined to produce the unique national value structure that Lipset has analyzed with immense subtlety. Americans are dominated by what he labels an achievement-egalitarian syndrome. The American devotion to equality is tempered by a similar commitment to individual achievement, and the resultant tension, or dialectic, between equality and individualism has caused the lower-class American "to drive *himself* to get ahead," unlike the working-class European, who tends to emphasize "collective modification of the class structure."[6] Hence, once again, peculiar American values preclude the possibility of a radical or socialist tradition.

Still, I would hazard to argue that during the lifetimes of Tom Mann and William D. Haywood, such differences between English and American society were more apparent than real and, to these two men, at least, insubstantial.

To begin with, we have the question of whether history is to be written, or indeed viewed, from the top down or the bottom up. For industrialists, the implications of a feudal tradition are clear enough: societies with aristocratic traditions preserve ruling-class values that are not necessarily gratifying to capitalists; aristocratic values are not those of economic man, particularly his scientific-technological variant. Moreover, industrialists must struggle to establish their values as preferable and often themselves can rise to the top of society only by assimilating aristocratic traditions.[7] But workers, in either case, are still ruled by factory masters, who set the terms of work and the rewards for labor. Mann and Haywood, perceiving society from the bottom up, viewed their respective "masters" in much the same way.

Social mobility also looks quite different, whether viewed from the bottom or the top of society. Asa Briggs's successful mid- and late-Victorian men and women, for example, sound remarkably like Lipset's Eisenhower-era Americans. Briggs's middle-class Victorians saw a society in which a marked degree of individual mobility existed; where the dividing line between classes was extremely difficult to draw; and in which divisions within class lines were often more significant than conflicts between classes. And Beatrice Webb in her autobiography remembers values inculcated during her childhood that are notably congruent with Lipset's ideal-type American values: "It was the bounden duty of every citizen to better his social status; to ignore those beneath him, and to aim steadily at the top rung of the ladder. Only by this persistent pursuit by each individual of his own and his family's interest would the highest general level of civilization be attained."[8] But down at the bottom of society in both England and the United States, what Haywood and Mann saw was mass insecurity, squalor, and poverty; the fortunate few might indeed rise, but only at the expense of the vast majority, who were doomed to remain in the class of their birth.

Furthermore, during the lifetimes of Mann and Haywood, labor politics in England and America perhaps did not appear as different as later historians have perceived it. In both nations, socialism and radicalism touched a relatively small minority, yet the ruling classes dreaded social turmoil and even revolution. If England had a Labour party before World War I, America had a Socialist party that seemed equally a potential threat to the political hegemony of the two dominant parties. That English labor would rise as American socialism declined, neither Mann nor Haywood could foresee before 1918, by which date they had formed their fundamental notions about labor, radicalism, and politics.

Let me now turn away from abstraction and examine more closely the lives and thoughts of Mann and Haywood. In both cases, however, a dearth of historical sources complicates the task of comparison and analysis.[9] The lack of sources notwithstanding, we can piece together enough about the lives of Mann and Haywood to reveal a similar developmental pattern.[10] Both men lost one parent at an early age,[11] lacked formal education, and turned to wage earning early—Mann started work in a coal mine at age nine and remained in the pit for four years; Haywood, scrambling for the various jobs available to an uneducated, working-class youth, spent his preadolescent days around Salt Lake City and several Utah mining camps. When Mann's father moved the family to Birmingham, Tom, fifteen, was apprenticed to a toolmaking firm, where he learned the engineering craft. Haywood at fifteen also discovered his primary occupation: together with his stepfather, he went down into the silver mines of Nevada, and he would stay a hard-rock miner until 1900. Mann, the skilled engineer, and Haywood, the skilled nonferrous miner, seldom remained long enough in one place to establish roots. After completing his Birmingham apprenticeship in 1877, Mann spent the next five years working in various capacities in London and Brooklyn, New York, and visiting Paris. Haywood, during the initial years of his working life, drifted about the widely scattered mining camps of Utah, Colorado, Nevada, and Idaho, finally settling down for a time in Silver City, Idaho.

Both men encountered the labor movement at various stages in their early working lives but at first committed themselves to it less than enthusiastically. Indeed, Mann would not become a truly active member of the Amalgamated Society of Engineers (ASE) until socialism touched his heart and mind. In Haywood's case, we have no substantial evidence of interest in trade unionism before 1896. But in that year, the president of the Western Federation of Miners (WFM) visited Silver City to charter a local, which Haywood joined. Over the succeeding decade, he was to rise within the union hierarchy and serve as a conscientious official until socialism became his new passion.

Mann and Haywood turned to socialism for similar reasons. Their experiences with bread-and-butter forms of unionism convinced them of its inability to solve the essential social problem; equally important, non-working-class socialists transformed both men into prominent public personalities. Mann and Haywood would also find at roughly the same time that socialism was less than a complete solution to industrial society's ills; and, disillusioned with the prospects of socialist revolutions, they became syndicalists.

Syndicalism in turn propelled Mann and Haywood into the communist movement. Mann, a charter member of the British Communist party, remained loyal to it until his death in 1941. For Haywood, communism led to political exile in the Soviet Union, where he died in 1928, having failed to promote radicalism in the land of his birth or to build his version of the new society in the land of his exile.

There are several other striking similarities in the lives of Mann and Haywood. Though they had families, evidence indicates that they were not family men. Indeed, Mann scarcely mentions his wife and children in his memoirs, and there is the distinct possibility that he in fact maintained two separate and distinct families. Haywood, a physically attractive man wed to a frail and increasingly superstitious woman, took to satisfying his sexual needs outside the home.[12]

Also notably congruent in the careers of Mann and Haywood was their commitment to internationalism in theory and practice. Mann, for example, twice visited the United States and South Africa; spent a decade in Australasia; traveled in the Soviet Union; and devoted considerable effort to establishing European trade-union federations. Haywood, in 1910 and again in 1913, toured Europe and Great Britain, where he addressed various trade-union and socialist audiences. And, of course, he spent the last eight years of his life in the Soviet Union.

It is indeed noteworthy how, despite their dissimilar immediate environments, their quite different crafts, and the divergent character of the trade unions to which they belonged, Mann's and Haywood's careers and values followed parallel paths. Birmingham and London were obviously worlds apart from Salt Lake City and Silver City. Practically the same can be said of the Amalgamated Society of Engineers and the Western Federation of Miners. The ASE, which Mann joined in the 1870s, was a proven success. Despite enormous changes in the social and economic environment of England, the society maintained its traditional posture of craft exclusiveness and union moderation. Representing the aristocrats of the British labor movement, it functioned within the limits set by Victorian working-class respectability and lower-middle-class morality.[13] The Western Federation was another matter. The union, which Haywood joined in 1896, had barely survived the first three years of its life and had a future that looked anything but healthy. But Haywood's recruitment coincided with an upturn in the union's prospects, an improvement that proceeded hand in glove with radicalism. Committed to militant notions of class struggle, the union practiced as well as preached solidarity. Its practices and beliefs cut against the grain of the American labor movement, most of whose affiliated unions were cut out of the same cloth as the English Amalgamated Society of Engineers.[14] In other words, Mann became a radical despite his union affiliation, while Haywood learned his radicalism in union service.

Nothing in the early union careers of Mann and Haywood hinted at the distance that they would travel in their radicalism. Before leaving Birmingham for London, Mann had devoted himself to temperance and viewed life from an orthodox Christian perspective. Even after his conversion to socialism early in the 1880s, he essentially remained moderate. During the famous London dock strike of 1889, which made him a national personality, Mann served more as the conscientious union official than the militant agitator. His moderation won him appointment to the Royal Commission on Labour, a position he held for three years. During that time, he spoke regularly to middle-class reform and church groups and indeed seemed so close to clergymen that rumors arose that Mann was about to take church orders. It was such behavior that caused Friedrich Engels to write: "Of their leaders, Tom Mann is upright but boundlessly weak, and he has been made half-crazy by his appointment as a member of the Royal Commission on Labour."[15]

Similarly, Haywood, the Silver City, Idaho, trade unionist, concentrating on job security, higher wages, shorter hours, and union-sponsored protection against illness, injury, and death, cautiously led his fellow workers along the accepted route of American trade unionism from 1896 to 1900. No wonder the chief engineer of the mine at which Haywood worked considered "Big Bill" a model citizen.[16] After 1900, when he left Silver City to become secretary-treasurer of the WFM, Haywood, by then a socialist, still acted moderately and cautiously. Confining his radicalism mostly to editorials in the union journal, Haywood, on the eve of the most brutal conflict in his union's history, remarked: "We are not opposed to employers. . . . it is our purpose and aim to work harmoniously and jointly with employers as best we can under this system, and we intend to change the system if we get sufficiently organized and well enough educated to do so."[17] Mann, at a comparable stage in his own career, had observed that the work of trade unionists was "to organize ourselves and to get workers generally so effectively organized, that we can insist on the necessary changes taking place."[18]

Yet even during the moderate phases of their respective socialisms, the factors that would later transform two conscientious union officials into radical gadflies were in gestation. This is much clearer in Mann's case and has been documented both in his memoirs and in Dona Torr's biography. Haywood's public arrival as an agitator was much more sudden, if equally understandable. After toiling as a worker and union official for some ten years in what Englishmen would refer to as the provinces, Haywood was suddenly catapulted into the national spotlight. Arrested for his part in the alleged conspiracy to assassinate ex-Governor Frank Steunenberg of Idaho and brought to trial for murder, he became a martyr to the cause of labor and radicalism. From his Boise prison cell, he stood in 1906 as the Socialist party candidate for governor of Colorado. Thereafter, he seldom drifted far from the radical limelight. Four years before his arrest, however, Haywood had premonitions of what his future role would be. Writing in the union journal, Haywood extolled the contributions of the agitator to civilization and asserted that the agitator "is the advance agent of social improvement and fully realizes that reforms are not achieved by conservative methods."[19] A decade earlier, Mann, in more biblical terms, had written similarly of his own function: 'Cry aloud, spare not, lift up thy voice like a trumpet, and show My people their transgressions. Upon the agitators rests the stupendous task of awakening the nation . . . to yearnings for a worthier life. For all effective agitators . . . we have cause to be devoutly thankful."[20]

These two self-proclaimed prophets of radicalism carried the same message to their respective societies. Fastening their gazes, as all good prophets are wont to do, on society's disinherited, those unable to adjust to industrialism or destroyed by it, they warned, in the words of Haywood at the founding convention of the Industrial Workers of the World (IWW): "society can be no better than its most miserable."[21] But the Anglo-American labor movement, at least as perceived by Mann and Haywood, neglected the disinherited. They observed nations in which capital was concentrating into immense industrial combines whose technology obliterated traditional skills, while trade unions remained devoted to crafts that had lost social and economic significance. As early as 1886, Mann had bemoaned the typical trade unionist of his time, whom he characterized as "a man with a fossilized intellect, either hopelessly apathetic or supporting a policy that plays directly into the hands of the capitalist exploiter."[22] Four years later, he and Ben Tillet ridiculed the deadly stupor of such tight craft unions as the Amalgamated Society and pleaded that "clannishness in trade matters must be superseded by a cosmopolitan spirit, brotherhood must not only be talked of but practiced."[23] Haywood proved equally severe in his condemnation of American trade unions, which represented a small minority of workers inculcated with the spirit of craft selfishness that tried to monopolize union benefits for the favored few. And Haywood, like Mann, asserted that the true friend of labor should see that "the diversity of labor is incapable of craft distinction. . . . The machine is the apprentice of yesterday, the journeyman of today. But the industrial union is the evolution of the labor movement confronting and competing with the strides of the machine in industrial progress. . . . it is also the open door of organized labor."[24]

Separated by three thousand miles of water and another twenty-five hundred miles of land, never having met personally (at least at this point in their lives), Mann and Haywood nevertheless shared thoughts about the labor movement, expressed those thoughts in comparable ways, and consistently sought to practice their theories of industrial unionism and labor solidarity.

Their transcendent faith in the value of workers' organizations also made both men uncertain socialists. Socialists largely by instinct, their politics were more of the heart than the mind. As socialist agitators, they stirred the emotions of workers with glowing pictures of a new and better world to be, not with learned exegeses of Marxian economics or politics. And their roles as agitators playing on the emotions of crowds made them uncomfortable with socialists primarily concerned with the finer points of theory or the gathering of an additional vote or two. As self-taught, working-class intellectuals, Mann and Haywood sometimes had strained relations with university-educated radicals.

From the first, Mann never believed that socialist politics was as important as working-class economic organizations. During his active years in the Social Democratic Federation (SDF), roughly 1884 to 1890, Mann was uneasy about the founder Henry Mayers (H. M.) Hyndman's hostility toward trade unions. Irked by the SDF's neglect of the labor movement, Mann quietly ceased his work for the federation. His subsequent relationship with the Independent Labour Party (ILP) also troubled him. Though Mann served as secretary of the ILP from 1894 to 1896, collaborated amicably with Keir Hardie, the Scottish former coal miner, union official, founder and cochair of the ILP, and later member of Parliament (1892–95, 1900–1915). Mann stood as an ILP candidate in several elections, but he was never secure in a party that veiled its socialist paternity and that seemed to him to be a vote-grabbing machine. In the period between his break with the SDF and his activity within the ILP, Mann expressed his fundamental attitude toward politics in these words: "The real worker for the people is the man who is changing their habits and thought, and he must work amongst the rank and file. Always remember that Parliament will not change the people, but as the people are changed, they will very soon change the Parliament."[25] And nine years of almost continuous agitation for socialism in Australasia, where he observed Labour governments in action, reinforced Mann's suspicions about politics. "It was plain to me," he wrote just before leaving Australia in 1909, "that economic organization was indispensable for the achievement of economic freedom. The policy of the various Labour parties gave no promise in this direction, nor did the superadding of political activities to the extant type of trade-union organization seem any more hopeful."[26] Taking note of syndicalism in France and Italy, as well as of the IWW in the United States, he observed: "Whether parliamentary action was to be dropped or not, increasing importance would evidently attach to industrial organization."[27]

Haywood's relationship to socialism proved more strained than Mann's and for comparable reasons. In a party eager to appear respectable, Haywood publicly gloried in his disdain for the capitalist law. The implications of the dynamiting of the *Los Angeles Times* building in 1911, which frightened many socialists, led Haywood to plead for more direct action and sabotage. To the Socialist party, many of whose leaders were professional men and women, Haywood challenged: "To understand the class struggle you must go into the factory and you must ride on top of the boxcars or underneath. . . . you must go down with me into the bowels of the earth. . . . there by the rays of a tallow candle you will understand something about the class struggle."[28] Worse yet, Haywood derided parliamentary reforms and declared instead: "I want to say . . . it is decidedly better . . . to be able to elect the superintendent in some branch of industry than to elect a congressman."[29] As a result of such declarations and his public actions, Haywood was recalled from the Socialist party's National Executive Committee in 1913; thereafter, he devoted himself to the IWW and to syndicalism.

For both Mann and Haywood, the transformation from socialist to syndicalist entailed no violent rupture with their earlier beliefs. Indeed, continuities in their patterns of thought were more apparent than discontinuities. Throughout the 1880s and 1890s, as he agitated for socialism, Mann constantly asserted that organization of the working class remained the single most important radical objective. It was so, too, in Haywood's case. At the moment he became an active socialist, Haywood noted: "The essential thing for the producing class is to control and supervise the means of production and distribution. . . . This can only be accomplished by workers themselves organizing an industrial government."[30]

In such comments lay the seeds of syndicalism: faith that the workers, by organizing themselves fully and engaging in direct action at the point of production, without the mediation of political parties or parliaments, could seize industry and operate it in the best interests of society. Again, it should be stressed that neither Mann nor Haywood presented blueprints detailing how workers would attain total organization, oust the capitalists from economic and political power, and run their new society. Theory and analysis were not their strong points; agitation was, and the style and content of their agitation for syndicalism was indeed similar.

Both men advised workers to ignore politics, because it only served to confuse and divide labor, fomenting sectarianism where solidarity was required. Traditional trade unionism was equally to be disdained. In place of politics and business unionism would arise the revolutionary union, which, in Mann's words, "would make possible concerted action whereby the workers may be enabled to decide the conditions under which production shall be carried on."[31] The essence of the revolutionary union was its unremitting adherence to the class struggle. In Haywood's words: "We deny that any identity of interest can exist between the exploiter and the exploited."[32] Or, as Mann noted: "The object of the unions is to wage the Class War and take every opportunity of scoring against the enemy."[33] Mann and Haywood thus opposed binding agreements with employers, which could only serve to paralyze the will of the labor movement and vitiate labor solidarity. Workers and their unions had to remain free at all times to act as fighting organizations, willing and ready to use any means of direct action necessary to achieve the social revolution.

Although Mann and Haywood never explained precisely how direct action would usher in the revolutionary commonwealth, their scenarios for revolution were basically similar. Mann simply advised workers to "cease to function as workers and this would force the employers to make the required concessions, including the complete capitulation."[34] Haywood concurred: "If labor was organized and self-disciplined it could stop every wheel in the United States tonight—every one—and sweep off your capitalists and State legislatures and politicians into the sea."[35] One could only wonder: Why, if employers and governments were superfluous, had they dominated society so long? And if, instead, they were powerful and essential, why they would meekly surrender their powers and privileges to an organized working class?

Vaguer still were Mann's and Haywood's notions concerning the administrations of a syndicalist society. Of one thing we can be sure: parliamentary politics had no place in their utopia. Industrial government would replace parliamentary institutions, trade unions would substitute for political parties, and union officials would take over from civil-service bureaucrats. Trade unions, as the primary social institutions, would, in the words of Mann, "assume the responsibilities of provisioning, clothing, and housing the people."[36]

Paradoxically, for syndicalists who asserted the primacy of industrial democracy and rank-and-file participation in all matters, Mann and Haywood shared a singular penchant for the type of scientific-efficiency approaches then so popular among English Fabians and American Progressives.[37] References to the efficient, scientific organization of society form a recurrent theme in the writing and remarks of both men. As early as the 1889 London dock strike, Mann's solution to the problems of waterside labor was the scientific reorganization of the London docks under municipal control. Six years later, in an ILP pamphlet, he asserted:

"What is now imperatively demanded is a national scientific supervision of the Nation's Work . . . scientifically adjusting our own energy so as to harmoniously balance the nation."[38] Indeed, the struggle for his syndicalist utopia was to be waged scientifically, by scientifically organized industrial unions.[39] Haywood's allusions to scientific efficiency scarcely differ; again and again, he reverted to the theme that workers would not be emancipated until their unions were established on a scientific basis and that his syndicalist state would be organized along lines more scientific and more efficient than those of anarchistic capitalism.

Not surprisingly, Mann and Haywood never resolved the contradictions inherent in their images of a revolutionary rank-and-file, working-class movement that would achieve power scientifically or of a syndicalist society that would be founded on absolute democracy and individual participation in decision-making and yet be totally scientific and efficient. Such beliefs placed them closer to middle-class technocrats and bureaucrats than to less-militant social democrats or ordinary rank-and-file workers. Perhaps this explains part of their inability to form mass movements among English and American workers and also their final turn to communism.

One can only hypothesize that in Lenin and the Bolshevik Revolution, Mann and Haywood saw a revolution actually achieved by nonparliamentary means, by what indeed could be considered direct action, and that Lenin personified the efficient, scientific revolutionary who coolly displaced the capitalists and their bureaucratic henchmen. The "dictatorship of the proletariat," it could be argued, was simply a preliminary stage in which the revolution was defended against counterrevolutionary terror while the scientific basis was laid for a future society of free men and women.

Mann had no apparent difficulty in reconciling communism and syndicalism. Of the Bolsheviks, he could simply say: "They hold that parliament is outworn, and that the growing economic power of the workers must fashion new forces of political expression." Of himself, he stated: "We should not rigidly adhere to past policies for the sake of consistency when these no longer make for perfect solidarity." The experience of world war and revolution had altered Mann's beliefs, leading him now to conclude that "the Communist International is the unifying force that must bring together and organize all the militant workers in their right relationship, so that each can play his part in the common struggle."[40] To that conception, Mann remained true until his death in 1941.

Haywood's switch to communism had a less rationalized base. Whether he went into exile because of his attraction to communism or simply out of a desire to avoid imprisonment is unclear. Most likely, his flight resulted from a combination of the two. Whatever the reasons for his flight to Russia, his exile was not a happy one. Out of his depth in the new society being created by such men as Lenin and Trotsky, not really a Bolshevik, and in fact seriously ill, Haywood saw his dream of building a Wobbly utopia in Russia quickly sour. By 1923 he was in semi-, if not permanent, retirement in Moscow, a desperately lonely man who remained something of a character in the world of American exiles in Russia. Ailing and frequently hospitalized, he finally died on May 28, 1928.[41]

What conclusions, then, can one draw about the comparability of the English and the American experience in the industrial era from such a brief glance at the lives of Mann and Haywood? Obviously, one cannot and should not make too much of similarities in transnational experience derived solely from a comparison of two individuals, exceptional as they both may have been. Still, there are so many obvious similarities in their careers, their perceptions of society, and their patterns of thought that one must question David Shannon's assertion that "it is natural to expect the Baltimore truck driver to think differently from the Newcastle shipyard worker" (indeed, one might also observe that it would be just as natural to expect the Yorkshire coal miner to think differently from the Cornish tin miner). For here we have a Birmingham engineer and a western American hard-rock miner who shared a common rhetoric and value system. Until we examine in more detail the rhetoric and value systems of other Anglo-American leaders and trade unions and choose leaders, individual unions, and federations of unions that are at least comparable, we are in no position to assume ipso facto that American working-class values differed fundamentally from English ones. The same caution holds for Lipset's assertions about the uniqueness of the general American value structure: his achievement-egalitarian syndrome. To Mann, the tension between equality and individualism was as intense among organized sectors of the English working class as among their American counterparts and caused workers on both sides of the Atlantic to drive themselves ahead rather than joining together collectively with all other workers to modify the class structure. Indeed, the history of Anglo-American labor movements is rife with examples of the tension between individualism and equality, selfishness and self-sacrifice, as even a cursory reading of the sources must indicate. Again, until we examine individuals and institutions on both sides of the Atlantic in comparable social situations, we are in no position to draw firm conclusions about fundamental differences or similarities.

The lives of Mann and Haywood do, however, reveal one clear similarity in the Anglo-American experience—and one sharp difference. Their careers certainly disclose how marginal a place the principled and militant working-class radical has held in Anglo-American society. The more radical both Mann and Haywood became, the more they led or spoke for organizations out of touch with the mass of workers, except in times of unusual crisis. But English society has always maintained that extra measure of tolerance for deviancy that America has lacked, indicating an English tolerance for eccentricity that Kenneth McNaught in his suggestive essay on the failure of American socialism has posited as the cause for the tenacity of English radicalism in contrast to the evanescence of American radicalism.[42] Tom Mann, the English radical and communist, could end his life in his native land after receiving birthday tributes from Emmanuel Shinwell and Clement Attlee. Haywood died a miserable exile, having to be satisfied that American communists distorted and romanticized his contributions to the American labor movement and to radicalism.

Notes

An earlier version of this essay appeared in *Toward a New View of America: Essays in Honor of Arthur C. Cole,* ed. Hans L. Trefousse (New York: Burt Franklin Publishers, 1977), 189–208.

1. Melvyn Dubofsky, "The Origins of Western Working-Class Radicalism, 1890–1905," *Labor History* 7 (Spring 1966): 154.

2. Seymour M. Lipset, *The First New Nation: The United States in Historical and Comparative Perspective* (New York: Basic Books, 1963); Louis Hartz, *The Liberal Tradition in America* (New York: Harcourt, Brace, 1955); idem, *The Founding of New Societies* (New York: Harcourt, Brace, and World, 1964), 69–122; Daniel Boorstin, *The Genius of American Politics* (Chicago: University of Chicago Press, 1953); idem, *The Americans* (New York: Random House, 1958, 1965), vols. 1 and 2.

3. Lipset, *First New Nation;* Hartz, *Liberal Tradition.*

4. Cited in Daniel Bell, *Marxian Socialism in the United States* (Princeton, N.J.: Princeton University Press, 1967), 4.

5. David Shannon, "Socialism and Labor," in *The Comparative Approach to American History,* ed. C. Vann Woodward (New York: Basic Books, 1968), 249. Carl Degler cites Shannon's essay as "one of the most incisive and fresh explanations for American exceptionalism in print" (untitled review in *Journal of Southern History* 34 [Aug. 1968]: 429). Cf. John Laslett, *Labor and the Left* (New York: Basic

Books, 1970), 304. See also Kent and Gretchen Kreuter, *An American Dissenter: The Life of Algie Martin Simons, 1870–1950* (Lexington: University Press of Kentucky, 1969), for the following remark: "Socialism was a fragment torn from the culture of another continent, and to live successfully in a new environment it had to unite itself with indigenous forms of life that were already thriving. . . . Yet he [Simons] underestimated the vigor of the life to which he sought to attach this foreign graft. It was socialism that was choked out" (220).

6. Lipset, *First New Nation,* 175.

7. For the problems of businessmen-capitalists in an aristocratic society, see David Landes, "French Entrepreneurship and Industrial Growth in the Nineteenth Century," *Journal of Economic History* 9 (1949): 49–61; idem, "French Business and the Businessman: A Social and Cultural Analysis," in *Modern France: Problems of the Third and Fourth Republics,* ed. E. E. Mead (Princeton, N.J.: Princeton University Press, 1951), 334–53.

8. Asa Briggs, "The Language of 'Class' in Early Nineteenth-Century England," in *Essays in Labour History,* ed. Asa Briggs and John Saville (London: Macmillan, 1967), 43–73, esp. 70–71, quoting Webb.

9. In Mann's case, we are more fortunate than Haywood's. Although there is no substantial collection of Mann's private papers and documents, we do have his own understated and quite believable autobiography, *Memoirs* (London: Labour Publishing Co., 1923). There is also Dona Torr, *Tom Mann and His Times,* vol. 1, *1856–1890* (London: Lawrence and Wishart, 1956); idem, *Tom Mann* (London: Lawrence and Wishart, 1936); Edward Thompson, "Tom Mann and His Times, 1890–1892," *Our History* 26–27 (Summer–Autumn 1962). For Haywood, we are less fortunate. His autobiography, about which there is still some dispute as to authorship, is exaggerated and at places clearly not in accord with the facts of his life. See William D. Haywood, *Bill Haywood's Book: The Autobiography of William D. Haywood* (New York: International Publishers, 1929). A biography that scarcely transcends the insights of the autobiography and can be equally misleading (though it contains some new information, particularly on Haywood's Russian exile) is Joseph R. Conlin, *Big Bill Haywood and the Radical Union Movement* (Syracuse, N.Y.: Syracuse University Press, 1969). For a somewhat different version of Haywood's life and career, see Melvyn Dubofsky, "The Radicalism of the Dispossessed: William Haywood and the IWW," in *Dissent: Explorations in The History of American Radicalism,* ed. Alfred F. Young (DeKalb: Northern Illinois University Press, 1968), 177–213.

10. Unless otherwise cited, the material for the biographical sketches comes from Mann's *Memoirs;* Torr's *Tom Mann and His Times* and *Tom Mann;* Haywood's *Bill Haywood's Book;* and Dubofsky, "Radicalism of the Dispossessed."

11. Mann lost his mother when he was only two and a half; Haywood's father died when Bill was three.

12. Confidential information on Mann from English sources; for Haywood's extramarital activities, see "Relating to the Western Federation of Miners, 1906–1907," Pinkerton Reports, microfilm, Idaho State Historical Society, Moscow; Mabel Dodge Luhan, *Intimate Memories,* vol. 3: *Movers and Shakers* (New York: Harcourt, Brace, 1936), 89, 186–87.

13. J. B. Jefferys, *The Story of the Engineers* (London: Lawrence and Wishart, 1946).

14. Melvyn Dubofsky, "Origins of Western Working-Class Radicalism"; Vernon Jensen, *Heritage of Conflict* (Ithaca, N.Y.: Cornell University Press, 1950).

15. Engels to F. Sorge, Aug. 9–11, 1891, in Karl Marx and Friedrich Engels, *Letters to Americans, 1848–1895* (New York: International Publishers, 1953), 235.

16. *The State of Idaho v. William D. Haywood, et al.,* microfilm, Idaho State Historical Society, Moscow.

17. "Stenographic Report of the Advisory Board Appointed by Governor James H. Peabody to Investigate and Report upon Labor Difficulties in the State of Colorado and More Particularly at Colorado City," 80, 81, 84, 109, 118, in James H. Hawley Papers, Idaho State Historical Society, Boise.

18. Mann, *Memoirs,* 106.

19. *Miner's Magazine* 3 (Feb. 1902): 6.

20. Tom Mann, *The Programme of the I.L.P. and the Unemployed* (London: n.p., 1895), 1–2.

21. *Proceedings of the First Annual Convention of the Industrial Workers of the World* (New York: Labor News Co., 1905), 18.

22. Torr, *Tom Mann and His Times,* 218.

23. Tom Mann and Ben Tillett, *The "New" Trade-Unionism: A Reply to Mr. George Shipton* (London: n.p., 1890).

24. *Miner's Magazine* 6 (May 11, 1905): 6; cf. ibid. 7 (Nov. 30, 1905): 10.

25. *Yorkshire Factory Times,* Aug. 28, 1891, cited in Thompson, "Tom Mann," 32.

26. Mann, *Memoirs,* 239.

27. Ibid., 243.

28. William D. Haywood, "Socialism the Hope of the Working Class," *International Socialist Review* 12 (Feb. 1912): 464.

29. Ibid., 462.

30. Haywood to Officers and Delegates at the 1906 WFM Convention, May 24, 1906, in WFM, *Official Proceedings of the 1906 Convention* (Denver: WFM, 1906), 17–22.

31. Tom Mann, "Forging the Weapon," *Industrial Syndicalist* 1 (Sept. 1910); idem, "Foreword," in Emile Pataud (Emile Pouget), *Syndicalism and the Co-operative Commonwealth* (Oxford: New International Publishing, 1913).

32. Haywood to Officers and Delegates at the 1906 WFM Convention, 17–22.

33. Mann, "Forging the Weapon," 7.

34. Mann, *Industrial Syndicalist* (Apr. 1911), cited in Torr, *Tom Mann and His Times,* 36–37.

35. *U.S. Commission on Industrial Relations, Final Report and Testimony,* vol. 11 (Washington, D.C., 1915), 10, 578.

36. Mann, "Foreword."

37. E. J. Hobsbawm, "The Fabians Reconsidered," in *Labouring Men,* ed. E. J. Hobsbawm (New York: Basic Books, 1964), 250–71; Robert Wiebe, *The Search for Order, 1877–1920* (New York: Hill and Wang, 1967), 145–63.

38. Mann, *Memoirs,* 127; idem, *The Programme of the I.L.P. and the Unemployed,*

3; idem, "Forging the Weapon," 4; idem, "The Transport Workers' Strike in England," *International Socialist Review* 12 (Dec. 1911): 355.

39. Ibid.

40. Tom Mann, *Russia in 1921* (London: n p., n.d.), esp. 15, 24, 38, 43; idem, *Memoirs,* 323–24; Torr, *Tom Mann and His Times,* 45–48.

41. Conlin, *Big Bill Haywood,* 194–209.

42. Kenneth McNaught, "American Progressives and the Great Society," *Journal of American History* 53 (Dec 1966): 504–20.

PART 2

Workers, Politics, and the State

THESE three essays, written over a fifteen-year period from the mid-1970s through the late 1980s, explore common terrain. Like the ones that precede them, these three were originally written as papers presented at scholarly conferences. Actually, I wrote the essay on the New Deal first, initially for an early meeting of the Columbia University Seminar on Labor and Working-Class History (1976) and subsequently in the form in which it was published for the German Society for American Studies annual conference in February 1978. I prepared the first essay in this section for another university seminar, a yearlong seminar (1982) sponsored by the history department at the University of Pennsylvania on the theme of workers and industrialism. I presented the final essay at a conference on the political party in Europe and the United States sponsored by the Gramsci Institute in Bologna, Italy, in May 1989, the proceedings of which, including my essay, were published subsequently in Italian.

In these essays, I try to explain the forces and factors that over the course of the twentieth century drew the American labor movement and masses of unorganized workers into the Democratic party. They serve as a triptych that formulates my version of the role of unions and workers in creating what Karen Orren has characterized as "modern American liberalism."[1] The third essay, to be sure, segues from the high point of modern American liberalism—during the Great Society years—to its collapse during the Ronald Reagan era, when the Democratic party could no longer rely on its coalition with workers and unions, nor could the labor movement look to Democratic administrations for assistance (and salvation).

The essays build on conventional wisdom about the relationship between workers and politics and also, in part, shatter that wisdom. The first essay explores why the concept of "voluntarism," so frequently cited by those scholars who assert that the American Federation of Labor (AFL) opposed positive state action on behalf of workers and disdained partisan politics, distorts the historical record. The more recent scholarship of Julie Greene, Joseph McCartin, and others strengthens my contention that in the era of Woodrow Wilson, Samuel Gompers vigorously led the AFL into the political arena and that the labor movement expected to benefit materially from its support of a Democratic administration and from positive state intervention on behalf of workers.[2] But the essay also hints at aspects of the uneasy relationship between organized labor and the Democratic party that would become evident only after the coalition grew firmer from the New Deal of Franklin Roosevelt to the Great Society of Lyndon Johnson. The sore points that opened between Wilson and his labor friends in 1919–20 foreshadowed similar developments that occurred in the administrations of Roosevelt, Truman, Johnson, and Carter (today one might also say Clinton) and that have been delineated so well in the scholarship of Steve Fraser, Nelson Lichtenstein, and Kevin Boyle.[3]

Once again, I must repeat that "Not So 'Turbulent Years'" should not be read to suggest that the New Deal Era lacked labor militancy or failed to transform the polity, society, and economy substantially. Rather, I sought to define the limits to the New Deal revolution and to locate them neither in the taming of labor militants by corporate liberals nor in their betrayal by unscrupulous labor leaders but instead in the essence of working-class culture.[4] The essay, I think, hints at the "moral economy of capitalism" that Lizabeth Cohen suggests motivated workers to make a New Deal; at the "working-class Americanism" that Gary Gerstle believes enabled workers to surmount the ethnoreligious identities that previously separated them; at the intrinsic weaknesses within the Congress of Industrial Organizations (CIO) that rendered it, in Robert Zieger's apt words, "a fragile juggernaut;" and at the divisions between union leaders and the rank and file that plagued the labor movement, which has been so well described by Steve Fraser and Nelson Lichtenstein in their respective biographies of Sidney Hillman and Walter Reuther.[5] It also intimates how ethnic and racial divisions persisted in dividing workers, a theme taken up more recently by Bruce Nelson, Kevin Boyle, and Michael Honey, among others.[6]

My recent experience at a scholarly conference to commemorate the twentieth anniversary of the Carter administration at the Jimmy Carter Presidential Library, at which I was commissioned to prepare a paper on the Carter administration and organized labor, convinced me that the themes outlined in my essay on workers and politics from Roosevelt to Reagan were right on target. The files on labor in the Carter Library were filled with material concerning how unions had lost touch with their members; how workers had become more concerned with prices, taxes, and inflation than with expansive public policy programs, and why they were drifting away from the New Deal–Great Society formula; how racial animosities fractured labor's united front and left the Carter administration unable to satisfy simultaneously its labor, African-American, and female constituents. All the paper presenters at the conference, myself included, who focused on Carter and domestic policy concluded that his presidency served as a bridge from the New Deal version of modern American liberalism to Ronald Reagan's Republican politics of free-market prosperity and Bill Clinton's "New Democrats." And, once again, the recent excellent scholarship of Kevin Boyle and Tom Sugrue demonstrates how and why workers deserted the labor leaders who constructed the AFL-CIO–Democratic party coalition.[7] The essay also presaged the story told more fully by James Gregory about how U.S. society and culture, especially the working-class component, became increasingly southernized after World War II, a reality disclosed graphically by George Wallace's political appeal to white northern workers.[8]

Taken as whole, then, the three essays in this section explore the political trajectory of American workers and their labor movement in the twentieth century from its rise in the Wilson years to its decline in the 1980s and thereafter. They also, each in its own way, suggest comparisons and contrasts between the history of workers in the United States and that of their brothers and sisters in Europe.

Notes

1. Karen Orren, "Organized Labor and the Invention of Modern Liberalism in the United States," *Studies in American Political Development* 2 (1987): 317–36; idem, "Union Politics and Postwar Liberalism in the United States," *Studies in American Political Development* 1 (1986): 215–52.

2. Julie Greene, *The Strike at the Ballot Box: The AFL and Electoral Politics, 1906–1916* (New York: Cambridge University Press, 1998); Joseph McCartin, *Labor's Great War: The Struggle for Union Democracy and the Origins of Modern American Labor Relations, 1912–1921* (Chapel Hill: University of North Carolina Press, 1998); Richard Schneirov, *Labor and Urban Politics: Class, Conflict, and the Origins of Modern Liberalism in Chicago* (Urbana: University of Illinois Press, 1998). For a history that stresses workers' political activism from a slightly different perspective, see Alan Dawley, *Struggles for Social Justice: Social Responsibility and the Liberal State* (Cambridge, Mass.: Harvard University Press, 1991).

3. Steven Fraser, *Labor Will Rule: Sidney Hillman and the Rise of American Labor* (New York: Free Press, 1991); Nelson Lichtenstein, *The Most Dangerous Man in Detroit: Walter Reuther and the Fate of American Labor* (New York: Basic Books, 1995); Kevin Boyle, *The UAW and the Heyday of American Liberalism, 1945–1968* (Ithaca, N.Y.: Cornell University Press, 1995).

4. For perspectives on the persistent effort to establish the militant, radical credentials manifested by the rank and file and how they were diluted by union officials and Democratic party manipulators, see *"We Are All Leaders": The Alternative Unionism of the Early 1930s,* ed. Staughton Lynd (Urbana: University of Illinois Press, 1996), esp. 1–26.

5. The tight links formed between organized labor and Democrats in the White House and Congress between 1935 and 1965 are discussed in Lizabeth Cohen, *Making a New Deal: Industrial Workers in Chicago, 1919–1939* (New York: Cambridge University Press, 1990); Gary Gerstle, *Working-Class Americanism: The Politics of Labor in a Textile City, 1914–1960* (New York: Cambridge University Press, 1989); Lichtenstein, *Most Dangerous Man;* Fraser, *Labor Will Rule;* Robert Zieger, *The CIO, 1935–1955* (Chapel Hill: University of North Carolina Press, 1995); David Plotke, *Building a Democratic Political Order: Reshaping American Liberalism in the 1930s* (New York: Cambridge University Press, 1996).

6. See the scholarly controversy in *International Labor and Working-Class History* 44 (Fall 1993): 1–63, which features Michael Goldfield's essay "Race and the CIO: The Possibilities for Racial Egalitarianism during the 1930s and 1940s" and the responses by Gary Gerstle, Robert Korstad, Marshall F. Stevenson, and Judith Stein. See also Michael Goldfield, "Race and the CIO: Reply to Critics," *International Labor and Working-Class History* 46 (Fall 1994): 142–60; Michael E. Honey, *Southern Workers and Black Civil Rights: Organizing Memphis Workers* (Urbana: University of Illinois Press, 1993); Boyle, *UAW;* Thomas J. Sugrue, *The Origins of the Urban Crisis: Race and Inequality in Postwar Detroit* (Princeton, N.J.: Princeton University Press, 1996). Bruce Nelson's "Organized Labor and the Struggle for Black Equality in Mobile during World War II," *Journal of American History* 80 (Dec. 1993): 952–88, is part of a larger study of the impact of race on trade-union organizing in the 1930s and 1940s. Two recent books treat race relations in the meatpacking industry: Roger Horowitz, *"Negro and White Unite and Fight": A Social History of Industrial Unionism in Meatpacking, 1930–1990* (Urbana: University of Illinois Press, 1998); Rick Halpern, *Down on the Killing Floor: Black and White Workers in Chicago's Packinghouses* (Urbana: University of Illinois Press, 1998). Two collections of essays on southern labor history also include important essays on the subject: *Organized Labor in the Twentieth-Century South,* ed. Robert Zieger (Knoxville: University of Tennessee Press, 1991); *Southern Labor in Transition, 1940–1995,* ed. Robert Zieger (Knoxville: University of Tennessee Press, 1997).

7. Melvyn Dubofsky, "Jimmy Carter and the End of the Politics of Productivity," in *The Carter Presidency: Policy Choices in the Post New Deal Era,* ed. Hugh Davis Graham and Gary Fink (Lawrence: University Press of Kansas, 1998), 95–116; Boyle, *UAW;* Sugrue, *Origins of the Urban Crisis;* Plotke, *Building a Democratic Political Order.*

8. See James Gregory, "Southernizing the American Working Class: Post-War Episodes of Regional and Class Transformation," *Labor History* 39 (May 1998): 135–54. See also the ensuing commentary and response between three scholars and Gregory, ibid., 155–68.

· 5 ·

Abortive Reform:The Wilson Administration and Organized Labor, 1913–20

FASHIONS in history sometimes seem as fashionable as those in dress. In the 1950s and early 1960s, the Progressive Era was an exciting intellectual frontier for scholars and was still largely interpreted as the "Age of Reform." More recently, however, a growing number of historians have perceived Progressive reforms as the limited triumphs of a group of emerging professionals and bureaucrats that was seeking to rationalize and stabilize a turbulent society. For such scholars, Frederick Winslow Taylor and John B. Watson serve as the chief surrogates for the age. In a somewhat similar, if partially divergent, interpretive vein, the New Left historians of the late 1960s and 1970s portrayed the Progressive Era as the moment when "monopoly capital" (to use the term that they were usually loath to apply) used the national state to solidify its dominance in the marketplace. For them, corporatism emerges as the central reform motif, and George W. Perkins (J. P. Morgan's right-hand man), Ralph Easley (secretary of the National Civic Federation), and ultimately the National Industrial Conference Board appear as the era's brain trusts. In all these interpretations, however, labor-capital conflict at best lurks in the background.[1]

To slight the centrality of labor-capital conflict in Progressive America and the role of the labor movement in the era's history seems to me a mistake. We would do better to recall the contemporary judgment of an ardent Wilsonian, Ray Stannard Baker, who, in a series of magazine articles published in 1904–5, described labor-capital relations as the central national political issue of his time. For of all the questions that embroiled politics in the early twentieth century, the labor question was the most sensitive and divisive and the least amenable to compromise. Indeed, the issue was so contentious that most politicians preferred to evade it. Nevertheless, as Bruno Ramirez has observed, the battle between labor and capital, between workers and employers, dominated the hidden agenda of Progressivism. At no time was this more true than during the presidency of Woodrow Wilson, the subject of this essay.

Many aspects of the political struggle among trade unionists, employers, and Democrats in the Wilson years presaged comparable events during the turbulent 1930s.[2] Let me try to explain briefly why this was so. First, the labor movement challenged fundamental American traditions from two directions. Radicalism, whether of socialist or syndicalist variety, was a vital presence among organized workers during the Progressive years. Either form of working-class radicalism threatened the established order. Yet, however threatening labor radicals may have been, they represented only a minority of organized workers. But it is a grave mistake to see the nonradical majority as domesticated citizens in an emerging corporate-liberal system. If Samuel Gompers, John Mitchell, and the workers they represented rhetorically defended private property and free enterprise, their actual practices conflicted with established principles of property rights and circumscribed entrepreneurial freedoms. As David Brody has written, "power and interest can be issues of deadly conflict even in a system in which men agree on the fundamentals."[3] American business never willingly conceded any of its prerogatives to workers and unions.

Second, in the early twentieth century, organized labor for the first time in American history represented a durable mass movement. Between 1897 and 1903, the unions affiliated with the American Federation of Labor (AFL) grew more than sixfold, from 400,000 members to almost 3 million, as also did many independent unions. An aggressive employer counterattack, as well as the business contraction of 1907–9, thwarted the advance of unionism but failed, unlike similar conjunctures in the nineteenth century, to paralyze it. Then, in the years 1910–13, unions grew again and succeeded in organizing workers hitherto thought unorganizable, setting the foundation for the remarkable growth in membership during World War I. This increase was linked directly to a rising intensity in industrial warfare.[4]

Third, what was happening in the United States must be understood in the context of the entire Atlantic economy—if not the global economy. Similar forces and events were sweeping Italy, France, Germany, the Lowlands, Britain, Scandinavia, and even eastern Europe and Russia. This was indeed the age of the mass strike. It was also the golden age of working-class internationalism and its institution, the Second International. The rise of the European working classes and the waxing power of socialist parties did not pass unnoticed in the United States.[5]

Fourth, American unions and workers became more active in national politics than ever before. As unions grew in size and industrial conflicts spread over a larger arena, federal policies and actions often proved decisive to the success or failure of the labor cause. John Mitchell, one of the nation's more moderate labor leaders, put the case well when he wrote in 1903: "The trade union movement in this country can make progress only by identifying itself with the state."[6] In fact, his union, the United Mine Workers of America (UMWA) had just benefited from the actions of Theodore Roosevelt.

But it was not until the presidency of Woodrow Wilson that the labor question became a persistent, inescapable national issue. Wilson's predecessors, Roosevelt and Taft, occasionally grappled with the problem of labor. Yet their administrations lacked well-defined labor policies; built and maintained no regular, systematic relationship with the labor movement; and, in the case of Taft especially, opposed labor's primary political goal: relief from legal injunctions and exemption from the Sherman Act. All this changed with Wilson's election. From 1913 through 1920, labor had direct access to the White House and the cabinet, achieved its most desired legislative goals, and gained a share, however small, in national political power.

Before analyzing Wilsonian labor policy in detail, we should consider briefly what might be defined as its general dynamics. It is essential to keep in mind that at no point between 1913 and 1920 was there a clear, consistent federal policy toward workers and trade unions. The structural separation of power at times resulted in conflicting policies adopted by the executive, legislative, and judicial branches of government. Even within the executive branch, bureaucratic competition proved the rule, as different cabinet officers and their departments contended for supremacy—especially during World War I. Despite the confusion and conflicts among Democrats in Washington over policy, however, by the midpoint of the Wilson presidency, a firm political alliance had been built between the AFL, most of its affiliated unions, and the Democratic party. Wilsonian labor policy divided into three quite distinct stages. The first ran from the creation of the Department of Labor through the publication of the *Final Report* of the U.S.

Commission on Industrial Relations (CIR). It included the enactment of several laws dear to the hearts of labor lobbyists. The second stage occurred during the World War I years, when the government provided organized labor with opportunities for growth hitherto unimaginable to most labor leaders. In the last stage, the federal government retreated from its advanced position on the labor-capital front, and policymakers diluted their previous solicitude for independent trade unionism.

The political alliance between labor and the Democrats did not emerge suddenly with the election of Woodrow Wilson. Despite conventional notions concerning the AFL's apolitical traditions, the federation had in fact originated to defend and advance labor's political interests. That was why when unions expanded so rapidly between 1897 and 1903, the AFL moved its headquarters from Indianapolis, a center of trade unionism, to Washington, D.C., the locus of national politics. The issue for such labor leaders as Gompers and the chiefs of the independent railroad brotherhoods was never whether or not labor should be active politically. Rather, it was to find a mode of political action that would produce the fewest divisions among the rank and file. Labor leaders had to maintain loyalty and solidarity among a membership split three ways: the AFL comprised traditional Republicans and Democrats, plus a growing number of independents and socialists. It is difficult to estimate in what proportions organized workers split among the three, but it would seem that the great majority of workers (70 to 80 percent) preferred either Democratic or some form of independent labor/socialist politics and that the remainder, mostly American-born Protestant workers whose allegiances derived from a political culture formed during the Civil War and Reconstruction, leaned toward Republicanism.[7]

Whatever the political inclinations of the rank and file, leaders realized that federal policies and actions vitally affected the security of trade unions. Railroad union leaders had learned that lesson by 1900, after almost three decades of industrial warfare punctuated by federal intervention.[8] As the economy continued to nationalize, many unions found their actions coming under federal scrutiny. The boycott, the secondary strike, and the sympathetic strike—essential weapons in labor's arsenal—were all at one time or another declared illegal by federal courts. Sections of the Sherman Antitrust Act, the Interstate Commerce Act, and the federal proscription of common law conspiracies in restraint of trade combined to imperil the future of trade unionism.[9] A comparable situation in Britain had pushed workers and their unions toward more independent forms of political action and ultimately to the founding of the Labour party. American union leaders were aware of British developments and were made more so by pressure from their followers. Not only was socialism making substantial inroads among workers—especially in such core unions as the mine workers, the machinists, and the brewery workers—but city centrals and state federations of labor were also flooding headquarters with petitions and letters demanding the creation of an American labor party and often citing the British example.[10]

In response, Gompers and his associates devised a political strategy that would mollify their followers while causing the least political dissension. First, AFL officials in 1906 drew up "Labor's Bill of Grievances" and presented it to leaders of both parties in Congress for action. They then established a Labor Representation Committee (patterned after the British model) to seek the election of trade unionists and union sympathizers to Congress. They even targeted specific members of the House, all Republicans, for defeat. Finally, Gompers went to the 1908 conventions of both major parties, demanding that they incorporate labor's primary goals into their platforms.[11]

The AFL's political assertiveness served primarily to forge an alliance between labor and the Democrats. In Congress, Democrats responded more sympathetically to the Bill of Grievances. The trade unionists elected to the House were mostly Democrats (of fifteen elected in 1910, thirteen were Democrats). And in 1908, the Democratic party agreed to incorporate the AFL's demands into its platform. As a consequence, Gompers and other labor leaders cooperated with the Democratic National Committee in campaigning for William Jennings Bryan. For their part, the Democrats had good reason to seek union support. As a minority party nationally, they needed allies wherever they could be found. Moreover, as a party whose strength was concentrated in the South and West, Democrats shared labor's antagonism to big capital. Thus, political calculation and sentiment increasingly bound Democrats and labor together.[12]

Ironically, however, the emergence of Woodrow Wilson as a national political figure at first threatened the Democratic-labor alliance. Though Southern-born, Wilson was discovered and promoted politically by what remained of the old northern Democratic financial community, the "gold bugs." Wilson brought to Democratic politics a distaste for organized labor and the principles it personified. A "Credo" written by the future president in 1907 defended the absolute right to freedom of contract from its union critics, whom he defined as men "who have neither the ideas nor the sentiments needed for "the maintenance or the enjoyment of liberty." Only two years later, he declared to an antilabor banquet audience: "I am a fierce partizan [sic] of the Open Shop and of everything that makes for industrial liberty." Not surprisingly, then, when Wilson ran for governor of New Jersey in 1910, the state's labor movement united against him. To quiet the voices of his trade-union critics, Wilson in 1910 changed his line. "I have always been the warm friend of organized labor," he assured trade unionists, and he defended their right to organize independent unions.[13]

Still, at the 1912 Democratic convention, labor held firm in the anti-Wilson camp, much preferring the candidacy of Missouri's Champ Clark. Once the nomination was Wilson's, though, he had little choice but to further his rapprochement with labor. Nor did Gompers have much choice other than to accept Wilson's overtures, unless he preferred to see the labor vote move more swiftly toward Debs and the socialists or Roosevelt and the Progressives. In 1912, the Democratic party once again incorporated the AFL's primary demands into its platform. Although Gompers asserted in his 1925 autobiography that he played no active role in the 1912 election, and the public record in fact shows only circumspect labor support for Wilson and the Democrats, the AFL national office served as a clearinghouse for Democratic National Committee efforts to woo the labor vote. The party chairman contacted Gompers about sending AFL organizers to different parts of the country on behalf of the Wilson campaign. John L. Lewis, for example, campaigned for the Democrats in New Mexico and Arizona.[14]

AFL assistance surely did not harm Wilson's prospects. Although it is impossible to apportion a labor vote among the parties and candidates, circumstantial evidence suggests that union endorsements brought Wilson a good many votes. He owed his victory primarily, of course, to the split within the Republican party; but the election returns proved how vital labor would be for future Democratic successes. The Taft Republicans, the only party among the four major ones contesting the election that offered nothing to workers and unions, received less than 25 percent of the popular vote. Wilson could interpret the results as well as anyone. It was not only the influence of Louis Brandeis that encouraged Wilson to show more sympathy for organized labor. What Brandeis perhaps did was to accelerate the speed at which Wilson was already moving, owing to political realities and electoral calculus.[15] In any event, after his election, the new president worked to solidify the Democratic-labor alliance.

Unlike any previous chief executive, Wilson opened his administration wide to the leaders of trade unionism. Cabinet officials, especially the secretary of labor, conferred regularly with the AFL Executive Council. Gompers and other labor leaders corresponded often and at length with the president, who made them feel their counsel was sought. Wilson made sure to appear personally at the July 4, 1916, dedication of the new AFL headquarters building and to say the proper ceremonial words. He also sought the AFL's advice of pending judicial appointments, up to and including the Supreme Court, a matter of no small importance to organized labor. Finally, one year after his reelection, in November 1917, Wilson became the first president to address an annual convention of the AFL. Surely, American labor now had a friend in the White House.[16]

Organized labor reciprocated Wilson's attentions. At no time was this clearer than in the election of 1916. The reunification of the Republican party boded ill for Democratic chances that year. Thus, Gompers called out the troops for Wilson, and he himself campaigned publicly for the Democrats. Such unions as the United Mine Workers (UMW) and the International Association of Machinists, which had leaned toward socialism before 1916, now fell in line behind Wilson. The railroad brotherhoods, special beneficiaries of Wilsonian largesse, were perfervid in their support for the President. In the western states, which were to prove so decisive in Wilson's reelection, labor united behind the president, and its votes were probably critical to his victory. By November 1916, organized labor had become a core constituency of the Democratic party.[17]

That connection, however, was built on more than symbolism. The Department of Labor, which was established as a cabinet-level agency in Wilson's first term, advocated trade unionism's case within the administration. The secretary of the department, William B. Wilson, an ex-UMWA officer and former Democratic congressman from Pennsylvania, considered himself and acted as a partisan of trade unionism. As he wrote to Gompers after eight years of service as secretary, the most important of the Labor Department's many duties was to have someone as its directing head who could carry the viewpoint of labor into the councils of the president. That was a task to which William Wilson dedicated himself. As he told the 1914 AFL convention: "If securing justice to those who earn their bread in the sweat of their faces constitutes partisanship, then count me as a partisan of labor." One year earlier, he had informed the same audience, much to the consternation of many conservatives, that absolute rights in private property did not exist. Society, he explained, has a perfect right to modify such rights "whenever in its judgment it deems it for the welfare of society to do it."[18]

In staffing the new department, William Wilson acted on these principles. Whenever possible, he chose officials sympathetic to labor or drawn directly from trade unions. The newly established federal conciliation service selected many of its mediators from the UMWA. In their capacity as mediators/conciliators, these Labor Department agents not only sought to eliminate the sources of industrial conflict; they also promoted the recognition of the AFL and other unions.[19]

Equally positive in their effects on the development of organized labor were the fieldwork, public hearings, and final report of the U.S. Commission on Industrial Relations. Originally conceived in the waning days of the Taft administration as a federal response to labor-capital violence, the CIR functioned as an advocate for the poor, the oppressed, and the unorganized. This was primarily because of the person William Wilson chose as the chairperson, Frank P. Walsh, a Kansas City attorney and left-wing Democrat. Otherwise balanced among representatives of enlightened capital, responsible labor (the AFL and the railroad brotherhoods), and the public at large, the commission was driven to the left by Walsh and his lieutenant, Basil Manly.[20]

For more than two years, the CIR conducted public hearings across the nation at which witnesses from management, labor, and the community testified about industrial violence, labor relations, and exploitation. Almost invariably, the public hearings—whether concerned with the 1913 Paterson, New Jersey, silk strike, labor policy in the Chicago packinghouses, or the shopmen's strike on the Illinois Central Line—offered unions a friendly forum in which to state their case. In dealing with capitalists, however, Walsh played the prosecutor. He pilloried John D. Rockefeller Jr. and held him personally responsible for the company policies that had resulted in the infamous Ludlow, Colorado, massacre. While castigating capital, Walsh publicly and more so privately extended a comradely hand to radicals— not only such "respectable" socialists as Morris Hillquit but also such "notorious" Wobblies as Vincent St. John and William D. Haywood. While the CIR held its public hearings, scores of field investigators filed unpublished reports. These, too, generally made the case for organized labor. Equally important, these unsung investigators later played prominent roles in implementing World War I and New Deal labor policies.[21]

Walsh's radicalism ensured that the CIR would divide internally when the time came to issue a final report and recommendations, which was precisely what happened. The commission split three ways. The representatives of capital essentially leaned to a middle way. They condemned equally irresponsible capital and radical labor, calling on enlightened businessmen and responsible trade unionists to bargain reasonably. They also defended the open-shop principle and drew no distinction between independent and company unions. The public representatives, John R. Commons and Florence Harriman, stood midway between the representatives of capital and the Walsh majority. More sympathetic to independent trade unions than the employers on the commission, Commons and Harriman found the majority too condemnatory of business, too soft on labor radicals, and too favorably inclined to positive state action. They preferred to have experts chair impartial, joint labor-management boards that would bring law and order to the anarchy of industrial relations. If corporate liberalism existed anywhere in Wilsonian America, it was among such people, whose recommendations were rejected by both capital and labor. The majority report, by contrast, prepared by Manly and signed by Walsh and the three labor commissioners, was perhaps the most radical document ever released by a federal commission. It blamed industrial violence and exploitation on the gross maldistribution of wealth and income, the ubiquity of unemployment, and corporate denial of workers' human rights, especially the right to organize unions of their own choosing. "Relief from these grave evils cannot be secured by petty reforms," declared the majority. "The action must be drastic." Among the drastic reforms proposed were federal laws and agencies to protect the rights of workers to organize and bargain collectively. Independent unionism was to be made a central objective of federal policy, as was a panoply of measures aimed at securing working people against unemployment, illness, and indigent old age. As Walsh himself wrote to a UMWA leader after the CIR submitted its final report, it was "more radical than any report upon industrial subjects ever made by any government agency."[22]

Trade unionists and radicals were much impressed. A railroad brotherhood journal proclaimed that the report would "go down in history as the greatest contribution to labor literature of our time." The socialist *Appeal to Reason* described it as peeling the hide off capitalism, and the *Christian Socialist* compared it to the Declaration of Independence and the Emancipation Proclamation. Finally, the *Masses* saw it as "the beginning of an indigenous American revolutionary movement."[23] Indeed so, for the Walsh-Manly recommendations of July 1915 incorporated a labor program that encompassed every reform of the New Deal and others that have never been enacted. In fact, the combination of a split commission and a radical majority report ensured that nothing substantive would come immediately from the CIR's work. But less than three years later, Frank Walsh would serve as cochair of the National War Labor Board (NWLB), a position from which he sought to implement many of his 1915 proposals.

Strangely enough for an administration that otherwise did so much for organized labor, the Wilsonians stocked the barest of legislative cupboards. On no issue was this truer than on the one closest to the heart of labor, relief from legal injunctions and antitrust legislation. Rather than describe in detail the complicated legislative politics and history of the Clayton Act controversy and its labor clauses, let me simply conclude that on the issue of injunctive relief, Wilson refused to defer to labor's requests or even to compromise. In his view, any statute that exempted labor from judicial review was a form of class legislation alien to the American way.[24] Nevertheless, for exigent political reasons, Wilson did in the summer of 1916 endorse an effort to abolish child labor through federal legislation (the Keating-Owens Act) and recommended passage of the Adamson Act to award operating railroad workers the basic eight-hour day at their previous ten-hour wage. This legislation proved an essential element in Wilson's 1916 political strategy and his electoral coalition.[25]

What had been mostly tendencies or halfway measures toward a new labor policy became a reality during World War I. One part of that reality, the AFL's cooperation in Wilsonian diplomacy, has been described and analyzed by Ronald Radosh and Frank L. Grubbs Jr.[26] The other and far more important part—domestic labor policy—has received no comparable treatment. James Weinstein touches several vital aspects of the subject in his book *The Corporate Ideal in the Liberal State,* as does David Kennedy in *Over Here.* But Weinstein forces Wilsonian labor policy into the Procrustean bed of his "corporate liberal" interpretation of American history, and Kennedy deals with it largely from the perspective of corporate planners and those members of the administration least sensitive to organized labor.[27]

Wartime labor policy was shaped by two distinct factors: the new realities of social and economic power, and the absence of a uniform, central direction in administration policy. The demands of war magnified labor's power. With unemployment eliminated, workers and unions felt free to press their claims against capital, whether through voluntary quits or collective action. Both labor turnover and the number of strikes reached unprecedented levels in 1917.[28] As for policy, what Robert D. Cuff has shown to be true for the War Industries Board—the existence of bureaucratic infighting and the absence of any accepted central plan—was also true for labor policy.[29] By and large, the president allowed subordinate officials, departments, and boards to make policy. Except for the heavy-handed repression of labor and political radicals, he rarely tried to coordinate actions on the labor front. The Labor Department, under William Wilson, and the War Department, under Newton D. Baker, generally favored trade unionism, as did the NWLB and the War Labor Policies Board (WLPB). The Commerce, Agriculture, and Justice Departments, as well as the separate military branches, the WIB, and corporate dollar-a-year men, often equated unionism with radicalism (subversion) and sympathized with open-shop principles. Added to this confusion, the federal judiciary handed down several decisions that conflicted with vital aspects of Wilsonian policy. In February 1918, the journalist Robert Bruere succinctly noted these contradictions. "Here were three branches of the Federal Government," he wrote:

> pursuing three radically divergent and hopelessly conflicting policies towards the wageworkers at the very moment when the nation was making a patriotic appeal to the workers to get cut a maximum production. . . . The United States Department of Justice was arresting them, the President's Mediation Commission was telling them that they must organize into unions, and the United States Supreme Court was announcing that if they attempted to organize under certain conditions they would be guilty of contempt of court.[30]

Despite the confusion in Washington, trade unionism clearly gained from the prevailing drift in federal policy. In this sense, David Kennedy is wrong to assert that federal labor policy did not alter the existing lines of power in society but instead scrupulously followed them and set them more rigidly in place. He is equally wrong in insisting that reformers and labor leaders had little success in winning federal support for trade unionism or that Gompers himself perceived such a goal as unrealistic by agreeing to an unpublished Council of National Defense (CND) statement stipulating "that employers and employees in private industries should not attempt to take advantage of the existing abnormal conditions to change the standards which they were unable to change under normal conditions."[31]

The evidence suggests a far different reality than the one limned by Kennedy. Of course, if one focuses primarily on the policies of Bernard Baruch, Walter S. Gifford, Louis B. Wehle, and Colonel Brice P. Disque, unions seemed to get short shrift in wartime.[32] But if one examines the records of the labor department, the President's Mediation Commission, the NWLB, the WLPB, and union leaders' own role in setting wartime policies, a quite different picture emerges. For example, on the CND statement concerning the maintenance of standards during the war, Labor Secretary Wilson interpreted that as applying only to working conditions and not to the question of unionization. He defined the right to organize as the "burning issue" of the day, and asserted: "capital has no right to interfere with working men organizing." And he convinced the president to write as follows to the director of the antiunion Alabama coal operators' association: "It is generally acknowledged that our laws and the long established policy of our Government recognize the right of workingmen to organize unions if they so desire."[33]

Moreover, many officials in Washington found labor more amenable to federal policies and goals than capital. President Wilson publicly told unionists at the 1917 AFL convention: "you are reasonable in a larger number of cases than the capitalists." More revealingly, War Secretary Baker confided to the president: "I confess I am more concerned to have industry and capital know what you think they ought to do in regard to labor than to have labor understand its duty. In my own dealings with the industrial problem here, I have found labor more willing to keep step than capital."[34]

As unrest swelled in the summer of 1917 and strikes disrupted war production, employers and patriots demanded they be suppressed. The administration, however, preferred a different prescription for quelling the eruption. As the Labor Department defined the situation, unrest was primarily an expression "of revolt at low wages and hard conditions in industry and impatience with the slow evolution of economic democracy through the organized labor movement." The Labor Department seconded Gompers's advice to the president, which maintained that if employers recognized bona fide AFL unions, the labor unrest would diminish. The problem was that capital refused to keep step with federal labor policy. And capitalist resistance to unionism grew as employers increasingly expected assistance from their many friends in Washington, whose policies were seldom directly overruled by the president.[35]

To overcome employer antiunionism and also to define more clearly a federal labor policy, Secretaries Wilson and Baker joined with Gompers in August 1917 to urge the president to appoint a special commission to investigate the wartime upheaval and to make recommendations for its resolution. The result was the appointment in September of the President's Mediation Commission. Chaired by Secretary Wilson and composed of two

AFL representatives and two employers, the commission was in fact dominated by Felix Frankfurter, who shared his friend Walter Lippmann's conviction that the war provided an unsurpassed opportunity to reform American society.[36]

Even before the commission began its task, Frankfurter laid down its guiding principles. He agreed with the Wilson-Gompers diagnosis of the labor troubles—that is, that most strikes resulted from a combination of real material grievances and employer antiunion practices. Frankfurter thus proposed that the mediators conduct in-depth investigations of working conditions in the troubled industries, that they recommend the creation of formal conciliation machinery to ameliorate grievances, that they urge employers to deal responsibly with their employees, and that they convince American workers that the war was not only to defend democracy abroad but also to establish industrial justice at home. Like Gompers and William Wilson, Frankfurter believed that these objectives could best be accomplished through peaceful bargaining between employers and AFL unions.[37]

Guided by Frankfurter's principles, the commission investigated disputes in the southwestern copper industry, the Pacific Northwest's woods, the West Coast telephone business, and the Chicago packinghouses. In January 1918, it recommended that: (1) a form of collective relationship between management and men is essential and that the recognition of this principle by the government should form an accepted part of the national labor policy; (2) employers should immediately establish grievance machinery to handle real problems equitably before they precipitate strikes; (3) the eight-hour day be established as national policy; and (4) unified direction of wartime labor policy be established.[38]

Acting on the commission's recommendations, President Wilson charged his labor secretary with directing labor policy. Secretary Wilson promptly invited representatives of capital, labor, and the public to meet as a War Labor Conference Board to devise a program to govern labor-management relations. In March 1918, the board approved recommendations comparable to those of the commission, defending the principle of workers' right to form trade unions unimpeded by employers. But it still equivocated by also recommending that management be required to bargain with shop committees, not with union representatives, and that unions coerce neither workers to join nor employers to grant the union shop.[39]

In April 1918, the president created the National War Labor Board, which was patterned after the composition of the War Labor Conference Board. As important as the policy principles enunciated and implemented by the NWLB were the practices of the cochairs, William Howard Taft and Frank P. Walsh, especially the latter. Walsh convinced Taft that the right of workers to organize should be sacrosanct and free of all employer interference. The board, as a matter of policy, ordered reinstatement and back pay for employees discharged for union activities. It also ruled that a whole host of traditional employer antiunion tactics were in violation of federal labor policy. Walsh, moreover, privately cooperated with labor leaders seeking to unionize the meatpacking and steel industries. Paradoxically, he also offered what assistance he could to labor radicals (mostly Wobblies), whom the federal government sought to put "out of business."[40]

The NWLB instituted a minor revolution by making the right to unionize real. Some of its specific orders introduced a whole new concept of property rights consonant with those William B. Wilson had enunciated before the 1913 AFL convention. As one business journal said of an NWLB order: "We know of no legislation authorizing the [NWLB] . . . to require private business concerns to revolutionize their business methods. We cannot see that the War Labor Board or the War Department has any more right to prescribe collective bargaining instead of individual bargaining than it has to prescribe red ink instead of black ink for the firm's letterheads."[41]

This legal revolution also was endorsed by another agency created in the spring of 1918 to implement labor policy: the War Labor Policies Board. And this was no wonder, for its head was Felix Frankfurter. Indeed, an unpublished document in the files of the WLPB proposed "to create in industry a condition of collective bargaining between employer and employee. It contemplates, and is based upon the existence of unions of employees and unions of employers."[42] Together, these agencies were responsible for transforming labor-management relations from a totally private arena to a semipublic one and, in the process, upsetting the historical balance of power in many industries between workers and bosses. As William Z. Foster, the leader of the meatpacking and steel organizing campaigns, observed about the spring and summer of 1918: "the Federal administration was friendly; the right to organize was freely conceded by the government and even insisted upon. . . . The gods were indeed fighting on the side of Labor. It was an opportunity to organize the [steel] industry such as might never again occur."[43]

Labor took full advantage of the opportunity. The growth in union membership was truly remarkable, increasing by over two million between 1917 and 1920, a gain of almost 70 percent. For the first time, total union membership approached 20 percent of the civilian, nonagricultural labor force, a level more than twice as high as any previous peak. Along with this growth went steady rises in wage rates and the general achievement of the eight-hour day.[44]

Union advances could be seen wherever the federal government intervened directly and regularly and wherever effective labor organizations or aggressive organizers functioned. In the men's clothing trade, which prospered on wartime federal contracts, Sidney Hillman, the president of the industry's union, the Amalgamated Clothing Workers of America, established excellent relations with federal contract administrators. As a result, his union, barely two years old when the United States entered the war, more than doubled its membership.[45] In two industries controlled by the federal government during the war (the railroads, directly; coal, indirectly), unions also flourished. The United Mine Workers won equal participation with employers on the wartime Fuel Administration and used its influence there to advance the union into the previously nonunion southern Appalachian coalfields. By war's end, the UMWA claimed more than a half million members, making it far and away the nation's largest union.[46] The story was much the same on the railroads. William McAdoo, the federal railroad czar, put out the welcome mat for labor leaders. Federal Railroad Administration orders increased wages, standardized work rules, and improved conditions. Unions grew rapidly, especially the previously smaller, nonoperating unions. Between 1914 and 1920, for example, the Brotherhood of Railway Carmen expanded from 28,700 to 182,000 members. "A worker . . . with a union card in his pocket," reported one carman, "will be looked after and has been assured by the government of this great country of ours that he will get a square deal."[47]

The most surprising gains occurred in industries with strong traditions of antiunionism: meatpacking and steel. In both cases, the labor organizers (John Fitzpatrick and William Z. Foster were primarily responsible for initiating both campaigns) looked to the federal government for support and received it. Between September 1917, when the Stockyards Labor Council was created in Chicago, and January 1918, organized labor succeeded in increasing dues-paying membership from about 8,000 to 28,229, and claimed between 25 and 50 percent of the industry's workers. Unable to stop their employees from joining the union, the owners drew the line at recognition and collective bargaining. But federal pressure compelled the owners to negotiate with union representatives (if not to recognize unionism). At the end of January 1918, the owners conceded union demands on employment and shop conditions, leaving other issues to be resolved by formal federal arbitration. In the arbitration hearings, Frank Walsh, soon to serve as cochair of the NWLB, represented the unions. On March 30, 1918, the arbitrator, Judge Samuel Alschuler, handed down his award. He granted workers a basic eight-hour day with ten hours' pay, substantial wage increases, and overtime premiums. The union took credit for the award and, in its wake, unionization swept across the meatpacking industry. Beginning in April, the NWLB delivered specific rulings and awards, which added impetus to the union drive. By November 1918, the Amalgamated Meat Cutters reported 62,857 dues-paying members, over twice as many as nine months earlier, and over ten times as many as three years earlier. "I think the foundations of unionism have been laid in the packing industry for a long time to come," Foster informed Walsh. Although the companies still refused formally to recognize the unions, in David Brody's words, "under the Alschuler administration, the unions assumed an important role both for the employees and management."[48]

A similar story repeated itself in steel. There, too, as the journal of the Amalgamated Association of Iron, Steel, and Tin Workers reported: "The Government stands firmly behind the organized labor movement in its right to organize, and that is why it [the union], is going to push its work of organization into the steel industries." Foster transferred his attention from meatpacking to steel and took command of an AFL-sponsored, joint-union organizing campaign (modeled after the multiunion Stockyards Labor Council). In the summer and fall of 1918, steelworkers joined the unions by the thousands. Foster claimed between 250,000 and 350,000 members. The balance of power in steel had surely shifted. Judge Elbert Gary of U.S. Steel recognized as much when he observed that the best that employers could hope for was that labor questions be evaded until the war was over.[49]

To summarize the impact of the federal government's wartime labor policies: wherever unions had real strength or solid footholds before the war crisis, they made enormous membership advances and often won de facto recognition, bargaining rights, and even the union shop. Where able and dedicated organizers worked to spread the union gospel, as in meatpacking, steel, and the railroad shops, labor's gains were equally substantial. Only where unions had been absent in the prewar period, fought among themselves, or lacked able organizers did the employers prevail. In those cases, war and federal intervention caused no fundamental alteration in relations between labor and capital. But even there, the war produced some changes. Nonunion workers won the eight-hour day, vastly improved working conditions, and formal grievance procedures. The *New Republic* was not far off when it observed at the war's end: "We have already passed to a new era, the transition to a state in which labor will be the predominating element. . . . The character of the future democracy is largely at the mercy of the recognized leaders of organized labor."[50]

Federal wartime labor policies and Wilsonian democratic rhetoric had fired the imagination of labor leaders. "What labor is demanding all over the world today," asserted Sidney Hillman, "is not a few material things like more dollars and fewer hours of work, but a right to a voice in the conduct of industry." In January 1918, Hillman was moved to write to his young daughter: "Messiah is arriving. He may be with us any minute. . . . one can hear the footsteps of the Deliverer—if only he listens intently. Labor will rule and the world will be free."[51] In more prosaic language, Harold Ickes described the postwar situation thus: "The chief issue is likely to be the relationship between capital and labor. . . . We sense disturbances way down underneath our social structure."[52]

Ickes was right; so was Hillman. In 1919, both labor and capital awaited "the Deliverer." For radical trade unionists, the Messiah appeared in the guise of the Bolshevik Revolution, or of the British Labour party's plan for a New Social Order, or more simply as the triumph in America of trade unionism and industrial democracy. For employers, the Messiah came as the armistice, with its promise of the restoration of the status quo antebellum. Of such conflicting visions was industrial warfare made.

The year 1919 was one like no other in American history. Industrial conflict reached unprecedented levels as more than three thousand strikes involved over four million workers. Even police walked out. Race riots and bomb scares proliferated. Not one but three American communist parties were formed. The world had been turned upside down. So thought Warren G. Harding, who wrote to a friend in the fall of 1919: "I really think we are facing a desperate situation. It looks to me as if we are coming to a crisis in the conflict between the radical labor leaders and the capitalistic system under which we have developed the republic. . . . I think the situation has to be met and met with exceptional courage."[53] So, too, thought Joe Tumulty, President Wilson's close and confidential adviser, who observed of the February 1919 Seattle general strike: "It is clear to me that it is the first appearance of the Soviet in this country."[54]

In this highly charged and tense situation, American labor faced a new set of economic and political realities. Fears abounded of labor made surplus in a depressed economy. Yet wartime inflation continued unabated, sparking consumer resistance to union wage demands. Wilsonianism seemed discredited politically. The Republicans had swept into control of Congress in the 1918 election, and their triumph flowed as much from disenchantment with Wilson's domestic policies, especially his alleged truckling to labor, as from his diplomacy. The 1920 election seemed destined to confirm Republican national political dominance, a dominance now more threatening than ever to organized labor. Small wonder, then, that during the spring and summer of 1919, all the federal agencies that had governed wartime labor policy were dismantled. Trade unionists could no longer look to a Frank Walsh or a Felix Frankfurter to defend their interests in Washington.[55]

These new realities quickly made themselves felt in the Wilson administration. Tumulty, for one, advised that high wages were bad for consumers and hence for Democrats. As workers walked off their jobs by the millions, Tumulty suggested: "One way labor can help is to increase production." The new Attorney General, A. Mitchell Palmer, sounded a similar note. During the autumn of 1919 coal strike, he recommended against any concessions to the miners' unlawful behavior because "concessions . . . will insure unreasonably high prices in all commodities for at least three years to come." And Tumulty spelled out the political implications lucidly for the president. Wilson had already assured the Democrats of labor's political support through enactment of the Clayton and Adamson Acts as well as wartime labor policies. If the administration continued to befriend unionists, advised Tumulty, "the country at large would think that we are making a special appeal to labor at this time. If there is any class in this country to which we have been overgenerous it has been labor. I think that this class owes us more than they have been willing to give."[56]

This is not to say that the Wilson administration completely deserted its friends in the labor movement. Quite the contrary was true. Administration officials still believed in the right of workers to organize unhindered by employer coercion and in basic trade-union principles, and they still encouraged employers to recognize unions and bargain with them. But now they also feared labor radicalism, took the AFL's support for granted, and declined to pressure or compel employers to deal with unions.[57]

With the war over and Republicans in control of Congress, Judge Gary and other corporation leaders could now deal with the labor question— and on the terms they preferred. In the packinghouses and railroad shops, employers refused to extend recognition or bargain collectively. In both places, the unions were unable to perfect the organization begun during the war. And they could no longer turn to Washington for support. If unions in the two industries did not collapse absolutely in 1919–20, they were much weakened by 1922.[58]

Even more revealing was what happened in steel and coal. In the former, the union suffered a stillbirth; in the latter, the largest and most powerful union in the country bore the full brunt of a federal antistrike campaign. In steel, union leaders had believed, in the words of John Fitzpatrick, that "the Government would intervene and see to it that the steel barons be brought to time, even as the packers were. . . . President Wilson would never allow a great struggle to develop between the steel-workers and their employers." Wilson indeed sympathized with the unions' plight in steel and desired to avert a strike. But he would neither rebuke steel management publicly nor compel it to meet with labor. For with the war over, the president lacked the law or precedent to do so. Thus, when the strike came on September 22, 1919, federal troops helped break it, and the unionization of steel failed.[59]

The situation in coal was both more complicated and less decisive in its outcome. Unlike in steel, unexpired wartime federal legislation still governed the industry, and the UMWA had a friend in the secretary of labor. Also, the UMWA, unlike the steel unions, had a large and loyal dues-paying membership with a long union tradition. Yet when the miners actually left the pits, the administration officials most involved in the situation, William B. Wilson excepted, defined the strike "as not only unjustifiable but unlawful." They insisted that the walkout was directed against the government, not the mine owners. "I am sure," wrote Tumulty, "that many of the miners would rather accept the peaceful process of settlement . . . than go to war against the Government of the United States." But go to war the miners did. As a result, the administration sought and obtained a stringent antistrike injunction. It also readied troops for duty in the coalfields, tapped the telephones of union leaders, sent federal agents to spy on the union, and threatened alien strikers with summary deportation. In the end, union leaders had no choice but to call off the strike. Because the UMWA was a large, stable union, it ultimately won a compromise wage award through the assistance of William B. Wilson. Yet as a result of the 1919 struggle, it lost most of its footholds in southern Appalachia, a precondition for its subsequent national collapse in the 1920s.[60]

The record of the immediate postwar years confirms David Brody's observation that "depending on their own economic strength, American workers could not defeat the massed power of open-shop industry. Only public intervention might equalize the battle." In two years, the labor movement lost 1.5 million members and was forced to retreat to its prewar bastions. After 1919, the great mass-production industries again operated without unions.[61]

How great a distance remained in 1919 between the aspirations of organized labor and the desires of corporate capital was revealed by the Industrial Conference that President Wilson convened in October 1919. Conceived to resolve the postwar labor-capital upheaval and avert the steel strike, Wilson's First Industrial Conference did neither. It deadlocked over irreconcilable union-management positions. The AFL unionists in attendance sought an equal role with management and government in the control of industry. The business delegates, on the contrary, advocated the extirpation of unionism root and branch. It was the union movement, not the specter of violent revolution, that frightened most businessmen. Hence, they wanted the government to curb the unions' drive for industrial power. And the essence of the open-shop principle, which remained their benchmark throughout the conference, was, in Haggai Hurvitz's words, "the 'utmost freedom' of management to act without outside interference and not labor's freedom to be employed without discrimination."[62] In the absence of a countervailing government presence on behalf of labor, management's principles and programs prevailed throughout the 1920s.

All in all, however, the Wilson years had provided a full dress rehearsal for the labor program of the New Deal. The political coalition between organized labor and the Democrats, constructed from 1912 to 1916, was perfected and strengthened in the Roosevelt years. The recommendations contained in the Walsh CIR report bore fruit in the advanced New Deal reforms of 1933–37. The labor policies that the Wilson administration implemented during a war crisis were set in place by the Roosevelt administration in peacetime. Even the political dynamics of the two eras bore striking resemblances. By 1938, Roosevelt's advisers were warning him that the labor question had become political dynamite, that the administration had already granted labor too much, and that the Democrats had the labor vote in their pocket. But 1938 was not 1919. War was yet to come; and when it came, it lasted more than twice as long as World War I and necessitated many more elaborate and stringent domestic regulations. That, in many respects, was the fundamental difference in labor politics between the Wilson and Roosevelt years. The great labor reforms of the Wilson era occurred in the midst of war and collapsed in the disillusionment of peace. Roosevelt's reforms were introduced in peacetime, were stabilized and routinized during the war, and then developed enough resiliency to enable organized labor to survive the postwar retrenchment.

Notes

An earlier version of this essay appeared in *Work, Community, and Power: The Experience of Labor in Europe and America, 1900–1925,* ed. James F. Cronin and Carmen Sirianni (Philadelphia: Temple University Press, 1983), 197–220. © 1983 by Temple University Press. All rights reserved. Reprinted by permission of Temple University Press.

1. For these themes, see, among other works: Robert Wiebe, *The Search for Order, 1877–1920* (New York: Hill and Wang, 1967), chaps. 5–8; Gabriel Kolko, *The Triumph of American Conservatism* (Glencoe, Ill.: Free Press, 1963); James Weinstein, *The Corporate Ideal in the Liberal State* (Boston: Beacon Press, 1968); Harry Braverman, *Labor and Monopoly Capital* (New York: Monthly Review Press, 1974), chaps. 4 and 5; Daniel Nelson, *Managers and Workers: Origins of the New Factory System in the United States, 1880–1920* (Madison: University of Wisconsin Press, 1975); idem, *Frederick W. Taylor and the Rise of Scientific Management* (Madison: University of Wisconsin Press, 1980); James B. Gilbert, *Work without Salvation* (Baltimore, Md.: Johns Hopkins University Press, 1977); Martin J. Sklar, "Woodrow Wilson and the Political Economy of Modern United States Liberalism," in *For a New America,* ed. James Weinstein and David W. Eakins (New York: Random House, 1970), 46–100.

2. Ray Stannard Baker, "Parker and Theodore Roosevelt on Labor," *McClure's* 24 (Nov. 1904): 41; Bruno Ramirez, *When Workers Fight: The Politics of Industrial Relations in the Progressive Era, 1898–1916* (Westport, Conn.: Greenwood Press, 1978).

3. David Brody, *Workers in Industrial America* (New York: Oxford University Press, 1980), 127.

4. Graham Adams Jr., *Age of Industrial Violence, 1910–1915* (New York: Columbia University Press, 1966).

5. Cf. Georges Haupt, *La Deuxieme Internationale, 1889–1914* (Paris: Editions Cujas, 1964); idem, *Socialism and the Great War: The Collapse of the Second International* (Oxford: Clarendon Press, 1972).

6. Cited in Marc Karson, *American Labor Unions and Politics, 1900–1918* (Carbondale: Southern Illinois University Press, 1958), 90.

7. For the historical and cultural roots of working-class politics, see Alan Dawley and Paul Faler, "Working-Class Culture and Politics in the Industrial Revolution: Sources of Loyalism and Rebellion," *Journal of Social History* 9 (Summer 1976): 466–80; Richard Jensen, *The Winning of the Midwest* (Chicago: University of Chicago Press, 1971); Paul Kleppner, *The Cross of Culture* (New York: Free Press, 1970); and Samuel P. McSeveney, *The Politics of Depression* (New York: Oxford University Press, 1972).

8. Gerald Eggert, *Railroad Labor Disputes* (Ann Arbor: University of Michigan Press, 1967).

9. Charles O. Gregory, *Labor and the Law* (New York: Norton, 1946), chaps. 4–6, 8, 10; Karson, *American Labor Unions,* 29–41; Bernard Mandel, *Samuel Gompers* (Yellow Springs, Ohio: Antioch University Press, 1963), 263–83.

10. See AFL Papers, Office of the President, File A, State Historical Society of Wisconsin, Madison (hereafter cited as SHSW), for the many boxes of correspondence and petitions concerning political action. See also John H. M. Laslett, *Labor and the Left* (New York: Basic Books, 1970); David Montgomery, *Workers' Control in America* (New York: Cambridge University Press, 1979), 48–90.

11. *American Federationist* 12 (May 1906): 293–96; 12 (Aug. 1906): 529–31; 15 (Aug. 1908): 589, 598–605; Karson, *American Labor Unions,* 42–70; Mandel, *Samuel Gompers,* 284–95.

12. Dallas Lee Jones, "The Wilson Administration and Organized Labor, 1912–1919" (Ph.D. diss., Cornell University, 1954), 1–33.

13. Arthur S. Link, *Wilson: The Road to the White House* (Princeton, N.J.: Princeton University Press, 1947), 112, 127, 158–59.

14. Ibid., 470–71; Karson, *American Labor Unions,* 70–73; Mandel, *Samuel Gompers,* 295–97; J. J. Keegan to Samuel Gompers, Oct. 11, 1912; Gompers to Keegan, Oct. 14, 1912; Keegan to Gompers, Oct. 15, 1912, all in AFL Papers, Office of the President, File A, Box 17, SHSW; Samuel Gompers, *Seventy Years of Life and Labor,* vol. 2 (New York: E. P. Dutton, 1925), 282–83.

15. Jones, "Wilson Administration," 50.

16. Ibid., 312–20; John S. Smith, "Organized Labor and the Government in the Wilson Era, 1913–1921," *Labor History* 3 (Fall 1962): 267–68, 272; Memorandum, R. Lee Guard, July 14, 1916, AFL Papers, Office of the President, File A, Box 22, SHSW. See also Gompers to John L. Lewis, Nov. 19, 1916; Lewis to Gompers, Nov. 20 and 21, 1916; Gompers to William B. Wilson, Nov. 23, 1916, all in AFL Papers, Box 23, SHSW.

17. This led Cyrus McCormick, in a letter to his brother Harold, to criticize the president: "he has alienated almost the entire business community because of the way he openly espoused the cause of labor and yielded to the threats of labor leaders" (cited in Robert Ozanne, *A Century of Labor-Management Relations at McCormick and International Havester* [Madison: University of Wisconsin Press 1967], 114).

18. For the letter to Gompers, see Jones, "Wilson Administration," 88; for the two quotations, see John Lombardi, *Labor's Voice in the Cabinet: A History of the Department of Labor from its Origins to 1921* (New York: AMS Press, 1968), 104–7, 75–95 (on William B. Wilson).

19. The files of the United States Mediation and Conciliation Service, Record Group 280, National Archives, show how Wilson used former union colleagues; cf. Smith, "Organized Labor," 276, and Jones, "Wilson Administration," 85–90.

20. The best history of the commission remains Adams, *Age of Industrial Violence;* a brief, more tendentious summary is in Weinstein, *Corporate Ideal,* chap. 7.

21. In 1916, the commission hearings and final report were published in eleven volumes as *Final Report and Testimony Submitted to Congress by the Commission on Industrial Relations,* 6th Cong., 1st sess., S. Doc. 415. More material can be found in the Frank P. Walsh Papers, New York Public Library; the reports of the investi-

gators in the National Archives, Department of Labor. Record Groups 1 and 174; and the Commission on Industrial Relations records at the SHSW, as well as twenty separate publications based on the field reports.

22. Commission on Industrial Relations, *Final Report*, 1–91; Adams, *Age of Industrial Violence,* 215–17; Weinstein, *Corporate Ideal,* 188, 190–91, 208–10; John R. Commons, *Myself: "The Autobiography of John R. Commons* (Madison: University of Wisconsin Press, 1964), 166–67, 172–73. Weinstein nevertheless concludes that Walsh had no intention of transforming social relations.

23. Adams, *Age of Industrial Violence,* 219–20.

24. Arthur S. Link, *Wilson: The New Freedom* (Princeton, N.J.: Princeton University Press, 1956), 428–31; idem, *Woodrow Wilson and the Progessive Era, 1910–1917* (New York: Harper, 1954), 69–70; Mandel, *Samuel Gompers,* 297–300; Gompers, *Seventy Years,* 2:298–99.

25. Link, *Woodrow Wilson and the Progressive Era,* 235–37; Edward Berman, *Labor Disputes and the President of the United States* (New York: Columbia University Press, 1924), 106–25; K. Austin Kerr, *American Railroad Politics, 1914–1920* (Pittsburgh, Pa.: University of Pittsburgh Press, 1968), 33–34.

26. Ronald Radosh, *American Labor and United States Foreign Policy* (New York: Random House, 1969); Frank L. Grubbs Jr., *The Struggle for Labor Loyalty* (Durham, N.C.: Duke University Press, 1968).

27. Weinstein, *Corporate Ideal,* chap. 8; David Kennedy, *Over Here: The First World War and American Society* (New York Oxford University Press, 1980).

28. Montgomery, *Workers' Control,* 95–98.

29. Robert D. Cuff, *The War Industries Board* (Baltimore, Md.: Johns Hopkins University Press, 1973).

30. Robert Bruere, "Copper Camp Patriotism: An Interpretation," *Nation* 6 (Feb. 1918): 236; Robert D. Cuff, "The Politics of Labor Administration in World War I," *Labor History* 21 (Fall 1980): 546–69; Berman, *Labor Disputes,* 126–53; J. Lombardi, *Labor's Voice,* 228–59.

31. Kennedy, *Over Here,* 266–67.

32. Kennedy's interpretation seems drawn heavily from three articles by Louis B. Wehle: "The Adjustment of Labor Disputes," *Quarterly Journal of Economics* 32 (1917): 122–41; "Labor Problems in the United States," ibid. 32 (1918): 333–92; and "War Labor Policies," ibid. 33 (1919): 321–43. Bernard Baruch succinctly states Kennedy's view: "While I am in favor of making every possible concession, at the same time we certainly should preserve the *status quo* and not permit anything to be used as a leverage to change conditions from the standpoint either of the employers or the employees" (cited in Baruch to William B. Wilson, June 30, 1917, Department of Labor, Record Group 280, File 33/493).

33. Jones, "Wilson Administration," 343; Mandel, *Samuel Gompers,* 366–68.

34. Lombardi, *Labor's Voice,* 238; Jones, ' Wilson Administration," 350–51.

35. Gompers to Wilson, Aug. 10, 1917, in Gompers Letterbooks, 5:237, Library of Congress. Newton D. Baker to William B. Wilson, Aug. 1, 1917; Wilson to Baker, Aug. 3, 1917, both in Department of Labor, Record Group 280, File 33/574; *Survey* 38 (Aug. 11, 1917): 429.

36. Gompers to Baker, Aug. 22, 1917, Gompers Letterbooks. See also Gompers

to W. B. Wilson, Aug. 27, 1917; W. B. Wilson, memo to President Wilson, Aug. 31, 1917; Woodrow Wilson to N. Baker, Sept. 19, 1917; Woodrow Wilson to W. B. Wilson, Sept. 19, 1917, all in Department of Labor, Record Group 174, File 20/ 473. Cf. Meyer H. Fishbein, "The President's Mediation Commission and the Arizona Copper Strike, 1917," *Southwestern Social Science Quarterly* 30 (Dec. 1949): 175–82.; Weinstein, *Corporate Ideal,* 214; Ronald Steel, *Walter Lippmann and the American Century* (Boston: Little, Brown, 1980), 112–15.

37. F. Frankfurter, memo to the commission, Oct. 5, 1917, Department of Labor, Record Group 174, File 20/473.

38. *Report of the President's Mediation Commission to the President of the United States, January 9, 1918;* the unpublished hearings and reports of the commission can be found in Department of Labor, Record Group 280, File 33/517. For more on Frankfurter's role, see Harlan B. Phillips, *Felix Frankfurter Reminisces* (New York: Reynal, 1960), 117–21.

39. David Brody, *Labor in Crisis: The Steel Strike of 1919* (Philadelphia: J. B. Lippincott, 1965), 53; Jones, "Wilson Administration," 363–70.

40. Jones, "Wilson Administration," 372; Weinstein, *Corporate Ideal,* 248; H. F. Pringle, *The Life and Times of William Howard Taft,* vol. 2 (New York: Farrar and Rinehart, 1939), 916; see also Walsh Papers, Box 18; Bureau of Labor Statistics, *National War Labor Board, Bulletin No. 287* (Washington, D.C., 1922).

41. Jones, "Wilson Administration," 381.

42. Brody, *Labor in Crisis,* 58; Lombardi, *Labor's Voice,* 265–92.

43. Brody, *Labor in Crisis,* 61.

44. *Historical Statistics of the United States,* ser. D 735–40 (Washington, D.C., 1960), 97; Montgomery, *Workers' Control,* 95–101; Brody, *Labor in Crisis,* 50–51, 60–61; Stanley Shapiro, "The Great War and Reform," *Labor History* 12 (Summer 1971): 334–35.

45. Matthew Josephson, *Sidney Hillman* (New York: Doubleday, 1952), 162–76.

46. *United Mine Workers Journal,* June 21, 1917, 4; ibid., Aug. 30, 1917, 6; Melvyn Dubofsky and Warren W. Van Tine, *John L. Lewis: A Biography* (New York: Times Books, 1977), 35–37, 42.

47. *Railway Carmen's Journal* 23 (June 1918), 347–48, cited in Stephen Freedman, "The Union Movement in Joliet, Illinois, 1870–1920: Organization and Protest in a Steel-Mill Town," ms., 20; Kerr, *American Railroad Politics,* 91–92.

48. David Brody, *The Butcher Workmen: A Study of Unionization* (Cambridge, Mass.: Harvard University Press, 1964), 76–83.

49. Brody, *Labor in Crisis,* 60–61, 63–77.

50. Cited in Shapiro, "Great War and Reform," 340.

51. Josephson, *Sidney Hillman,* 190–93.

52. Cited in Kennedy, *Over Here,* 287.

53. Warren G. Harding to F. E. Scobey, Oct. 25 and Nov. 3, 1919, Harding Papers, Reel 21, Ohio Historical Society, Columbus.

54. John Morton Blum, *Joe Tumulty and the Wilson Era* (Boston: Houghton Mifflin, 1951), 206.

55. Berman, *Labor Disputes,* 154–209; Lombardi, *Labor's Voice,* 306–15; Jones, "Wilson Administration," 436–40.

56. A. Mitchell Palmer to the Chamber of Commerce, Moberly, Missouri, Dec. 1, 1919, Department of Labor, Record Group 174, Box 207; Blum, *Joe Tumulty,* 148–49.

57. On this point, see Brody, *Labor in Crisis,* 103–4, 127–28.

58. Brody, *Butcher Workmen,* 85–91; Robert Zieger, *Republicans and Labor, 1919–1929* (Lexington: University Press of Kentucky, 1969), 129–43.

59. Brody, *Labor in Crisis,* 102–3, 147–78.

60. Dubofsky and Van Tine, *John L. Lewis,* 53–61.

61. Brody, *Workers in Industrial America,* 45.

62. Haggai Hurvitz, "Ideology and Industrial Conflict: President Wilson's First Industrial Conference of October, 1919," *Labor History* 18 (Fall 1977): 516–17, 518–19, 521–22. For a more benign view of the conference, see Brody, *Labor in Crisis,* 127–28. On a second Wilson Industrial Conference and its failure, see Gary Dean Best, "President Wilson's Second Industrial Conference, 1910–1920," *Labor History* 16 (Fall 1975): 505–20.

· 6 ·

Not So "Turbulent Years":
Another Look at America in the 1930s

OUR conventional view of the 1930s was aptly caught in the title of Irving Bernstein's history of American labor during that decade, *Turbulent Years,* a title that the author borrowed from Myron Taylor's annual report to the board of directors of the U.S. Steel Corporation in 1938. That liberal historians and corporate executives perceive the 1930s as a "turbulent" decade should today occasion no surprise. For the American business elite especially, their social, economic, and political world had turned upside down during the Great Depression and New Deal. After nearly a full decade of corporate hegemony, class collaboration, and trade union retreat, the United States during the 1930s seemed chronically beset with class conflict, violence, and ubiquitous labor radicalism. In the words of one of the decade's radicals, Len DeCaux, a "new consciousness" awakened workers from lethargy: "There was light after the darkness in the youth of the movement," exulted DeCaux. "Youth that was direct and bold in action, not sluggish and sly from long compromise with the old and the rotten. There was light in the hopeful future seen by the red and the rebellious, now playing their full part in what they held to be a great working-class advance against the capitalist class. There was light, and a heady, happy feeling in the solidarity of struggle in a splendid common cause."[1]

The picture one has of the 1930s, then, whether painted by a liberal scholar such as Bernstein, an activist like DeCaux, or a tycoon like Taylor, is of conflict and struggle. The foreground is filled with militant and radical workers, the masses in motion, a rank and file vigorously, some-

times violently, reaching out to grasp control over its own labor and existence. Given the conventional portrait of the American 1930s, conventional questions arise, the most obvious of which are the following: (1) Why
did labor militancy decline? (2) Why did militant, radical rank-and-file
struggles produce, in many cases, old-fashioned, autocratically controlled
trade unions? (3) Why did the turbulence create no lasting, mass radical
political movement? Before seeking to answer such questions, even assuming they are the best ones to ask about the 1930s, I am reminded of a lesson contained in an American cartoon strip. A caveman reporter informs
his stone-age editor that he has both good news and bad news. "Let's have
the bad news first," says the editor. "There's only good news," responds
the reporter. Need I add that American journalists had a field day during
the 1930s and that their editors rejoiced in an abundance of "bad news?"
Front-page headlines shrieked class war and wire photos depicted strikers in armed conflict with police and troops.

But were class war and violent pitched battles the reality of the 1930s?
And, if they were, how do we explain the absence of a mass radical political movement?

Frankly, all of us realize how difficult it is to create or grasp historical
reality. As historians, we work with the available evidence, always, to be
sure, seeking to discover more about the past, but always aware that the
total record of what happened is beyond our recall or recreation. Ultimately,
then, just as man through his thoughts and actions makes history, historians, in the process of research and writing, create their own history.

In examining the 1930s, how should we go about creating the history
of that era? Two convenient models are at hand. In one, we can seek lessons for the present in an instrumental view of the past. That approach
suggests the might-have-beens of history. If only communists had behaved
differently; if nonsectarian radicals had pursued the proper policies; if the
militant rank and file had been aware of its true interests (as distinguished
from the false consciousness inculcated by trade-union bureaucrats and
New Deal Democrats); then the history of the 1930s would have been different and *better*.[2] The second approach to our turbulent decade has been
suggested by David Brody. "The interesting questions," writes Brody, "are
not in the realm of what might have been, but in a closer examination of
what did happen."[3] Brody's approach, I believe, promises greater rewards
for scholars and may even be more useful for those who desire to use the
past to improve the present and shape the future. As Karl Marx noted in
The Eighteenth Brumaire man indeed makes his own history but only

"under circumstances directly encountered, given and transmitted from the past. The tradition of all the dead generations weighs like a nightmare on the brain of the living."[4]

One more preliminary observation must be made about recreating the past in general and the American 1930s in particular. We must be zealously on guard against falling victim to what Edward Thompson has characterized as the "Pilgrim's Progress" orthodoxy, an approach that, in his words, "reads history in the light of subsequent preoccupations, and not fact as it occurred. Only the successful . . . are remembered. The blind alleys, the lost causes, and the losers themselves are forgotten."[5] In light of what I intend to say below—and also of what such theorists of "corporate liberalism" as Ronald Radosh and James Weinstein have written about the history of the American labor movement—it is well to bear in mind Thompson's comment that history written as the record of victors and survivors is not necessarily synonymous with the past as experienced by all of those who lived it and created it.[6]

Let us now see if we can uncover or glimpse the reality of the American 1930s. Certainly, the turbulence, militancy, and radicalism of the decade existed. From 1929 through 1939, the American economic and social system remained in crisis. Despite two substantial recoveries from the depths of depression, unemployment during the decade never fell below 14 percent of the civilian labor force or 21 percent of the nonagricultural workforce.[7] Those workers who once believed in the American myth of success, who dreamed of inching up the occupational ladder, acquiring property of their own, and watching their children do even better occupationally and materially had their hopes blasted by the Great Depression. As Stephan Thernstrom's research shows for Boston, the Great Depression thwarted occupational and material advancement for an entire generation of workers.[8] And what was true in Boston most likely prevailed elsewhere in the nation. If, in the past, American workers had experienced marginal upward social and economic mobility, during the 1930s, they could expect to fall rather more often than to climb.

The thwarted aspirations of millions of workers, combined with persistent mass unemployment, produced a decade of social unrest that encompassed every form of collective and individual action from mass marches to food looting. One historian has pointed out that between February 1930 and July 1932, at least seventeen separate incidents of violent protest occurred. In Chicago in 1931, after three persons were killed during an antieviction struggle, sixty thousand citizens marched on City Hall to protest police brutality. Indeed, in nearly every city in which the unemployed organized and protested, violent confrontations with the police erupted.[9]

More important and more threatening to the established order than protests by the unemployed and hungry, which punctuated the early Depression years, were the more conventional forms of class struggle that erupted with greater incidence after the election of Franklin Roosevelt and the coming of the New Deal. In 1934, after twelve years of relative quiet on the labor front, industrial conflict broke out with a militancy and violence not seen since 1919. In Toledo, Ohio, National Guardsmen teargassed and drove from the city's streets Auto-Lite Company strikers who had the support not only of the radical A. J. Muste's American Workers Party and Unemployed League but also of the citywide central labor council, an American Federation of Labor (AFL) affiliate. And the following month, July 1934, witnessed still more violent struggles. A strike by maritime workers in the San Francisco Bay area brought battles between police and longshoremen, the deaths of several strikers, and the dispatch of state troops. In protest, the San Francisco central labor council declared a citywide general strike for July 16. Here, too, a labor radical, Harry Bridges, an Australian immigrant and a Marxist, led a strike unsanctioned by the AFL. Only a day after the San Francisco general strike ended, Americans read in their July 21 newspapers that on the previous day in Minneapolis, Minnesota, fifty men had been shot in the back as police fired on strikers. Within a week of the bloody July 20 battle between police and teamsters in the city's main square, Minnesota Governor Floyd Olson placed the Twin Cities under martial law. Once again, in Minneapolis, as earlier in Toledo and San Francisco, left-wing radicals led the strike; in this instance, it was the Trotskyists Farrell Dobbs and the brothers Vincent, Miles, Grant, and Ray Dunne. And only a week after the shootings in Minneapolis, on July 28, 1934, deputy sheriffs in the company town of Kohler, Wisconsin, killed one person and injured twenty in what the *New York Times* characterized as a "strike riot."[10]

Few areas of the nation seemed untouched by labor militancy in 1934. In the spring, a national textile strike called by the United Textile Workers of America brought out 350,000 workers from Maine to Alabama, and violent repression of the strikers proved the rule in the South's Piedmont mill towns. Throughout the spring, auto- and steelworkers flocked into trade unions, like coal miners the previous year, seeming almost to organize themselves. And when auto manufacturers and steel barons refused to bargain with labor, national strikes threatened both industries. Only direct presidential intervention and the equivocal actions of AFL leaders averted walkouts in the auto and steel industries.[11]

If 1934, in Irving Bernstein's chapter title, amounted to an "Eruption," 1937 experienced an epidemic of strikes. The year began with the famous Flint sitdown strike, in which the United Auto Workers (UAW) conquered General Motors; saw U.S. Steel surrender to the Steel Workers Organizing Committee (SWOC) without a struggle less than three weeks after the General Motors strike ended; and culminated in the late spring with perhaps the most violent and bloodiest national strike of the decade: the Little Steel conflict that led to the Memorial Day "massacre" outside Republic Steel's South Chicago plant. In between Flint and Little Steel, more than 400,000 workers participated in 477 sitdown strikes. Twenty-five sitdowns erupted in January 1937, forty-seven in February, and 170 in March. "Sitting down has replaced baseball as a national pasttime," quipped *Time* magazine.[12]

The labor militancy and strikes of 1934 and 1937 created a solidarity that hitherto had eluded American workers. During the 1930s, it seemed, the United States had developed a true proletariat, more united by its similarities than divided by its differences. Mass immigration had ended in 1921; and hence, the last immigrant generation had had more than a decade to integrate itself into the social system and for its children to have been "Americanized" by the public schools and other intermediate social agencies. Male-female role conflicts appeared notable by their absence, and strikers' wives provided their husbands with substantial assistance as members of women's auxiliaries. "I found a common understanding and unselfishness I'd never known in my life," wrote the wife of one Flint sitdowner. "I'm living for the first time with a definite goal. . . . Just being a woman isn't enough any more. I want to be a human being with the right to think for myself."[13] A new type of woman was born in the strike," noted an observer of the struggle in Flint. "Women who only yesterday were horrified at unionism, who felt inferior to the task of speaking, leading, have, as if overnight, become the spearhead in the battle for unionism."[14]

Even racial tensions among workers seemed to diminish during the 1930s, especially after the emergence of the Congress of Industrial Organizations (CIO), whose "new unionists" often crusaded for civil rights as vigorously as for trade unionism. The changes wrought by the CIO led two students of black labor to conclude in 1939 "that it is easier to incorporate Negroes into a new movement . . . than to find a secure place in an older one." Surveying the impact of the Depression, the New Deal, and the CIO on black workers, Horace Cayton and George S. Mitchell suggested that "in the readjustment of social patterns and ideologies, we find reflected a profound transition in Negro life as well as in the economic outlook of American workers generally. What has been for generations a racial stratification in occupations is, under present-day conditions, in process of transformation. Class tensions and class solidarity have measurably relaxed racial tensions and, by so doing, have mitigated the divisive effects of racial antagonism."[15]

One must not, however, romanticize working-class solidarity and thus lose sight of the tensions that continued to pit American workers during the 1930s against each other rather than a common enemy. In New Haven, Connecticut, American-born workers still denigrated Italians as "wops"; "it's dog eat dog all right," retorted an Italian-American machinist, "but it's also Mick feeds Mick!"[16] A Hollywood film of the late 1930s, *Black Legion,* starring Humphrey Bogart as a frustrated, white, American-born Protestant machinist, captured the still-lingering resentment harbored by the American-born against the foreign-born (and even their children) and depicted the sort of worker more likely to listen *to* Father Coughlin than to John L. Lewis, Franklin D. Roosevelt, or perhaps William Z. Foster. Or there are the words of an official of an AFL union with jurisdiction in an industry that employed many Afro-Americans: "I consider the Negroes poor union men. You know as well as I do that they are shiftless, easily intimidated and generally of poor caliber. . . . What should have happened is what is being done in Calhoun County, Illinois, where Negroes are not allowed to stay overnight. As a result there are no Negroes there and no Negro problem."[17]

It was the CIO, however, not the AFL, that symbolized the labor upheaval of the 1930s. And in 1937, when the CIO organized the auto, steel, and rubber industries and other former bastions of the open shop, between 3.5 and 4 million workers joined the labor movement, a larger number than the entire AFL claimed as of January 1, 1937. Now, for the first time in its history, organized labor in America wielded power in the strategic core of mass-production industry, and it did so under the aegis of a labor federation, the CIO, whose leaders consciously repudiated the AFL tradition of class accommodation and collaboration. The CIO during the late 1930s exemplified solidarity rather than exclusiveness, political action in place of nonpartisanship, biracialism and bisexualism instead of racial and sexual chauvinism, and militancy rather than opportunism. "CIO started as a new kind of labor movement," recalled Len DeCaux in his autobiography, "a challenge to the old AFL and the status quo it complacently guarded. It was new in its youth and fervor, new in the broad sector of the working class it brought into action, new in the way it accepted and integrated its radicals, new in its relative independence of corporate and government control, new in its many social and political attitudes."[18]

DeCaux was not alone among radicals in looking to the CIO as the instrument through which to build a new America. Powers Hapgood, the Harvard-educated son of a wealthy midwestern family, and who worked as a coal miner to share the worker's plight, felt compelled in 1935 to seek an accommodation with his ancient enemy John L. Lewis, who was then organizing the CIO. "It's surprising how many radicals think I ought to see Lewis," Hapgood informed his wife, "saying it's much less of a compromise to make peace with him and stay in the labor movement than it is to get a government job and cease to be active in the class struggle." To reject a reconciliation with Lewis in 1935, concluded Hapgood, would let the left wing down.[19] After the CIO's first national conference in Atlantic City in October 1937, Adolph Germer, a former ally of Hapgood and then a social democrat evolving into a New Deal Democrat, wrote to an ex-associate in the Socialist Party of America: "I attended the Atlantic City conference and I assure you it was an educational treat. There was as much difference between that meeting and the A. F. of L. conventions I have attended as there is between night and day."[20] And Lee Pressman and Gardner Jackson, the former an ex-Communist and the latter a left-wing, socialist-inclined reformer, both of whom worked closely with Lewis from 1936 through 1940, observed that Lewis seemed a changed man in 1937 and that the CIO experience had transformed him from "a labor boss of the most conventional kind, and a discredited one at that" into an eager, dedicated leader of a movement encompassing blue- and white-collar workers, farmers, small professionals, and all sorts of "little people." In 1937, Pressman and Jackson believed that Lewis might well lead an independent populist or farmer-labor political movement in the event Roosevelt and the Democrats failed to implement full-employment policies and a welfare state.[21]

Had Lewis decided to lead such an independent political movement, the time never seemed riper. The Great Depression and the New Deal had wrought a veritable political revolution among American workers. Masses of hitherto politically apathetic workers, especially among first-generation immigrants and their spouses, went to the polls in greater numbers. And Roosevelt broke the last links that bound millions of workers across the industrial heartland from Pittsburgh to Chicago to the Republican party.[22] Lewis exulted at the results of the 1936 election, in which, for the first time since the depression of the 1890s, Democrats swept into power in the steel and coal towns of Pennsylvania and Ohio, winning office on tickets financed by CIO money and headed by CIO members. A new consciousness appeared to be stirring among the nation's industrial workers.[23] A social scientist sampling attitudes and beliefs among Akron rubber workers at the end of the 1930s discovered that the vast majority of CIO members valued human rights above property rights and showed little respect or deference for the prerogatives and privileges of corporate property. Akron's workers, and also many residents characterized as middle class, apparently distinguished between purely personal use-property and property as capital, which afforded its possessors power over the lives and labor of the propertyless.[24] Such an altered consciousness fed the dreams of popular fronters and third-party activists.

All this ferment, militancy, radicalism, violence, and perhaps even an altered working-class consciousness were part of American reality during the 1930s. Yet, as we know, American socialism expired during the Depression decade, communism advanced only marginally, Roosevelt seduced the farmer-laborites and populists, the CIO came to resemble the AFL, and John L. Lewis once again reverted to behaving like a "labor boss of the most conventional kind." Why? To answer that question, we have to examine other aspects of social, economic, and political reality during the 1930s.

Just as one can claim that the 1930s represented a crisis for American capitalism that expressed itself most overtly in the eagerness and militancy with which workers challenged their corporate masters, one might just as easily assert that for most Americans, workers included, events during the decade reinforced their faith in the "justness" of the American system and the prospects for improvement without fundamental restructuring. For many workers, capitalism never collapsed; indeed, for those employed steadily (always a substantial proportion of the work force), real wages actually rose as prices fell. For other workers, the tentative economic recovery of 1933–34 and the more substantial growth of 1937 rekindled faith in the American system. The two great strike waves of the decade, 1934 and 1937, erupted not in moments of crisis but when hope, profits, employment, and wages all revived. Crisis, in other words, induced apathy or lethargy; economic recovery, a sign that the system worked, stimulated action. And when the recovery of 1935–37 was followed by the "Roosevelt Depression," a more rapid and deeper decline than the Great Crash of 1929–33, the number of strikes diminished markedly and the more militant CIO affiliates concentrated in the mass-production industries suffered severe membership and financial losses.[25] Perhaps this final crisis of the Depression decade left unresolved might have snapped whatever bonds still tied workers to the American system. That, however, remains a problematic historical might-have-been, as the coming of World War II resolved the contradictions in American capitalism and substituted patriotic unity for class conflict.

An analysis of the statistics of working-class militancy during the 1930s—the incidence of strikes, the number of workers affected, the man-days lost—also leads to divergent interpretations. One can stress the high level of strike activity, the fact that only 840 strikes were recorded in 1932 but 1,700 erupted in 1933; 1,856 in 1934; 2,200 in 1936; and in the peak strike year, 1937, 4,740 broke out.[26] One can argue that no area of the nation and, more importantly, no major industry escaped industrial conflict. For the first time in U.S. history, strikes affected every major mass-production industry and paralyzed the towering heights of the economy: steel, auto, rubber, coal, electrical goods, and so forth. For the nation and its workers, the 1930s were indeed "turbulent years."

But the statistics of industrial conflict reveal another story, an equally interesting one. When the 1934 strike wave erupted, President Roosevelt sought to understand its origins and implications. He asked the commissioner of labor statistics, Isidore Lubin, to analyze and interpret the 1934 outbreak. Lubin prepared a report that he transmitted to the president in August 1934. Seeking to place the 1934 strikes in historical perspective, Lubin acted logically. He compared what had happened in the first half of 1934 to the last previous year in which the United States had experienced such massive labor militancy, 1919. He concluded that the 1934 strike wave could not match 1919 in intensity, duration, or the number of workers involved. More than twice as many strikes began each month in the first half of 1919, reported Lubin, than in the same period in 1934; moreover, more than two and one-half times as many workers were involved in the 1919 strikes. He then proceeded to assure the president that July 1934, the month of the San Francisco and Minneapolis general strikes, witnessed no mass working-class upheaval. Only seven-tenths of one percent, or seven out of every one thousand wage earners, participated in strikes. Only four-tenths of one percent of man-days of employment were lost as a result of strikes. "In other words," Lubin reassured the president, "for every thousand man-days worked four were lost because of strikes." Selecting ten major industries for analysis, Lubin observed that only one-half of one percent of the total number employed struck in July 1934. "Comparing the number employed with the number actually involved in strikes, one reaches the conclusion that for every thousand workers employed in those industries only five were affected by strikes. In terms of the number of man-days lost . . . it is estimated that for every thousand man-days worked . . . seven days of employment were lost because of strikes." And, in a final note of reassurance for the president, Lubin observed that the "recent strikes have been relatively short lived," lasting less than half as long as the average duration during 1927 (twenty-four compared to fifty-one days), a time of relative labor peace.[27]

But what of 1937, the decade's premier strike year, when more than twice as many workers struck as in 1934? According to official statistics, only 7.2 percent of workers were involved in walkouts (practically the same percentage as in 1934), and their absence from work represented only 0.043 percent of all time worked.[28]

Questions immediately arise from a reading of such strike statistics. What was the other 93 percent of the labor force doing during the great strike waves of 1934 and 1937? More important, how were they affected by the upsurge of industrial conflicts that did not involve or affect them directly?

Such questions are especially important when one bears in mind the continental size of the United States. Geography could, and did, easily dilute the impact of industrial conflict nationally. The United States lacked a London, Paris, Berlin, or Rome, where massive, militant strikes directly affected the national state as well as private employers. Few of the major strikes of the 1930s occurred even in state capitals, most of which were isolated from industrial strife. When teamsters tied up Minneapolis and longshoremen closed down San Francisco in July 1934, truckers continued to deliver goods in Chicago and Los Angeles, and waterfront workers remained on the job in New York, Baltimore, and San Pedro. For trade unionists and radicals, it was exceedingly difficult, as Roy Rosenzweig has shown for A. J. Muste's Unemployed League, to transform well-structured local and regional organizations into equally effective national bodies.[29] Just as the millions of unemployed during the 1930s did not experience the shock of joblessness simultaneously, so, too, different workers experienced industrial conflict at different times and in different places. As we will see below, what workers most often experienced in common—participation in the American political system—was precisely what most effectively diluted militancy and radicalism.

Despite the continental size and diversity of the American nation, it is possible to glimpse aspects of working-class reality in local settings that disclose uniformities in belief and behavior that do much to explain the dearth of durable radicalism in the United States. We are fortunate that two truly excellent, perceptive sociological field studies were completed during the 1930s that dissect the social structure and culture of two characteristic, smaller American industrial cities. We are even more fortunate that the two cities investigated—Muncie, Indiana, and New Haven, Connecticut—proved so unlike in their economic structures, population mixes, and regional and cultural milieus. Muncie was dominated by two industries—Ball Glass and General Motors—characterized by an almost totally American-born, white, Protestant population and was situated in the heartland of American agriculture, individualism, and evangelical Protestantism. New Haven, by contrast, claimed no dominant employers, encompassed a population differentiated by nationality, race, and religion as well as class, and was set in a region traditionally urban (also urbane) and nonevangelical in culture. Yet after one finishes reading Robert and Helen Lynd on Muncie and E. Wight Bakke on New Haven, one is more impressed by the similarities rather than the differences in working-class attitudes and behavior.[30]

Let us examine Muncie first. The Lynds had initially gone to Muncie in the mid-1920s to discover how urbanization and industrialization had affected American culture, how the city and the factory had altered beliefs and behavioral patterns developed in the country and on the farm.[31] They returned a decade later to see what impact, if any, the Great Depression had had on local culture and behavior. Surprisingly, for them at least, they found labor organization weaker in 1935 than it had been in 1925, yet the Muncie business class seemed more united and more determined than ever to keep its city open shop (nonunion). The Lynds discovered objectively greater class stratification in 1935 than in 1925 and even less prospect for the individual worker to climb up the ladder of success (see Thernstrom on Boston's Depression-generation workers for similar findings), yet they characterized Muncie's workers as being influenced by "drives . . . largely those of the business class: both are caught up in the tradition of a rising standard of living and lured by the enticements of salesmanship." As one Middletown woman informed the sociologists: "Most of the families that I know are after the same things today that they were after before the depression, and they'll get them the same way—on credit."[32]

Union officials told the Lynds a similar tale of woe. Union members preferred buying gas for their cars to paying dues and going for a drive to attending a union meeting. Local workers were willing to beg, borrow, or steal to maintain possession of their cars and keep them running. Despite seven years of depression, Muncie's workers, according to the Lynds, still worshiped the automobile as the symbol of the American Dream and, as long as they owned one, considered themselves content.[33]

"Fear, resentment, insecurity and disillusionment has been to Middletown's workers largely an individual experience for each worker," concluded the Lynds, "and not a thing generalized by him into a 'class' experience. Such militancy as it generates tends to be sporadic, personal, and flaccid; an expression primarily of personal resentment rather than an act of self-identification with the continuities of a movement or of a rebellion against an economic status regarded as permanently fixed. The militancy of Middletown labor tends, therefore, to be easily manipulated, and to be diverted into all manner of incidental issues."[34]

So it was for Muncie. But what was the experience in New Haven, with its more heterogeneous and less individualistic (culturally) working class, a working class that, in some cases, the investigator could interview and probe after the CIO upheaval of 1936–37? Again, we see in E. W. Bakke's two published examinations of the unemployed worker in New Haven an absence of mass organization, collective militancy, or radicalism, despite an apparent hardening of class lines. New Haven's workers, unlike Muncie's, apparently did not share the drives of the business class, and they did in fact develop a collective sense of class. "Hell, brother," a machinist told Bakke, "you don't have to look to know there's a workin' class. We may not say so—But look at what we do. Work. Look at where we live. Nothing there but workers. Look at how we get along. Just like every other damned worker. Hell's bells, of course there's a workin' class, and its gettin' more so very day."[35] Yet New Haven, like Muncie, lacked a militant and radical working class. Why?

Bakke tried to provide answers. He cited the usual barriers to collective action and working-class radicalism: ethnic heterogeneity; fear of the alien; fear of repression; and capitalist hegemony that was cultural as well as economic and political.[36] Yet he also discovered that answers to the absence of militancy and radicalism lay embedded deep within the culture of New Haven's workers. In most cases, their lives had disproved the American Dream; rather than experiencing steady upward mobility and constantly rising material standards of living, Bakke's interviewees had lived lives of insecurity and poverty. They regularly had to adjust their goals to actual possibilities, which almost always fell far below their aspirations. As one worker after another informed Bakke, life involved putting up with it, grinning and bearing it, and using common sense to survive. Explaining how the unemployed managed in a period of general economic crisis, a brass worker noted in a matter-of-fact fashion: "The poor are used to being poor."[37]

Eugene Genovese has remarked, in a different context, on an attempt to explain the absence of slave rebellions in North America:

> Only those who romanticize—and therefore do not respect—the laboring classes would fail to understand their deep commitment to "law and order." Life is difficult enough without added uncertainty and "confusion." Even an oppressive and unjust system is better than none. People with such rich experience as that of the meanest slaves quickly learn to distrust Utopian nostrums. As Machiavelli so brilliantly revealed, most people refuse to believe in anything they have not experienced. Such negativity must be understood as a challenge to demonstrate that a better, firmer, more just social order can replace the one to be torn down.[38]

It was just so with New Haven's workers. For the majority of them, alternatives to the existing social structure seemed most notable for their absence. The only alternatives the city's workers cited—German nazism, Italian fascism, and Soviet communism, none of which, to be sure, they had experienced—held no allurement, promised them "no better, more just social order." Workers repeatedly referred to Soviet Russia to explain both socialism's and communism's lack of appeal.[39]

Lacking an alternative to the existing system, New Haven workers grabbed what few joys they could in an otherwise perilous existence. One worker explained his own resistance to socialism in the following manner: he had fought enough losing battles in his life. But he knew one place where he could celebrate as a winner. As a Democrat or a Republican, at least once in a while, he could get drunk on election night and act the part of a winner. But socialists, he sneered, "when do you think they're goin' to have a chance to get drunk?"[40]

Thus, one might say that Muncie and New Haven were atypical and their working class populations more so. Look at Flint and Youngstown, Akron and Gary, Minneapolis and San Francisco. In those cities, workers acted collectively and militantly. But a closer look at even such foci of labor struggle reveals a much more complex reality than suggested by conventional romanticizations of working-class solidarity and rank-and-file militancy.

Without militants, to be sure, there would have been no Flint sit-down strike, no San Francisco general strike, no walkout by Akron's rubber workers. Without rank-and-file participation—that is, collective struggle—there would have been no union victories. Yet, in reality, solidarity rarely produced collective action; rather, more often than not, action by militant minorities (what some scholars have characterized as "sparkplug unionism"[41]) precipitated a subsequent collective response. And rank and filers frequently resisted the radicalism of the militant cadres that sparked industrial confrontations. In Flint, as Sidney Fine has shown, only a small minority of the local workers belonged to the UAW and paid dues on the eve of the strike, and the sitdown technique was chosen consciously to compensate for the union's lack of a mass membership base.[42] The story was the same in Akron. When that city's rubber workers gained the CIO's first major victory in March 1936, after a strike against the Goodyear Tire and Rubber Company, Powers Hapgood disclosed the following to John L. Lewis: "Confidentially, I can tell you that it was a minority strike, starting with only a hand full of members and gradually building a membership in that Local Union to a little over 5000 out of 14,000 workers."[43] Lee Pressman, general counsel to the Steel Workers Organizing Committee, recalls that as late as the spring of 1937, after the UAW's success at Flint and U.S. Steel's surrender to SWOC, labor organizers had still failed to enroll in SWOC more than a substantial minority of the steelworkers employed by firms other than U.S. Steel.[44] For most rank and filers, then, militancy consisted of refusing to cross a picket line and no more. As one observer noted of the Flint sitdowners, a group more militant than the majority of autoworkers: "Those strikers have no more idea of 'revolution' than pussycats."[45]

Even the most strike-torn cities and regions had a significantly internally differentiated working class. At the top were the local cadres, the "sparkplug unionists," the men and women fully conscious of their roles in a marketplace society that extolled individualism and rewarded collective strength. These individuals, ranging the political spectrum from social democrats to communists, provided the leadership, militancy, and ideology that fostered industrial conflict and the emergence of mass-production unionism. Beneath them lay a substantial proportion of workers who could be transformed, by example, into militant strikers and unionists, and, in turn, themselves act as militant minorities. Below them were many first- and second-generation immigrant workers, as well as recent migrants from the American countryside, who remained embedded in a culture defined by traditional ties of family, kinship, church, and neighborhood club or tavern. Accustomed to following the rituals of the past, heeding the advice of community leaders, and slow to act, such men and women rarely joined unions prior to a successful strike, when finally moved to act behaved with singular solidarity, yet rarely served as union or political activists and radicals. And below this mass were the teenage workers caught halfway between liberation from their parental families and the formation of their own new households, more attracted to the life and rituals of street gangs and candy-store cronies than to the customs and culture of persistent trade unionists and political activists.[46]

A word must now be added concerning those scholars who have argued that during the 1930s, a spontaneously militant and increasingly radical rank and file was either handcuffed or betrayed by bureaucratic and autocratic labor leaders. For those who accept the Leninist thesis that trade unions are, by definition, economist and hence nonrevolutionary, there is no problem in comprehending the behavior of American trade unions and their members during the 1930s. But for those who seek to understand why the militant beginnings of the CIO terminated in an ideological and institutional dead end, why, in David Brody's words, "the character of American trade unionism . . . made it an exploiter of radicalism rather than vice versa," questions remain.[47] And it may seem easiest to answer, as Art Preis, Ronald Radosh, James Weinstein, and Staughton Lynd have done, that the blame for the failure of radicalism rests with such labor leaders as John L. Lewis and Sidney Hillman, who sold out to the New Deal, collaborated with employers, and restrained rank-and-file militancy through the instrument of the nonstrike union contract. That hypothesis, commonly subsumed under the rubric "corporate liberalism", contains a grain of truth.[48] But the small truth tends to obscure a greater reality. As J. B. S. Hardman observed a half century ago, labor leaders are primarily accumulators of power; and, need it be said, no man was more eager to accumulate power than John L. Lewis.[49] A businessman's power flowed from his control of capital; a politician's from his influence over voters and his possession of the instruments of government; and a labor leader's power derived from his union membership. Thus, the more massive and militant the rank and file, the more influential was the labor leader. Bereft of a mass membership or saddled with a lethargic rank and file, the labor leader lost influence—and power. All labor leaders, then, necessarily played a devious and sometimes duplicitous game. Sometimes they rushed in to lead a rebellious rank and file; other times, they agitated the rank and file into action; whether they seized leadership of a movement already in motion or themselves breathed life into the rank and file, labor leaders obtained whatever power they exercised with employers and officials as a consequence of their followers' behavior. Yet, while they encouraged militancy, labor leaders also restrained their troops and, in John L. Lewis's phrase, "put a lid on the strikers." They did so for several reasons. First, not all rank-and-file upheavals promised success. And nothing destroyed a trade union as quickly or diluted a labor leader's power as thoroughly as a lost strike. Second, leaders had to judge at what point rank-and-file militancy would produce government repression, an ever-present reality even in Franklin D. Roosevelt's America. Third, and more selfishly, rank-and-file upheavals could career out of control and threaten a labor leader's tenure in office as well as strengthen his external power. Throughout the 1930s, labor leaders such as John L. Lewis alternately encouraged the release of working-class rebelliousness and put the lid back on. The labor leader was truly the man in the middle, his influence rendered simultaneously greater and also more perilous as a result of working-class militancy.[50]

A final word must also be said about the union contract, the instrument that allegedly bound workers to their employers by denying them the right to strike. With historical hindsight, this seems to be the end result of the union-management contract under which the union promises to discipline its members on behalf of management. But one must remember that during the 1930s, ordinary workers, the romanticized rank and file, risked their jobs, bodies, and lives to win the contract. And when they won it, as in Flint in February 1937, a sitdown striker rejoiced that it "was the most wonderful thing that we could think of that could possibly happen to people."[51]

Paradoxically, the one experience during the 1930s that united workers across ethnic, racial, and organizational lines—New Deal politics—served to vitiate radicalism. By the end of the 1930s, Roosevelt's Democratic party had become, in effect, the political expression of America's working class. Old-line socialists, farmer-labor party types, and even communists enlisted in a Roosevelt-led popular front. Blacks and whites, Irish and Italian Catholics, Slavic- and Jewish-Americans, uprooted rural Protestants, and stable, skilled workers joined the Democratic coalition, solidifying the working-class vote as never before in American history. Roosevelt encouraged workers to identify themselves as a common class politically as well as economically. As with David Lloyd George in Britain's pre–World War I Edwardian crisis, Franklin D. Roosevelt in the American crisis of the 1930s found revolutionary class rhetoric indispensable. It panicked the powerful into concessions and attracted working-class voters to the Democratic party. Just as Lloyd George intensified the earlier British crisis to ease its solution, Roosevelt acted similarly in New Deal America. By frightening the ruling class into conceding reforms and appealing to workers to vote as a solid bloc, Roosevelt simultaneously intensified class consciousness and stripped it of its radical potential.[52]

The dilemma of John L. Lewis showed just how well Roosevelt succeeded in his strategy. During the 1930s, no matter how much Lewis preferred to think of himself as an executive rather than a labor leader, however little he associated personally with the working class, he functioned as the leader of a militant working-class movement. Whereas Roosevelt sought to contain working-class militancy through reforms, militant workers pressured Lewis to demand more than the president would or could deliver. The more evident that the New Deal's economic failures became, the more heatedly labor militants demanded a fundamental reordering of the economy and society—demands that Lewis, as leader of the CIO, came to express more forcefully than any other trade unionist. "No matter how much Roosevelt did for the workers," recalls Len DeCaux, "Lewis demanded more. He showed no gratitude, nor did he bid his followers be grateful—just put the squeeze on all the harder."[53] But Lewis—unlike the British labor leaders of Lloyd George's generation, who found in the Labour party an alternative to the prime minister's "New Liberalism"—had no substitute for Roosevelt's New Deal. In the United States, the president easily mastered the labor leader.

Lewis's lack of a political alternative to the New Deal flowed from two sources. First was the refusal of most American leftists to countenance a third-party challenge to the Democrats and the intense loyalty most workers felt to Roosevelt. Between the winter of 1937–38 and the summer of 1940, however much Lewis threatened to lead a new third party, his public speeches and private maneuvers failed to create among workers a third-party constituency. It was Lewis's radical speeches that made his eventual endorsement in 1940 of Wendell Willkie so shocking to many of the labor leader's admirers. Had those Lewis sycophants known that in June 1940, the CIO president had plotted to win the Republican nomination for Herbert Hoover, they might have been even more startled.[54] And it was his support first of Hoover and then of Willkie that exposed the second source for Lewis's lack of a radical alternative to the New Deal. That was the extent to which Lewis, other labor leaders, and perhaps most workers had assimilated the values of a business civilization. This union, Lewis told members of the United Mine Workers at their 1938 convention, "stands for the proposition that the heads of families shall have a sufficient income to educate . . . these sons and daughters of our people, and they go forth when given that opportunity. . . . they become scientists, great clergymen . . . great lawyers, great statesmen . . . . Many of our former members are successful in great business enterprises." And two years later, in 1940, he told the same audience: "You know, after all there are two great material tasks in life that affect the individual and affect great bodies of men. The first is to achieve or acquire something of value or something desirable, and then the second is to prevent some scoundrel from taking it away from you."[55] Notice the substance of Lewis's remarks to a trade-union crowd, the combination of urging the children of the working class to rise above it, not with it, and the materialistic stress on possessive individualism. Lewis, the most militant and prominent of the Depression decade's labor leaders, remains too much the personification of vulgar pragmatism and business values to lead a third-party political crusade.

What, then, follows logically from the above description of the 1930s and the implied line of analysis? First, and perhaps obviously, however turbulent were the American 1930s, the Depression decade never produced a revolutionary situation. Second, one observes the essential inertia of the working-class masses. Once in motion, the mass of workers can move with great acceleration and enormous militancy—but such movement remains hard to get started. Such social inertia, combined with the inability of most workers and their leaders to conceive of an alternative to the values of marketplace capitalism—that is, to create a working-class culture autonomous from that of the ruling class—was more important than trade-union opportunism, corporate co-optation, or New Deal liberalism (though the last factor was clearly the most potent) in thwarting the emergence of durable, working-class radicalism. Third, and finally, it suggests that a distinction must be drawn between class struggle as a historical reality and workers as a class fully aware of their role, power, and ability to replace the existing system with "a better, firmer, more just social order [than] . . . the one to be torn down."

Notes

An earlier version of this essay appeared as "Not So 'Turbulent Years': Another Look at the American 1930s" in *Amerikastudien* 24 (1979): 5–20.

1. Len DeCaux, *Labor Radical* (Boston: Beacon Press, 1970), 230.

2. Staughton Lynd, "The Possibility of Radicalism in the Early 1930's: The Case of Steel," *Radical America* 6 (Nov.–Dec. 1972): 37–64; idem, "Guerilla History in Gary," *Liberation* 14 (Oct. 1969): 17–20. For a revised version of Lynd's views of the 1930s, one more in consonance with what actually happened—not what might have been—see Lynd, "The United Front in America: A Note," *Radical America* 8 (July–Aug. 1974): 29–37.

3. David Brody, "Labor and the Great Depression: The Interpretive Prospects," *Labor History* 13 (Spring 1972): 231–44; idem, "Radical Labor History and Rank-and-File Militancy," *Labor History* 16 (Winter 1975): 122.

4. Karl Marx and Friedrich Engels, *Selected Works* (London: Lawrence and Wishart, 1968), 97.

5. E. P. Thompson, *The Making of the English Working Class* (London: Victor Gollanz, 1963), 12.

6. Ronald Radosh, "The Corporate Ideology of American Labor Leaders from Gompers To Hillman," in *For a New America,* ed. James Weinstein and David W. Eakins (New York: Random House, 1970), 125–52; idem, *American Labor and United States Foreign Policy* (New York: Random House, 1969), 18–29; James Weinstein, *The Corporate Ideal in the Liberal State* (Boston: Beacon Press, 1968).

7. Stanley Lebergott, *Manpower in American Economic Growth* (New York: McGraw-Hill, 1964), 512.

8. Stephan Thernstrom, *The Other Bostonians* (Cambridge, Mass.: Harvard University Press, 1973), 56, 59, 90, 203, 207, 233, 240, 249.

9. Bernard Sternsher, *Hitting Home: The Great Depression in Town and Country* (Chicago: Quadrangle Books, 1970), 10; John A. Garraty, "Radicalism in the Great Depression," in *Essays on Radicalism in Contemporary America,* ed. Leon B. Blair (Austin: University of Texas Press, 1972), 89; Roy Rosenzweig, "Radicals and the Jobless: The Musteites and the Unemployed Leagues, 1932–1936," *Labor History* 16 (Winter 1975): 52–77; Daniel J. Leab, "United We Eat: The Creation and Organization of the Unemployed Councils in 1930," *Labor History* 8 (Fall 1967): 300–315.

10. Irving Bernstein's *Turbulent Years* (Boston: Houghton Mifflin, 1969), chap. 6, remains the best description of the 1934 "Eruption." *New York Times,* July 17, 20, 21, 27, 28, 1934, all on p. 1.

11. Lynd, "The Possibility of Radicalism," 38, 49–51; Sidney Fine, *The Automobile under the Blue Eagle: Labor, Management and the Automobile Manufacturing Code* (Ann Arbor: University of Michigan Press, 1963), 298–315.

12. Sidney Fine, *Sit-Down: The General Motors Strike of 1936–1937* (Ann Arbor: University of Michigan Press, 1969), 331.

13. Ibid., 201.

14. Ibid.

15. Horace R. Cayton and George S. Mitchell, *Black Workers and the New Unions* (Chapel Hill: University of North Carolina Press, 1939), vi, viii.

16. E. Wight Bakke, *The Unemployed Worker* (New Haven, Conn.: Yale University Press, 1940), 87.

17. Cayton and Mitchell, *Black Workers,* 268.

18. DeCaux, *Labor Radical,* 303.

19. Powers Hapgood to Sweetheart, July 24, 1935, Powers Hapgood Papers, Lilly Library, Indiana University at Bloomington.

20. Adolph Germer to Harry Hauser, Oct. 29, 1937, Adolph Germer Papers, Box 4, State Historical Society of Wisconsin, Madison.

21. Gardner Jackson, 727–28, Columbia Oral History Collection, Columbia University, New York (hereafter Columbia Oral History Collection); Lee Pressman, 96–97, Columbia Oral History Collection.

22. See Paul Kleppner, *The Cross of Culture: A Social Analysis of Midwestern Politics* (New York: Free Press, 1970), chaps. 5 and 7; Richard Jensen, *The Winning of the Midwest* (Chicago: University of Chicago Press, 1971), chaps. 9 and 10.

23. "Notes on CIO Meeting, November 7–8, 1938," Katherine Pollack Ellickson Papers, microfilm, Franklin D. Roosevelt Library, Hyde Park, N.Y.

24. Alfred Winslow Jones, *Life, Liberty, and Property* (Philadelphia: J. B. Lippincott, 1941), 250–79, 350–51, 354.

25. Walter Galenson, *The CIO Challenge to the AFL* (Cambridge, Mass.: Harvard University Press, 1960), 585; Philip Taft, *The A. F. of L. from the Death of Gompers to the Merger* (New York: Harper, 1959), 199–200; W. Jett Lauck, Diary, Dec. 13, 1937, W. Jett Lauck Papers, University of Virginia Library; John Frey to A. Appleton, Apr. 13 and Aug. 1, 1938, John Frey Papers, Box 1, File 8, Library of Congress.

26. See, for example, James R. Green, "Working-Class Militancy in the Depression," *Radical America* 6 (Nov.–Dec. 1972): 2–3.

27. Isidore Lubin, Memorandum to the President, Aug. 29, 1934, Franklin D. Roosevelt Papers, OF 407B, Box 10, Franklin D. Roosevelt Library, Hyde Park, N.Y.

28. Calculated from *Historical Statistics of the United States, Colonial Times to 1957,* ser. D 764–78 (Washington, D.C., 1960), 99.

29. Rosenzweig, "Radicals and the Jobless," 60.

30. Bakke, *Unemployed Worker;* idem., *Citizens without Work* (New Haven, Conn.: Yale University Press, 1940); Robert S. and Helen M. Lynd, *Middletown in Transition* (New York: Harcourt. Brace, 1937).

31. Robert S. and Helen M. Lynd, *Middletown: A Study in American Culture* (New York: Harcourt, Brace, 1929), 3–6.

32. R. and H. Lynd, *Middletown in Transition,* 42–43, 73, 203, 447–48.

33. Ibid., 26–28; cf. R. and H. Lynd, *Middletown in Transition,* 254.

34. R. and H. Lynd, *Middletown in Transition,* 41–44.

35. Bakke, *Citizens without Work,* 102; cf. ibid , 89–99.

36. Ibid., 59–66.

37. Ibid., 69.

38. Eugene D. Genovese, *Roll, Jordan, Roll: The World the Slaves Made* (New York: Pantheon, 1974), 115.

39. Bakke, *Citizens without Work,* 57–59.

40. Ibid., 64.

41. Edward Shorter and Charles Tilly, *Strikes in France, 1830–1968* (London: Cambridge University Press, 1974).

42. Fine, *Sit-Down,* 117. The UAW had signed up fifteen hundred out of more than twelve thousand autoworkers. Cf. Adolph Germer to John Brophy, Dec. 8, 1935, Germer Papers, Box 2, State Historical Society of Wisconsin, Madison.

43. Hapgood to Lewis, Mar. 29, 1936, Hapgood Papers, Lilly Library, Indiana University at Bloomington.

44. Pressman, 193–94, Columbia Oral History Collection; David J. MacDonald, Oral History Transcript, 11, Pennsylvania State University Labor Archives, University Park.

45. Fine, *Sit-Down,* 331.

46. Peter Friedlander, *The Emergence of a UAW Local, 1936–1939: A Study in Class and Culture* (Pittsburgh, Pa.: University of Pittsburgh Press, 1975), xiii–xx, 27–28, 119–31 passim.

47. Brody, "Labor and the Great Depression," 241.

48. See note 6 above and Lynd, "Possibility of Radicalism," 50–51; idem, "Guerilla History," 17–20; idem, "Personal Histories of the Early CIO," *Radical America* 5 (May–June 1971): 50; Alice and Staughton Lynd, *Rank and File* (Boston: Beacon Press, 1973), 4–5, 89–90. Cf. Mark Naison, "The Southern Tenant Farmers Union and the CIO," *Radical America* 11 (Sept.–Oct. 1968): 36–54; Art Preis, *Labor's Giant Step* (New York: Pioneer Publishers, 1964).

49. J. B. S. Hardman, "Union Objectives and Social Power," in *American Labor Dynamics,* ed. J. B. S. Hardman (New York: Harcourt, Brace, 1928), 104.

50. Melvyn Dubofsky and Warren Van Tine's *John L. Lewis: A Biography* (New York: Times Books, 1977) is a study of precisely that process and the dilemma of trade-union leadership. Cf. Friedlander, *Emergence of a UAW Local,* 119–31 passim.

51. Fine, *Sit-Down,* 307; Brody, "Radical Labor History," 125.

52. For the Edwardian British analogy, see Paul Thompson, *The Edwardians* (Bloomington: Indiana University Press, 1975), 260–62. On the working-class core of the Democratic party, see Samuel Lubell, *The Future of American Politics* (New York: Doubleday, 1965), 179–82; Jones, *Life, Liberty, and Property,* 314–17; Friedlander, *Emergence of a UAW Local,* 112–14.

53. DeCaux, *Labor Radical,* 295; Pressman, 91, 96–97, 188, 191, 352, Columbia Oral History Collection.

54. Pressman, 380, Columbia Oral History Collection; statement, Herbert Hoover Papers, June 1940, Post-Presidential Files, John L. Lewis, Box 98, Herbert Hoover Library, West Branch, Iowa.

55. United Mine Workers of America, *Convention Proceedings* (Washington, D.C., 1938), 172; idem, *Convention Proceedings* (Washington, D.C., 1940), 14. In *Life, Liberty, and Property,* Alfred Winslow Jones observed of Akron's workers in 1939, even the highly politicized ones: "Our measurements of opinion and the comments of workers indicate clearly that most of them do not want to feel that they have isolated themselves from the general run of 'middle class opinion.' The general climate of opinion bears in upon them and would make it impossible for them to turn decisively away into a workers' world, even if such a thing existed" (297).

7

American Industrial Workers and Political Parties from Roosevelt to Reagan: A Comparative Perspective

THE primary problem before us is to explore a political phenomenon in U.S. history that is usually described in one of two ways: (1) the absence of a mass-based socialist, social democratic, or labor party; or (2) the limited influence of American workers in the political arena and process as compared to those in other advanced industrial nations. The conventional explanation to account for that peculiarity of the American political experience has usually fallen under the rubric of "American exceptionalism," the concept that in certain fundamental respects, the economy, the society, and especially the culture of the United States have been unlike that of any other modern industrial democracy. The reasoning behind the concept of American exceptionalism, however, has been quite circular. Most often, for example, the absence of a socialist party and class consciousness has been taken to prove the existence of an American exceptionalism. And, then, the concept itself has been asserted as the reason for the absence of class consciousness and socialism in the United States.[1]

No student of the political history of the American working class can escape a confrontation with the issue of exceptionalism. Let me also say flatly that the methods with which historians treat their subject tend to reinforce the explanatory appeal of exceptionalism. As a group, we focus on the particular, not the general, the concrete rather than the abstract; that is, we examine what distinguishes the French past from the British one, or the German national experience and character from, let us say, the Italian (just as there is an American exceptionalism, there is also a German *sonderweg*). Historians may be the most "scientific" of humanists, but we remain the least scientific of social scientists.

The basis for "American exceptionalism" as laid out by most scholars is simple. It usually consists of all or some of the following characteristics: (1) the absence of a feudal or predemocratic experience in which people were categorized and defined on the basis of class, caste, or status (in Louis Hartz's phrase, Americans were "born free"); (2) the absence of impermeable class lines and the persistent movement of Americans up and down the occupational/income ladder, mostly up; (3) the remarkable spatial mobility of Americans; (4) the exceptionally high wage rates and standards of living (in Werner Sombart's formulation, the wrecking of the ship of socialism on reefs of roast beef and shoals of apple pie); (5) the diversity of ethnoreligious groups that made class solidarity impossible to achieve and instead created a society in which ethnicity rather than class was the decisive fault line.[2] This, to be sure, is not a complete list of the attributes that characterize American exceptionalism.

Of the characteristics listed above, all save the first, which is not a self-explanatory notion, were scarcely singular to the history of the United States. Nineteenth- and twentieth-century European history is filled with examples of working-class mobility, both spatial and occupational (or class). As more and more research has been done on the subject, the alleged U.S. superiority in wage rates and living standards has grown less obvious. Few European nation-states, moreover, had unitary, solidified working classes. In Europe as well as the United States, workers could be distinguished from one another on the basis of nationality, religion, language, and politics.[3]

In fact, one can make a strong case for arguing that between 1870 and 1919, and latterly from 1946 to the present, working-class political behavior in the United States was a variety of the more general pattern in industrial nations and not an exception to the rule. In the former time period, for example, especially in the last one-third of the nineteenth century, instances of independent working-class politics at the local and state levels abounded. Moreover, the two national labor federations that appeared in the era, the Knights of Labor and the American Federation of Labor (AFL), were created as much to voice the political aspirations of American workers as to unionize them. Then, in the first part of the twentieth century, the halcyon years of the Second International, the Socialist Party of America (SPA) seemed a flourishing institution destined to claim for itself a major share of political power nationally. Some of the nation's largest trade unions and at least one-third of all the members of the AFL were committed to some form of socialism. And just as was the case in France, Italy, Spain, and—to some degree—Britain, the United States had its own boisterous and militant exponents of direct action, the exponents of syndicalism and anarcho-syndicalism.[4] And after 1946, a case can be made for arguing that in the advanced European industrial nations, workers and working-class institutions began to adopt a more American model of behavior. Although socialist and labor parties remained the rule, beginning with the Federal Republic of Germany in 1955, such parties began to eliminate programmatic references to class conflict and the revolutionary seizure of power (the British Labour party never stressed class war nor promoted revolutionary politics). As in the United States, so it was in western Europe that an economics of abundance and a culture of consumption transformed working-class politics.[5] The interwar years, 1919–39, however, were a time when U.S. working-class politics diverged from the European pattern, and the main body of this essay will bridge the exceptional interwar years and the more "normal" postwar era.

In what follows, I would like to proceed on the assumption that there were indeed differences between the United States and Europe in the development and practice of working-class politics but that they flowed more from historical contingency than from inherent, fundamental, or essential differences between U.S. workers, their labor organizations, and their forms of political belief and behavior than that of their European brothers and sisters.

The political history of American industrial workers from 1933 to the present naturally was shaped by the inheritance of the past. In the United States, unlike Europe, political democracy and mass political parties preceded the emergence of a modern proletariat with its own institutions and forms of organization. By the time American workers built their first truly national labor movement in the late nineteenth century, most male citizens had already formed their political consciousness and loyalties as Republicans or Democrats. In Europe, by contrast, the growth of political democracy, labor unions, and socialist and labor parties proceeded hand in glove.[6]

A second salient factor distinguished U.S. from European political realities in the late nineteenth century. In the words of Stephen Skowronek, the United States was a state of "courts and parties." The American nation lacked an effective public administrative apparatus to which people could turn to use public power to regulate and improve their conditions

of life. Instead, political parties, which were private and voluntary institutions, and party leaders, who were often private individuals holding no
public position, substituted for bureaucrats and administrators. This gave
the two dominant national political parties singular influence and power,
further reinforcing existing working-class loyalties either to the Republicans or Democrats.[7]

Thus, as several historians have argued, political parties in the United
States acted as the "graveyard of class-based politics." Alan Dawley and
Anthony F. C. Wallace have suggested that antislavery and the Civil War
(the war for union) united Protestant, American-born workers and their
factory masters in a common cause: "free labor" and the Republican party.[8]
As voluntary private institutions, moreover, the two dominant political
parties regularly recruited the natural leaders of the working class into
positions of influence, power, and substantial income. Careers in party
politics replaced a commitment to trade unionism and the labor movement.[9] By the end of the nineteenth century, not only had the Republicans
and the Democrats won the loyalties of most working-class voters and
stripped the labor movement of some of its "best" men; the parties also
successfully practiced a form of politics that substituted ethnoreligious
loyalties for class-based distinctions.[10]

Between the 1870s and World War I, however, an alternative, or
countertradition, of working-class politics persistently made its presence
felt. During the 1870s and 1880s, municipal labor parties frequently challenged for power locally and often won at the ballot box. Most often, such
local, class-based political action was precipitated by antistrike actions
taken by judicial and police officials.[11] Then, in the 1890s, in several parts
of the nation, most especially the mining states of the Mountain West, the
coal-mining regions of Illinois, Ohio, and southern Appalachia, and also
in Wisconsin, Minnesota, Kansas, and on the Pacific Coast, unions and
workers served as the cutting edge of the Populist revolt.[12] The defeat of
Populism did not spell the end of independent labor politics. As the People's
party vanished from the political arena, the Socialist Party of America grew
as the primary challenger to Republican and Democratic hegemony. From
1900 to 1912, and again in 1917–18, the SPA voiced the aspirations of
America's most militant and radical workers as the party's membership
rolls and voting returns swelled.[13] Partly to counter the growth of socialism, partly to retard the development of independent labor parties, and
partly to counter the antilabor animus of the federal judiciary, the AFL
between 1906 and 1912 became more actively involved in partisan poli-

tics. Indeed, between 1912 and 1916, the leaders of the AFL fashioned a close political alliance with the Democratic party and the administration of Woodrow Wilson.[14]

Despite the reality of this long and persistent countertradition of independent working-class politics, one must also take note of the actual structural barriers to effective action by workers in the political arena. First, many of the procedural voting reforms associated with the Progressive Era disfranchised workers. These reforms either directly stripped workers of the right to vote or did so indirectly by diluting the power of political bosses and ward heelers who had acted as intermediaries between working people and the political process.[15] The character and residential habits of working-class voters also diluted their political presence. Composed in largest part of immigrants and their children, the blue-collar workforce included millions of men ineligible for the franchise. Women, an increasing bloc in the waged labor force, lacked the franchise, as did male workers under twenty-one years of age and most nonwhite wage earners. Although we lack precise estimates of the number and proportion of workers eligible to vote, there is no doubt that a substantial proportion lacked the franchise. Even among those theoretically eligible to vote, a large proportion lost the right as a result of frequent residential moves across legal voting boundaries.[16] One must also remember the link between organizational affiliation and voting behavior. Members of trade unions were more likely than unaffiliated workers to vote and ballot independently. Yet at no time before World War I did trade unions ever effectively organize more than 10 percent of the eligible labor force (usually that figure fell beneath 10 percent). Finally, until the years of the New Deal revolution, the national state had a minimal impact on the lives of most working people. The United States remained preeminently a "state of courts and parties." However weakened by progressive reforms, the ward heeler, not the public official (the party, not the state), acted as the mediator between the private and public realms, between citizens and their government.

If a variety of factors combined to attenuate the political power of American workers in the half century from the end of the Civil War to the end of World War I, those factors assumed added force during the 1920s. Socialism practically disappeared as a real presence in the political arena. Communism, which came to dominate the political left, built no mass following in the trade unions or among the working class. The labor movement steadily shrank from its wartime peak membership and lost whatever militancy it had once evinced. In 1924, progressive forces inside and outside the labor movement joined together for one last hurrah, the third-party presidential campaign of Robert LaFollette. For labor and the left, the campaign practically aborted itself. Communists, socialists, and trade unionists fought among themselves. The AFL endorsed LaFollette, yet many of the federation's most prominent trade-union leaders backed the Republican party. If organized workers diluted their political influence by dividing among themselves, larger masses of American workers simply withdrew from the political arena, as attested by all the data on voting turnout.[17]

"Fordism" had triumphed, as most workers, like those Robert and Helen Lynd studied in the mid-sized industrial city of Muncie, Indiana, seemingly conspired in their own subjugation to the hegemony of capital. They chose a culture of consumption over a politics of class.[18] And when greater numbers of workers chose to vote, as they did in the presidential election of 1928, ethnoreligious factors appeared far more potent than class affiliations, especially among the working-class voters of the Roman Catholic and Orthodox persuasions, who cast their ballots for the Democratic candidate Al Smith, whose campaign was run by John J. Raskob of the General Motors and Dupont corporations, two of the most notorious antilabor enterprises in the nation. Several labor leaders had no difficulty endorsing the Republican candidate, Herbert Hoover, who personified the "new capitalism" of the 1920s, a capitalism built on scientific management as practiced by responsible employers and unions committed to mass production, high wages, and mass consumption. American-born trade unionists and workers, especially those of the Protestant faith or those without religious affiliations, probably also preferred Hoover.[19]

The Great Depression and the New Deal of the 1930s ended Fordism and American workers' consent to their own subordination in society, economics, and politics. The reforms of the Roosevelt administration also penetrated the state into the lives of ordinary working people. Whether or not the New Deal weakened the power of urban political machines—and on that question there is much disagreement and dispute—it did at least give coercive public agencies coequal power with voluntary private political parties. Whether it was at first to the Works Progress Administration (WPA), the Public Works Administration (PWA), the Civil Works Administration (CWA), or the Civilian Conservation Corps and later to the Social Security Administration and the National Labor Relations Board (NLRB) that working people looked for relief and assistance (the latter two agencies bypassed local party leaders and typified the routinized, bureaucratized, modern administrative state), they identified their welfare with public policies set in Washington. Whether it was the Lynds revisiting Muncie in 1935, E. W. Bakke studying unemployed workers in New Haven, Connecticut, during the Depression, or Alfred Winslow Jones surveying opinions and attitudes among workers of Akron, Ohio, at the end of a turbulent decade, they all found a new relationship between workers and the state. In all three cities, workers identified positively with the national state as represented by the welfare policies and prolabor tendencies of the Roosevelt administration. Where once political loyalties had been cemented through the private patronage and favors of ward heelers, it now owed as much or more to the public policies enacted by the national government and implemented by public administrators.[20]

The presence of an active national state committed to reforming and regulating the economy, to fashioning a welfare state of sorts, and even to promoting trade unionism and collective bargaining refashioned both the labor movement and labor politics. Organized labor could neglect politics only at its own peril. The Roosevelt administration, first of all, shaped the universe in which trade unions functioned and, second, created a political milieu, in which workers identified with the Democratic party, with a president who mastered the rhetoric of class politics and who, with language as well as action, could frighten the powerful into concessions and attract the ruled to the Democratic party. As one worker put it colloquially: "Mr. Roosevelt is the only man we ever had in the White House who would understand that my boss is a son-of-a-bitch."[21]

Those labor leaders most attuned to the new politics and the new opportunities sought to rebuild the labor movement and to do so in coalition with the Democratic party of Franklin D. Roosevelt. Led by John L. Lewis of the United Mine Workers and Sidney Hillman of the Amalgamated Clothing Workers of America, they struggled to unionize workers never before a part of the labor movement—the mass-production workers who toiled for the largest and most powerful corporations in the nation. And they believed that they could do so only as an integral part of the New Deal political coalition, as labor leaders who could deliver the labor vote to Roosevelt in return for policies that fostered trade unionism and the welfare state.

In the spring, summer, and fall of 1936, these labor leaders built a firm coalition with the president. In simplest terms, the president promised to assist their campaign to organize mass-production workers, especially in the steel industry. In return, the labor leaders promised to support

Roosevelt with money, manpower, and votes. Lewis and Hillman established Labor's Non-Partisan League as a trade-union adjunct to the Democratic party, and Lewis donated more than a half million dollars from his union's treasury to the Roosevelt presidential campaign, the largest single contribution until then ever offered a national political party. In regions of the country where Lewis's mineworkers, Hillman's men's clothing workers, and both men's agents were actively organizing industrial workers, the local Democratic party and the union grew indistinguishable. In some places, labor provided not only money, personnel, and votes; it also volunteered its own cadres as Democratic candidates for office.[22] In other regions of the country, where workers and radicals found it difficult to vote Democratic either because of traditions of socialism or the persistent conservatism of local Democratic party leaders, union radicals provided an alternative through which workers could vote for Roosevelt without casting a Democratic ballot. In Minnesota, Wisconsin, and Washington State, a form of Farmer-Labor Democratic party provided the alternative. In New York, clothing trades workers and their socialist allies created the American Labor party. Even communists, especially the ones active in the trade unions, while committed on paper to their own independent presidential candidate, by and large supported the reelection of Roosevelt.[23]

The 1936 election results delivered everything that Roosevelt and his labor allies could have desired. Throughout the industrial states and wherever blue-collar workers formed a substantial bloc of voters, the Democrats swept the canvass. States and cities that had been Republican since the political realignment of the 1890s went for Roosevelt and also elected Democrats, many of whom were trade unionists, to local office. The vast majority of industrial workers, composed in the main of immigrants and their children and grandchildren of Roman Catholic faith, voted Democratic, as did an overwhelming proportion of Jewish-Americans, whether of working-class, socialist, or bourgeois background. Even African Americans broke irrevocably with their Republican heritage for the first time since they had been emancipated, decisively choosing the former party of slavery, the Democrats. Almost as soon as the votes had been counted, John L. Lewis of the Congress of Industrial Organizations (CIO) told his supporters on the executive board what the results meant: "We . . . must capitalize on the election. The CIO was out fighting for Roosevelt, and every steel town showed a smashing victory for him. . . . We wanted a President who would hold the light for us while we went out and organized."[24]

At first, it seemed that the election of 1936 and its immediate aftermath would transform the coalition between a part of the labor movement and the Democratic party into an American version of European social democracy. Between January and March 1937, the Democrats in power enabled John L. Lewis's CIO to wrest union recognition and collective bargaining contracts from General Motors and U.S Steel, as well as from scores of smaller, less obdurate, antiunion firms. Lewis himself used a newspaper cartoon to illustrate the meaning of the new politics. In the midst of tense negotiations among Lewis, corporation executives, and the Democratic governor of Michigan, Frank Murphy, to settle the General Motors sit-down strike of 1937, Lewis showed the cartoon to the governor. It portrayed Murphy as labor's ally, a figure swelling in size and stature as contrasted to the Republican, anti-CIO governor of New Jersey, a tiny figure by comparison. Befriend labor, Lewis implied to Murphy, and there would be no limits to the governor's political future, including the presidency. Elated by his victories over General Motors and U.S. Steel, Lewis also had the young economists he had appointed to staff positions in the CIO devise an elaborate welfare state program for enactment by the Roosevelt administration. The program called for the expansion of the new social security system to include all the workers neglected by the law of 1935 and to increase retirement benefits to a minimum health and decency level. The CIO demanded unemployment benefits that guaranteed a living wage and a public works program that would eliminate the need for benefits. It proposed national minimum-wage and maximum-hour laws that would be comprehensive in coverage. It suggested national education programs that would enable the children of workers to complete a secondary school education and even to enter colleges and universities. Not least important, staff economists designed a program of national health care that would entitle all citizens to basic health and medical treatment at public expense.[25]

In the late winter and early spring of 1937, such a welfare state appeared well within the realm of possibility. A president committed to the CIO occupied the White House, and he spoke openly of redressing the needs of a nation and its people, one-third of whom in 1937 remained ill-fed, ill-clothed, and ill-housed. Roosevelt's New Deal agenda indeed seemed consonant with the demands and needs of the CIO and of industrial workers.

Only one year later, by November 1938, the entire effort to tie the Roosevelt administration more tightly to the cause of organized labor and the general welfare state seemed a shambles. The evolution of the Democratic party toward social democracy had ground to a halt. In 1937 municipal elections in such important industrial cities and centers of CIO influence as Detroit and Akron, independent labor tickets (linked to the social-democratic wing of the Democratic party) lost badly in local elections as working-class voters split their ballots. A year later, in November 1938, several Democratic candidates closely tied to labor lost their bids for reelection, most notably Governor Murphy of Michigan. That same election saw Roosevelt's purge of reactionary Democrats fail and the Republicans gain a considerable number of congressional seats.[26] What had happened?

To begin with, the split in the labor movement between John L. Lewis's "new unionists" in the CIO and the old guard in the AFL carried over into the political arena. As a rule, the labor barons in the AFL opposed political candidates preferred by the CIO, at times to the point of endorsing antilabor Democrats in primaries and antilabor Republicans in general elections. By 1938, moreover, only about 15 to 20 percent of wage and salary earners belonged to the competing centers of the divided labor movement. The great majority of nonunion workers—white-collar employees, petty proprietors, and the growing managerial-professional class—had become fearful of labor militancy and the violence associated with it. The wave of sitdown strikes that followed the General Motors walkout of 1937 and the ensuing violent steel strike in the spring of that year measurably shifted popular opinion to the right. Roosevelt's advisers informed him that further close identification with John L. Lewis, the CIO, industrial warfare, and labor militancy would be political dynamite. He had the labor left in his hip pocket; now it was time to tack the ship of state to the right.[27] The extent to which Roosevelt had captured working-class voters, including those with a long tradition of social-democratic voting, was caught in the words of a Tammany Hall Democratic leader in New York who explained the new voting habits of the city's Jewish workers. For them, he said, there were three worlds: "Di welt, jener welt, und Roosevelt."[28]

Equally important for the inability of the CIO to push Roosevelt to the left and for Roosevelt to move his party in that direction was the exceptional strength of southerners in Congress and in the Democratic party nationally. A few mavericks notwithstanding (and most of them came from states or districts in which John L. Lewis's mineworkers were numerous—Kentucky, West Virginia, Tennessee, and Alabama), by 1938, the bulk of southern Democrats had become open enemies of the CIO and the welfare state. The new industrial unionism and an activist national state threatened the southern economic and social system, which was based on cheap, nonunion labor and racial segregation. Elected to office from a region in which African Americans and poor whites were equally disfranchised, southern Democrats did not have to fear political retribution at the polls. Moreover, as more Republicans entered Congress after the 1938 election, southern Democrats could coalesce with them to combat unionism and social reforms.[29]

The election of 1940 proved precisely how little room labor had to maneuver politically and also how successfully Roosevelt had captured the working-class vote for his party. When John L. Lewis hinted at a break with Roosevelt and flirted with a variety of left-wing groups, the president drew other CIO leaders more tightly into his circle, inviting Sidney Hillman to serve as labor's man in the administration. In the words of Lee Pressman, the CIO staff attorney and an intimate of Communist party members, Hillman served as Roosevelt's lieutenant in the labor movement rather than as labor's emissary to the White House.[30] Even Lewis's belated attempt to shift votes away from Roosevelt in several key industrial states where the labor leader felt his influence to be greatest by endorsing the Republican candidate Wendell Willkie proved an abysmal failure. More clearly than ever, in November 1940, industrial workers remained loyal to the Democratic ticket. Even Lewis's own mineworkers overwhelmingly cast their votes for Roosevelt.[31] The ties between industrial workers and the Democratic party had grown unshakeable.

During World War II, those ties grew firmer. Most trade-union leaders from affiliates of both the AFL and the CIO served the national administration in minor capacities. More important, their organizations grew and flourished as never before. Under the benevolent guardianship of the national government during a time of tight labor markets, trade unions came by 1945 to encompass one-third or more of the nonagricultural labor force and had wrested recognition from nearly every sector of corporate America.[32]

For a time, however, the death of Franklin D. Roosevelt in April 1945 threatened the future of the labor–Democratic party coalition. Roosevelt's successor, Harry S. Truman, lacked his predecessor's links to the labor movement and, moreover, came from the border state–southern wing of the Democratic party, a group not known for its commitment to the labor movement and the welfare state. During the postwar strike wave of 1945–46, labor's doubts about Truman grew. The new president implemented policies designed to end strikes quickly and strip labor of its militancy. In fact, Truman seemed more concerned about soothing business anxieties than allaying labor's fears.[33]

Soon, however, Truman rebuilt his relationship with labor leaders. If he wanted to run for the presidency in his own right in 1948, he had to have the support of organized labor and the votes of American workers. His closest advisers, Clark Clifford most especially, told him how to do so. First, Truman vetoed the Taft-Hartley Labor Act of 1947, which had been passed by the Republican majority in Congress with support from southern Democrats. In his veto message, the president referred to New Deal labor laws and trade unions in the most glowing terms. Although Congress overrode the presidential veto, Truman had scored his points. Next, Truman approved a campaign policy for the approaching Democratic national convention and subsequent election that ignored the interests of southern Democrats and antiunion reactionaries. The president supported equal rights for African Americans, the repeal of the Taft-Hartley Act, and an expansion of the New Deal welfare state under the rubric of the "Fair Deal." He risked a secession by segregationist southern Democrats to hold the labor vote in the North and West.

Truman's strategy worked perfectly. Not only did he win a close election in November, he made the labor-Democratic coalition firmer than ever. So fearful were CIO leaders about the prospects of a Republican victory that they made support of Truman a litmus test of labor loyalty. Largely as a result of decisions made during the election of 1948, the CIO purged eleven allegedly communist unions from its ranks, unions that had betrayed labor's cause in 1948 by supporting the presidential campaign of Progressive party candidate Henry A. Wallace. Although the AFL did not play as prominent a public political role as the CIO, most of its leaders and affiliates worked behind the scenes to ensure Truman's election. Labor had become completely captive to the Democratic party just as Democratic candidates for national office had become dependent on the votes of the working class and of African Americans.[34] Labor's submission to the dictates of the Democratic party and its bosses resulted partly from trade unionism's failure to reshape southern politics. The abject failure of the CIO's much-heralded "Operation Dixie," an effort to unionize the South, left reactionaries in full control of the Democratic party regionally; southern power in Congress undiminished; and black and white workers divided.[35]

For the next twenty years, from roughly 1948 through 1968, outside the South, the Democratic party and organized labor were virtually indistinguishable. Between 1948 and 1955, the CIO's Political Action Committee (PAC) supplied much of the Democratic party's precinct-level organizational strength. PAC enrolled voters; it brought them to the polling place on election day; it financed campaigns and distributed campaign literature. After the merger of the AFL and the CIO in 1955, the AFL-CIO Committee on Political Education (COPE) took over those roles. According to one political scientist, in many U.S. industrial states and cities, COPE had, in effect, become the Democratic party. According to the same scholar, the Democratic party had become—in practice, if not in name—an American variant of European social democracy.[36] In the arena of national politics, lobbyists from the AFL-CIO were largely responsible for congressional expansion of the welfare state. During the Eisenhower years, they used their political influence to widen the scope of the social security system (and its benefits), to increase the minimum wage and the workers it covered, and, in general, to broaden the category of those benefiting from what came to be called the "social wage." Under Presidents Kennedy and Johnson, union lobbyists not only continued to call for improvements in the social wage (labor support was decisive in the enactment of Medicare); they also provided the indispensable support for the passage of the great civil rights legislation of the 1960s. As David Brody has pointed out, time and again, labor spokespeople in Washington sacrificed the narrower interests of their own members for the benefit of workers, nonwhites, and poor people outside the unions. Only the labor movement functioned in a way that aggregated the votes of poor people and elaborated a political program that promoted the general interest of society.[37] Labor built the welfare state at home; it also enlisted in the Cold War abroad.

Throughout the two decades of labor influence in the Democratic party, and through the party in national affairs, labor leaders publicly decried any interest in transforming the party into a labor party. Walter Reuther explained why. "The essential problem for the labor movement," he said, "is to learn to work with a party without trying to capture it. . . . I think that at the point the labor movement captures the Democratic party, you then destroy the broad base that is essential to translate sound policy into governmental action."[38] Reuther spoke as he did because he remembered well the experiences of 1937, 1938, 1948, and other times when labor had experimented with independent politics. He also knew firsthand of the failure of Operation Dixie and of subsequent attempts to unionize the South. Southern Democratic politics remained unreconstructed and antilabor. As Mike Davis has argued, the Democrats had captured and domesticated labor rather than labor having converted their political allies to social democracy.[39] Worse was soon to come, however, as the factors that in the past had combined to strengthen working-class political influence began to weaken during the 1960s.

Beginning in the 1950s and then accelerating in the 1960s and 1970s, structural changes in the economy and society weakened the political influence of labor and fragmented the votes of working-class citizens. Those changes also decimated the ranks of trade unionism. At first, unions lost membership only relative to absolute growth in the waged labor force. As unions recruited members during the 1950s and 1960s, whenever the business cycle turned up, they found themselves representing an ever-decreasing proportion of the labor force. Then, in the decade of the 1970s, unions began to lose members, a process that grew most rapidly in the years of the Reagan depression (1981–82). Today, fewer than one in six wage workers belongs to a union. Worse yet, the membership losses hit hardest at those unions concentrated in the mass-production sector of the economy, which had formed the core of the CIO's new unionism and new politics. Between 1974 and 1978, unions in manufacturing lost over one million members—more than 11 percent of their total membership. In 1981 and 1982, unions in the automobile and steel industries suffered even heavier losses. In February 1982, for example, the United Automobile Workers (UAW) averaged 300,000 fewer members than in 1979. As total employment diminished in the mass-production sector of the economy, the unions were unable to take advantage of sharply rising employment in the non-manufacturing sector. Such developments led critics on the left and right to print obituaries for the American labor movement.[40]

These changes in the structure of the labor force were also linked to transformations in the beliefs and behavior of blue-collar workers. Partly as a result of the New Deal welfare state, partly as a result of the material benefits wrested from employers by the trade unions, and partly as a consequence of public policies that converted more Americans than ever from renters to homeowners, workers, including masses of union members, began to act the part of suburban consumers. As George Meany proudly proclaimed in a Labor Day interview in 1969 (based on the results of an opinion survey poll among union members), workers were now solid middle-class citizens who worried more about prices and taxes than about wages and working conditions.[41] Thus was laid the basis for the Republican party politics of deflation and tax reduction. Workers in the largely nonunion financial, consumer, and service sector, who by July 1982 outnumbered those employed in primary production (manufacturing, mining, and construction), had often been eager recruits in the politics of deflation and tax cuts. The more educated white-collar employees in that sector—accountants, bookkeepers, engineers, and technicians, among others—had usually identified themselves as part of a professional or management team.

They, too, proved more susceptible to the politics of Republicanism than of social democracy.[42]

Linked to this was what might be called the movement of the South to the north and west. That movement occurred literally and figuratively: literally in the sense that between 1950 and 1970, millions of southern blacks and whites moved north to seek better jobs and higher wages; figuratively to the degree that the southern politics of race found a new home to the north and west. At first, John F. Kennedy's personal appeal to the old, New Deal, blue-collar constituency and then Lyndon B. Johnson's landslide victory over Barry Goldwater veiled what was happening. The civil rights revolt of the 1960s and the urban riots that ensued had an impact on northern blue-collar workers that could not be controlled or predicted. The first hint came during George Wallace's campaign in the presidential primaries of 1964, when he garnered an unusually large degree of working-class support in such states as Michigan, Indiana, and Wisconsin, where old CIO unions and COPE had long been influential. The 1968 national election confirmed the deleterious impact of race on politics and working-class voting. The AFL-CIO and COPE worked as never before to keep the blue-collar vote in the Democratic camp, and their leaders later insisted that such efforts and working-class loyalty to the party of Roosevelt had nearly placed Hubert Humphrey in the White House. In truth, Humphrey came close to victory only because the independent candidacy of George Wallace siphoned white racist votes away from Richard Nixon and the Republicans. The combined total of votes for Wallace and Nixon overwhelmed the Democratic tally; and, moreover, had the union vote for Humphrey been disaggregated by race, it would have shown clearly a white working-class drift away from the Democratic party.[43] Thereafter, Nixon and his party learned to play the politics of race even more expertly.

Less than ten years after Nixon left the White House in disgrace, Ronald Reagan played the politics of race and deflation to perfection. In the election of 1980, Reagan won the votes of the bulk of white union members and their families (the AFL-CIO trumpeted the fact that a majority of union members still voted Democratic without stressing that nearly all its substantial nonwhite membership provided much of that vote). Once in office, Reagan implemented policies that weakened trade unionism but kept the loyalty of a majority of white workers, union as well as nonunion. Although he used coercion to smash a strike by air traffic controllers and to destroy their union, although he presided over the worst depression and most massive unemployment since the 1930s, Reagan did so, he convinced many workers, in the interest of lower prices and lower taxes. Rightly or wrongly, more workers believed that they benefited from Reagan's war against inflation and high federal taxes than they suffered from unemployment, reduced wages, and union givebacks. White workers also appreciated the president's coolness to African-American spokespeople, his condemnation of affirmative action, and his resistance to other forms of compensatory treatment for minorities. And they showed their appreciation in the election of 1984 by once again giving Reagan a majority of their votes, this despite the fact that the AFL-CIO's own candidate, Walter Mondale, carried the Democratic torch.

George Bush's race for the presidency in 1988 showed that he learned his lessons well at Reagan's side. Once again, a Republican campaign practiced the politics of race to perfection; once again, an appeal to white union members as homeowners and consumers (low prices and low taxes plus prosperity) had its intended impact. As in 1980 and 1984, so in 1988 a majority of white union members and their families voted Republican. One might also note that from March through July 1988, when nearly every respected opinion poll survey showed Bush trailing Dukakis (and sometimes by quite a wide margin), the Teamsters' own survey of their locals and members suggested that the Democratic candidate would not have a chance in November. Rank-and-file Teamsters were pleased with Republican prosperity, the success of Reagan's war against inflation, and the series of federal tax cuts. If they were white, and most were, Teamsters intended to vote Republican.[44] Today, American workers seem fragmented politically and also more depoliticized than at any time since the decade of the 1920s.

In conclusion, one might ask, how does the American situation compare to the contemporary political scene in Europe? In Europe, too, I think that we can see an attenuation of traditional working-class modes of political behavior, a process that is occurring most rapidly in Great Britain and more slowly on the Continent. European workers, like their American brothers and sisters, have become consumers who respond to the politics of deflation (lower prices) and lower taxes, a politics that is practiced far better by parties of the right than parties of the left. European societies are also experiencing a transformation of the labor force that reduces the number of classical, blue-collar, industrial proletarians and replaces them with increasing numbers of white-collar, technical, professional, and managerial employees—people, as a group, far more susceptible to the appeal of conservative politics. One also sees signs in Europe of the sort of racist sentiments that separate white workers from nonwhite, "native" from "foreign." The impact of racism has probably been greatest in the United Kingdom; but now one can see its influence in France, West Germany, and even Italy.

No wonder, then, that the British Labour party staggers from crisis to crisis and electoral defeat to defeat; that the Austrian Socialist party forms a coalition with its conservative People's party counterparts; that the French Socialist party switches from a policy of economic expansion and inflation to one of restraint and fiscal responsibility as Mitterand makes it the party of the center; that the Social Democrats in the Federal Republic of Germany can probably only return to national power through a coalition with the Greens; and that the PCI (the Italian Communist party) searches desperately for the policy mix that will enable it either to appeal to a larger proportion of Italian voters or be invited to join a coalition government.

Yet one also observes certain decisive differences between the contemporary political situation in the United States and that of Europe. First, the issue of race is neither as influential nor as decisive a factor in party politics. Second, the Greens, or environmentalists, probably have a greater influence on the political left and among working-class voters. Third, levels of participation in elections remain far higher in Europe, especially among working people. Fourth, one sees far greater resistance to the dilution of the welfare state.

How does one account for such differences? I am not sure. Perhaps, despite all the transformations of the past two decades in Europe's economy, society, and the structure of its labor force, European workers remain more organized and more integrated into national society than their less unionized and more anomic American brothers and sisters. Certainly, European political parties remain more structured and disciplined entities than their American counterparts, which today barely function as real institutions.

Yes, political parties and working-class politics in the United States are different than elsewhere. Are they exceptional? The answer depends on how we use language, understand the past, and perceive the present. For myself, I prefer to see the U.S. case as a variety of the more general model of working-class political behavior in industrial democracies.

Notes

An earlier version of this essay appeared in Italian as "Gli operai dell'industria statunitense e i partiti politici da Roosevelt a Reagan" in *Il partito politico americano e l'Europa,* ed. Maurizio Vaudagna (Milan: Giancomo Feltrinelli Editore, 1991), 211–35.

1. Louis Hartz, *The Liberal Tradition in America* (New York: Harcourt, Brace, 1955); Seymour Martin Lipset, *The First New Nation* (New York: Basic Books, 1977), 170–204; cf. two other works by Lipset, "Why No Socialism in the United States?" in *Radicalism in the Contemporary Age,* ed. S. Bialer and B. Sluzer (Boulder, Colo.: Westview Press, 1977), 31–149, 346–63, and *Conflict and Consensus* (New Brunswick, N.J.: Transaction Publishers, 1985), 187–252. See also David Shannon, "Labor and Socialism," in *The Comparative Approach to American History,* ed. C. Vann Woodward (New York: Basic Books, 1968).

2. See the sources above as well as the following: Selig Perlman, *A Theory of the Labor Movement* (New York: Macmillan, 1928); Stephan Thernstrom, *The Other Bostonians* (Cambridge, Mass.: Harvard University Press, 1973); Stephan Thernstrom and Peter Knights, "Men in Motion: Some Data and Speculations about Urban Population Mobility in Nineteenth-Century America," *Journal of Interdisciplinary History* 1 (Autumn 1970): 7–35; Peter Knights, *The Plain People of Boston, 1830–1860* (Cambridge, Mass.: Harvard University Press, 1971); Stephan Thernstrom, "Working-Class Social Mobility in Industrial America," in *Essays in Theory and History,* ed. Melvin Richter (Cambridge, Mass.: Harvard University Press, 1970), chap. 8.

3. For a comparative study of British and American wage rates, see Peter Shergold, *Working-Class Life: The "American Standard" in Comparative Perspective, 1899–1913* (Pittsburgh, Pa.: University of Pittsburgh Press, 1982). See also Mary Nolan, *Social Democracy and Society: Working-Class Radicalism in Dusseldorf, 1890–1920* (New York: Cambridge University Press, 1981); idem, "Working-Class Formation and Working-Class Politics in Imperial Germany," in *Technological Change and Workers' Movements,* ed. Melvyn Dubofsky (Beverly Hills, Calif.: Sage, 1985), 45–76; Eric Hobsbawm, *Workers: Worlds of Labour* (New York: Pantheon, 1984), 49–65; Peter N. Stearns, *Lives of Labor: Work in a Maturing Industrial Society* (New York: Holmes and Meier, 1975).

4. For the case against American exceptionalism argued from a variety of perspectives, see Sean Wilentz, "Against Exceptionalism: Class Consciousness and the American Labor Movement, 1790–1920," *International Labor and Working-Class History* 26 (1984): 1–24; Eric Foner, "Why Is There No Socialism in the United States?" *History Workshop Journal* 17 (Spring 1984): 57–80; Melvyn Dubofsky, "William D. Haywood and Tom Mann," in *New Perspectives on American History,* ed. Hans L. Trefousse (New York: Burt Franklin, 1977), 189–208; William E. Forbath, "The Shaping of the American Labor Movement," *Harvard Law Review* 102 (1989): 1118–26; Ira Katznelson, "Working-Class Formation: Constructing Cases and Comparisons," and Aristide Zolberg, "How Many Exceptionalisms?" both in *Working-Class Formation,* ed. Ira Katznelson and Aristide Zolberg (Princeton, N.J.: Princeton University Press, 1986), 13–44, 397–455.

5. Giovanni Arrighi, "The Labor Movement in 20th Century Western Europe," in *Labor in the World Social Structure,* ed. Immanuel Wallerstein (Beverly Hills, Calif.: Sage, 1983), 44–57; Giovanni Arrighi and Beverly Silver, "Labor Movements and Capital Migration: The U.S. and Western Europe in the World-Historical Perspective," in *Labor in the Capitalist World-Economy,* ed. Charles Bergquist (Beverly Hills, Calif.: Sage, 1984), 183–216; Research Working Group on World Labor,

"Global Patterns of Labor Movements in Historical Perspective," *Review* 10 (Summer 1987): 137–55.

6. Perlman's *Theory of the Labor Movement* is still worth reading on this point, esp. 78–79, 129–40, 162–76.

7. Stephen Skowronek, *Building a New American State: The Expansion of National Administrative Capacities, 1877–1920* (New York: Cambridge University Press, 1982), 39–46.

8. Alan Dawley, *Class and Community: The Industrial Revolution in Lynn* (Cambridge, Mass.: Harvard University Press, 1976); A. F. C. Wallace, *Rockdale* (New York: Knopf, 1978).

9. David Montgomery, *Beyond Equality: Labor and the Radical Republicans, 1862–1873* (New York: Knopf. 1967), 208–15; Richard Oestreicher, "Urban Working-Class Political Behavior and Theories of American Electoral Politics, 1870–1940," *Journal of American History* 74 (1988): 1257–86.

10. Oestreicher, "Urban Working-Class Political Behavior"; Paul Kleppner, *The Cross of Culture: A Social Analysis of Midwestern Politics, 1850–1900* (New York: Free Press, 1970); Richard Jensen, *The Winning of the Midwest: Social and Political Conflict, 1888–1896* (Chicago: University of Chicago Press, 1971); and Samuel McSeveney, *The Politics of Depression: Political Behavior in the Northeast, 1893–1896* (New York: Oxford University Press, 1972).

11. Leon Fink, *Workingmen's Democracy: The Knights of Labor and American Politics* (Urbana: University of Illinois Press, 1983), 52–58, 78–82, 119–31, 188–210; Alan Dawley, *Class and Community,* 196–201.

12. Robert Larson, *New Mexico Populism: A Study of Radical Protest in a Western Territory* (Boulder: Colorado Associated University Press, 1974); idem, *Populism in the Mountain West* (Albuquerque: University of New Mexico Press, 1986); James E. Wright, *The Politics of Populism: Dissent in Colorado* (New Haven, Conn.: Yale University Press, 1974), esp. 153–58, 226–30; Thomas A. Clinch, *Urban Populism and Free Silver in Montana* (Missoula, Mont.: n.p., 1970); Norman Pollack, *The Populist Response to Industrial America: Midwestern Populist Thought* (Cambridge, Mass.: Harvard University Press, 1962), 66–67; Lawrence Goodwyn, *Democratic Promise: The Populist Moment in America* (New York: Oxford University Press, 1976), 307–11; James Peterson, "The Trade Unions and the Populist Party," *Science and Society* 8 (Winter 1944): 143–60.

13. James Green, *Grass-Roots Socialism: Radical Movements in the Southwest, 1895–1943* (Baton Rouge: Louisiana State University Press, 1977); James Weinstein, *The Decline of Socialism in the United States* (Boston: Beacon Press, 1968); Richard Judd, *Socialist Cities: Municipal Politics and the Grass Roots of American Socialism* (Albany: State University of New York Press, 1989); Melvyn Dubofsky, "Success and Failure of Socialism in New York City, 1900–1918: A Case Study," *Labor History* 10 (Fall 1968): 361–75. See also Shelton Stromquist, "The Politics of Class: Urban Reform and Working-Class Mobilization in Cleveland and Milwaukee, 1890–1910"; Cecelia Bucki, "Craft Workers and Municipal Politics in the 1930s," both papers read at the Eighty-first Annual Meeting of the Organization of American Historians, Reno, Nevada, March 1988.

14. Julia Greene, "The Strike at the Ballot Box: The American Federation of La-

bor, Local Trade Union Leadership, and Political Action, 1881 to 1916" (Ph.D. diss., Yale University, 1990); Melvyn Dubofsky, "Abortive Reform: The Wilson Administration and Organized Labor, 1913–1920," in *Work, Community, and Power: The Experience of Labor in Europe and America, 1900–1925,* ed. James F. Cronin and Carmen Sirianni (Philadelphia: Temple University Press, 1983), 197–220.

15. J. Morgan Kousser, *The Shaping of Southern Politics: Suffrage Restriction and the Establishment of the One-Party System* (New Haven, Conn.: Yale University Press, 1974); Walter Dean Burnham, *Critical Elections and the Mainsprings of American Politics* (New York: Norton, 1970); idem, "The System of 1896: An Analysis," in *The Evolution of American Electoral Systems,* ed. Paul Kleppner et al. (Westport, Conn.: Greenwood Press, 1981), 147–202; Richard McCormick, *The Party Period and Public Policy* (New York: Oxford University Press, 1986), 171–81; Frances Fox Piven and Richard Cloward, *Why Americans Don't Vote* (New York: Pantheon, 1988), esp. 64–95; Samuel P. Hays, "The Politics of Reform in Municipal Government in the Progressive Era," *Pacific Northwest Quarterly* 55 (Oct. 1964): 157–69.

16. See Thernstrom, "Working-Class Social Mobility," and Thernstrom and Knights, "Men in Motion," for the argument that large numbers of the working class in Boston were permanent transients, many of whom were disfranchised by the residency requirements for voting in Massachusetts. Thernstrom also contends that while other "birds of passage" may have remained in Boston long enough to meet residency requirements for suffrage, they retained the *mentalité* of transients and thus were often politically indifferent.

17. David Montgomery, *The Fall of the House of Labor* (New York: Cambridge University Press, 1987), 406, 436; J. Weinstein, *Decline of Socialism,* 290–339; Paul Kleppner, *Who Voted? Electoral Turnout, 1870–1980* (New York: Praeger, 1982), 55–82; Alan Lichtman, "Critical Election Theory and the Reality of American Presidential Politics, 1916–1940," *American Historical Review* 81 (Apr. 1976): 317–51.

18. Robert and Helen Lynd, *Middletown: A Study in American Culture* (New York: Harcourt, Brace, 1965).

19. Samuel Lubell, *The Future of American Politics* (New York: Doubleday, 1965), 49–50, 54–55; Allan Lichtman, *Prejudice and the Old Politics: The Presidential Election of 1928* (Chapel Hill: University of North Carolina Press, 1979); Irving Bernstein, *The Lean Years: A History of the American Worker, 1920–1933* (Boston: Houghton Mifflin, 1960), 75–82; V. O. Key Jr., "A Theory of Critical Elections," *Journal of Politics* 17 (Feb. 1955): 3–18.

20. Robert and Helen Lynd, *Middletown in Transition* (New York: Harcourt, Brace, 1965); E. W. Bakke, *The Unemployed Worker* (New Haven, Conn.: Yale University Press, 1940); idem, *Citizens without Work* (New Haven, Conn.: Yale University Press, 1940); Alfred W. Jones, *Life, Liberty, and Property* (Philadelphia: J. B. Lippincott, 1941). For books by historians that take a more jaundiced view of the impact of the New Deal on local political machines and the practice of urban politics, see the following: Bruce Stave, *The New Deal and the Last Hurrah: Pittsburgh Machine Politics* (Pittsburgh, Pa.: University of Pittsburgh Press, 1970); Charles H. Trout, *Boston, the Great Depression, and the New Deal* (New York: Oxford University Press, 1977); Jo Ann E. Argensinger, *Toward A New Deal in Balti-*

more: *People and Government in the Great Depression* (Chapel Hill: University of North Carolina Press, 1988).

21. William E. Leuchtenberg, *Franklin D. Roosevelt and the New Deal, 1932–1940* (New York: Harper and Row, 1963), 188–89; Melvyn Dubofsky, "Not So 'Turbulent Years': Another Look at the American 1930s," *Amerikastudien* 24 (1979): 5–20; idem, "The New Deal and Labor," in *The Roosevelt New Deal: A Program Assessment Fifty Years After*, ed. Wilbur J. Cohen (Austin: University of Texas Press, n.d.), 73–82.

22. Melvyn Dubofsky and Warren Van Tine, *John L. Lewis: A Biography* (New York: Times Books, 1977), 248–52; Steven Fraser, "From the 'New Unionism' to the New Deal," *Labor History* 25 (Summer 1984): 405–30; idem, "Sidney Hillman: Labor's Machiavelli," in *Labor Leaders in America*, ed. Melvyn Dubofsky and Warren Van Tine (Urbana: University of Illinois Press, 1987), 207–33.

23. Irving Howe, *The World of Our Fathers* (New York: Harcourt Brace Jovanovich, 1976), 350–51, 391–92; Arthur Liebman, *Jews and the Left* (New York: Wiley, 1979), 65–66; John Haynes, *Dubious Alliance: The Making of Minnesota's DFL Party* (Minneapolis: University of Minnesota Press, 1984); idem, "Communists and Anti-Communists in the Northern Minnesota CIO, 1936–1949," *Upper Midwest History* 1 (1981): 55–73; Robert Ozanne, *The Labor Movement in Wisconsin* (Madison: University of Wisconsin Press, 1984), 133–38; Jonathan Dembo, *Unions and Politics in Washington State, 1885–1935* (New York: Garland, 1983); Kenneth Walzer, "The Party and the Polling Place: American Communism and an American Labor Party in the 1930s," *Radical History Review* 23 (Spring 1980): 104–35. See also Seymour Martin Lipset, "Roosevelt and the Protest of the 1930s," *Minnesota Law Review* 68 (Dec. 1983): 273–98.

24. Samuel Lubell, *Future of American Politics*, 55–68; John Allswang, *The New Deal and American Politics: A Study in Political Change* (Port Washington, N.Y.: Kennikat Press, 1978); idem, *A House for All Peoples: Ethnic Politics in Chicago, 1890–1936* (Lexington: University Press of Kentucky, 1971), 37–59; Kristi Anderson, *The Creation of a Democratic Majority, 1928–1936* (Chicago: University of Chicago Press, 1979); Nancy Weiss, *Farewell to the Party of Lincoln: Black Politics in the Age of FDR* (Princeton, N.J.: Princeton University Press, 1983); Dubofsky and Van Tine, *John L. Lewis*, 252–53.

25. For this welfare state program, see Dubofsky and Van Tine, *John L. Lewis*, 268, 326, 330.

26. Daniel Nelson, "The CIO at Bay: Labor Militancy and Politics in Akron, 1936–1938," *Journal of American History* 71 (Dec. 1984): 565–86; Samuel McSeveney, "The Michigan Gubernatorial Campaign of 1938," *Michigan History* 45 (June 1961): 97–127; Sidney Fine, *Frank Murphy: The New Deal Years* (Chicago: University of Chicago Press, 1979), 481–528; W. E. Leuchtenberg, *Franklin D. Roosevelt and the New Deal*, 272–73; Samuel Lubell, *Future of American Politics*, 30, 144.

27. *New York Times*, Oct. 7, 1938, 3; FDR Press Conferences, transcripts, vol. 9, 467, FDR Papers, Roosevelt Library, Hyde Park, N.Y.; Harry Hopkins to Franklin D. Roosevelt, with enclosure, July 2, 1937, FDR Papers, OF 407B, Box 27; and the following poll results as reported in *Fortune*: July 1937, 98–100; Oct. 1937, 162–64; Jan. 1938, 910–12; Apr. 1938, 100.

28. Irving Howe, *World of Our Fathers,* 393.

29. James Patterson, *Congressional Conservatism and the New Deal: The Growth of the Conservative Coalition in Congress, 1936–1939* (Lexington: University Press of Kentucky, 1967); idem, "The Failure of Party Realignment in the South, 1937–1939," *Journal of Politics* 27 (Aug. 1965): 602–17.

30. Steven Fraser, "Sidney Hillman"; Ronald Schatz, "Philip Murray and the Subordination of the Industrial Unions to the United States Government," in Dubofsky and Van Tine, *Labor Leaders,* 234–57; Dubofsky and Van Tine, *John L. Lewis,* 339–57.

31. Dubofsky and Van Tine, *John L. Lewis,* 357–61; Irving Bernstein, *The Turbulent Years: A History of the American Worker, 1933–1941* (Boston: Houghton Mifflin, 1970), 715–20; Samuel Lubell, "Post-Mortem: Who Elected Roosevelt?" *Saturday Evening Post,* Jan. 25, 1941, 9.

32. The best study of wartime labor politics, one that takes a more jaundiced view of public policy, is Nelson Lichtenstein's *Labor's War at Home: The CIO in World War II* (New York: Cambridge University Press, 1982). For an analysis of the war's impact on the consciousness of workers, see the same author's "Making of the Postwar Working Class: Cultural Pluralism and Social Structure in World War II," *Historian* 51 (Nov. 1988): 42–63.

33. On Truman and labor, see Alonzo Hamby, *Beyond the New Deal: Harry S. Truman and American Liberalism* (New York: Columbia University Press, 1973), 53–85; Bert Cochran, *Harry S. Truman and the Crisis Presidency* (New York: Funk and Wagnalls, 1973), 198–212; Barton Bernstein, "The Truman Administration and Its Reconversion Wage Policy," *Labor History* 6 (Fall 1965): 214–31; idem, "Walter Reuther and the General Motors Strike of 1945–46," *Michigan History* 49 (Sept. 1965): 260–77; idem, "The Truman Administration and the Steel Strike of 1946," *Journal of American History* 52 (Mar. 1966): 791–803.

34. Nelson Lichtenstein, "Labor, the Welfare State and the Fair Deal," paper in author's possession; Bert Cochran, *Labor and Communism, The Conflict That Shaped American Unions* (Princeton, N.J.: Princeton University Press, 1977), chap. 12; David Brody, *Workers in Industrial America* (New York: Oxford University Press, 1980), 223–28; Hamby, *Beyond the New Deal,* 215–17, 283–84; Dudley W. Buffa, *Union Power and American Democracy: The UAW and the Democratic Party, 1935–1972* (Ann Arbor: University of Michigan Press, 1984).

35. Barbara Griffith, *The Crisis of American Labor: Operation Dixie and the Defeat of the CIO* (Philadelphia: Temple University Press, 1988); Michael Honey, "Labor and Civil Rights in the South: The CIO in Memphis, 1937–1955" (Ph.D. diss., Northern Illinois University, 1987).

36. J. David Greenstone, *Labor and Politics* (New York: Knopf, 1969); see also James C. Foster, *The Union Politic* (Columbia: University of Missouri Press, 1975).

37. Brody, *Workers,* chap. 6; Greenstone, *Labor and Politics.*

38. Brody, *Workers,* 234–36.

39. Mike Davis, *Prisoners of the American Dream* (London: Verso, 1986).

40. Melvyn Dubofsky, "Which Side Are You On? The Contemporary Crisis and the Future of American Trade Unionism," in *Socialist Perspectives,* ed. Julius and Phyllis Jacobson (New York: Karz-Cohl Publishing, 1983), 21–40; Rob Wrenn, "The

Crisis of American Trade Unionism," *Socialist Review,* nos. 82–83 (1985): 89–117; *Barron's,* Apr. 10, 1989, 8–9, 59.

41. *New York Times,* Sept. 1, 1969.

42. Dubofsky, "Which Side Are You On?"

43. For the impact of race on the northern, working-class voter, see J. A. Lukas, *Common Ground* (New York: Knopf, 1986); see also Walter Dean Burnham, *The Current Crisis in American Politics* (New York: Oxford University Press, 1982).

44. It should be noted that these reports came in just when the Teamsters had reaffiliated with the AFL-CIO and agreed to follow national policies in politics, which meant endorsing the Democrats. Personal interviews with members of the Human Relations Department, International Brotherhood of Teamsters, May–June 1988.

PART 3
Theory and World Systems

THESE last three essays all grew out of my association with the Fernand Braudel Center for the Study of Economies, Societies, and Civilizations at Binghamton University, SUNY, and its director, Immanuel Wallerstein. From the late 1970s through the early 1990s, a research working group at the center, which I directed and codirected with Giovanni Arrighi, devoted itself to examining how the modern capitalist world-system affected the historical cycles of worker movements on a global scale from 1870 to the present. In the course of our research and study, we developed formal scholarly exchange relationships with a research institute on world labor in the Soviet Academy of Sciences, French economic historians associated with the Center for Research in Economic History and Development (GEMDEV) in Paris, and with students of Caribbean and Latin American labor history. Thus, two of the final three essays developed out of papers originally prepared under the auspices of the center, and the third put to use theories developed by Arrighi in collaboration with other members of our research working group.

The essay on technological change and trade unions in the United States applies to U.S. history a concept developed by Arrighi that posits that as heavily capitalized industrial production replaced labor-intensive artisanal modes of manufacture, workers' power shifted away from its location in the labor market toward its place at the direct point of production. The point of Arrighi's theory and my essay is that the history of the response of unions in the United States to technological change replicated cyclical patterns of worker behavior that were common across the capitalist world-system wherever and whenever more modern methods of production substituted for older forms of manufacture.

The second essay, written for a symposium held in Paris in the early summer of 1988, approached the same subject from a slightly different angle. Here, I took a theory developed by French economic historians, most especially Michel Aglietta and Robert Boyer, that defined "Fordism" as a regime of "regulation" that governed a new capitalist "mode of accumulation" and asked to what extent did the United States create a Fordist order of technologically advanced production and mass consumption. In answering that question, I found that Charles Maier, an American historian of modern Europe, had in a series of books and essays explained quite thoroughly and convincingly the links between U.S. and European managerial, labor, and public policies from the 1920s through the 1960s.[1] Once again, American working-class history, rather than being exceptional, fit neatly into the larger pattern of capitalist world history.

The final essay was written for a conference held at William Paterson College in December 1992 to commemorate two centuries of the history of Paterson, New Jersey. The conference organizers charged me with explaining the impact of Paterson on the scholarship of Herbert Gutman and the making of "new" labor history. My original paper, presented here in substantially revised form, enabled me to accomplish three objectives. First, I could pay proper homage and respect to Gutman for how he made historical scholarship in the United States a more inclusive enterprise, both for the sorts of people who made history in the past and for those who wrote it in the present. Second, I could also suggest where Gutman's approach to the past and his effort to write a new labor history—and perhaps even a new national narrative—fell short. Third, and most important, I could explicate how the history of Paterson fit neatly into world-system and world-economy paradigms and especially how that story might lead to new directions in the writing of labor history.

Note

1. Chapter 9 contains the complete citations to the relevant works by Aglietta, Boyer, and Maier, as well as to other French scholars of the "regulation" school.

8

Technological Change and American Worker Movements, 1870–1970

FERNAND Braudel has written that "technology is the queen: it is she who changes the world."[1] Few economic or modern historians would challenge that assertion. Indeed, two of the most comprehensive and significant histories of economic development and growth in the modern era—David Landes's *The Unbound Prometheus* (1969) and Alfred D. Chandler Jr.'s *The Visible Hand* (1977)—assign primary influence to technological innovations as the source of economic growth. Both Landes and Chandler see the past in much the same way. At some point in the late eighteenth century (in Landes's history of economic growth) and in the mid-nineteenth century (in Chandler's history of the development of corporate enterprise), human existence moved onto a new course. In Landes's words, which Chandler would undoubtedly second, "the industrial revolution marked a major turning point in man's history. . . . It was the Industrial Revolution that initiated a cumulative, self-sustaining advance in technology whose repercussions would be felt in all aspects of economic life."[2]

As economies grew and developed, and change begat change, the lives of working people inexorably altered. Industrialization and technological change created a new breed of worker, one habituated to the discipline of the time clock and the routines of the machine rather than the more irregular rhythms of nature and social tradition. If first-generation industrial workers had to learn a new way of life, their heirs did not have it easier. For one of the constants of economic development in the nineteenth and twentieth centuries was the cyclical regularity of technological innovation, which in changing how goods were produced transformed the way people labored. Not only did succeeding generations of workers tend to labor in different ways, fabricating new products with innovative machines; they toiled under changing systems of supervision for shifting forms of intrinsic and material rewards.

That technological change during the past two centuries has had an enormous impact on working people is without challenge. That trade unions have been simultaneously shaped by and themselves sought to control technology is also scarcely subject to serious doubt. Today, more clearly than ever, we can perceive aspects of that process. Two immediate examples may suffice as illustrations. In the late summer of 1983, employees of the American Telephone and Telegraph Company walked off their jobs when contract negotiations between their unions and the company collapsed. Although nearly 100 percent of the production workers (operators, installers, linespeople, and repairers) struck, most users of the company's services remained unaffected. Modern communications technology enabled a smaller number of managerial and supervisory employees to provide satisfactorily all the services ordinarily performed by the great mass of strikers. About the same time, a similar story repeated itself in New York City. There, the local utility workers struck; but they, too, failed to disrupt electrical and gas service to the city's consumers. Once again, computerized communications and control systems enabled the utility company to operate effectively despite its employees' solidarity as strikers. On the one hand, then, contemporary, computerized technology rendered organized workers' ultimate weapon, the strike, relatively harmless. But, on the other hand, the firms affected by the strikes, AT&T and Consolidated Edison, did not use their new technology to smash the unions as would undoubtedly have been the case at any other time between the 1870s and 1930s. Clearly, something decisive had changed that was related in as of yet little understood ways to the manner in which technology affected the distribution of power between capital and labor, employers and workers. Perhaps I can suggest some tentative hypotheses concerning the relationship between trade unions and technological change.

Today it can be said that we have a substantial body of literature concerning the impact of technology on work, although there is far less written on the relationship between technology and trade unions. Ever since Harry Braverman published *Labor and Monopoly Capital* in 1974, a veritable subfield of the social sciences dedicated to the study of what is labeled "the labor process" has boomed. By now, all must be familiar with Braverman's contention that the history of technological innovation under capitalism has been the unilinear story of labor's deskilling and the expropriation of workers' crafts and skills by managers and scientists in the service of capital. A whole school of scholars has built elaborations on Braverman's theory of the progressive degradation of labor under capitalism, from Stephen Marglin's analysis of English employers' attempts to deskill labor in the early industrialization of the seventeenth century to Katherine Stone's description of the tactics used by American steelmasters to eliminate all skills and autonomy possessed by their employees.[3] All of these students of the labor process, unlike Landes and Chandler, see the primary impetus for technological change in capitalists' urge to control labor and not in their desire to increase productivity through the application of science to industry.

Other scholars less prone to see technological innovation as a single-minded attempt by employers to deskill their workers and hence gain control over production nevertheless describe a similar process. Whether in David Brody's study of steelworkers in the nonunion era or Daniel Nelson's description of managerial reforms in the late nineteenth to early twentieth centuries, the result appears the same: innovation leads to the loss of skills, which in turn causes workers to lose all or part of their autonomy and power on the job.[4] Indeed, almost all of the literature on the history of work, in particular crafts or industries, describes a steady transformation of traditional patterns of work in which established skills are persistently diluted or erased.

Because most of the literature focuses on how old skills were diluted and not on how new ones emerged, much of what we know about the impact of technology on unions concerns traditional craft unions of skilled workers. We have case studies of the impact of technology on specific craft unions and their responses as well as more general models exploring the parameters of the craft unions' reactions to technological change. But we know less about the impact of technological change on the shape of the overall labor movement and how the labor movement as a whole has behaved under changing technologies.

At this point, I prefer to venture a hypothesis to explain trade-union behavior and how it relates to different historical periods. The strength of craft unions was based initially on their control over entry into the trades and hence on their ability to establish monopolies in the labor market. As long as employers could not produce profitably without the skills possessed by craft unionists, such workers could secure their jobs, statuses, and incomes through what Giovanni Arrighi defines as marketplace bargaining power (MBP). As technological change diluted existing skills, craft unionists lost both their strategic place in the shop or factory and their power in the labor market. In Arrighi's words:

> The process is completed in machinofacture, which turns upside down the relationship between the workman and the means of production, transforming the former into an appendage/instrument of the latter. The expansion of capital is thus freed from its previous dependence on the personal strength and personal skill with which the detail workmen in manufacture, and the manual laborers in handicraft, wielded their implements. The MBP of workers, that is, as sellers of labor-power, is thus progressively undermined by the very process of capitalist accumulation.[5]

Yet, as workers lose their bargaining power in the market (MBP), they ineluctably regain it at the point of production (WBP). The ever-growing division of labor in the factory, the increasing scale and complexity of factories and their machinery, and the concomitant concentration of workers in ever-larger productive units make capital (employers) more vulnerable to work stoppages and passive forms of resistance at the shop-floor level. Moreover, the greater the organic value of the capital in an establishment, the greater the damage created by an interruption or slowdown in production, even by a small number of workers. Again, in Arrighi's words: "The downward tendency of labor's MBP, emphasized by Marxist theory, is thus always matched by an upward tendency of its WBP."[6]

Arrighi's hypothesis, which I find convincing in the abstract, presents problems when set to the test of history. The major difficulty is that the history of capitalism is so uneven that its development pattern or trajectory does indeed seem to follow what many Marxists refer to as "combined and uneven development." Technological change occurs at varying rates of speed in different sectors of the economy. Some craft workers see their skills eliminated by technology; others simultaneously find that technological change intensifies the demand for their labor. Some firms use the most innovative production methods; other firms in the same industry resist change and even remain profitable, for a time at least, under the old regime. And even the most modern, technologically advanced economy exhibits large pockets of traditional production. Thus, it is impossible to state that from the 1870s, say, to the present, all workers experienced a decline in MBP and a rise in WBP. Or that all craft workers had MBP and all machine operators had WBP. But by examining the history of American workers and their trade unions since the mid-nineteenth century, we can see under precisely what conditions or circumstances the hypothesis fits.

In seeking to periodize the history of technology's impact on American unions, we cannot do better than use the eras suggested in David Gordon, Richard Edwards, and Michael Reich's recent economic history of American labor, *Segmented Work, Divided Workers* (1982). Their first period, the early 1800s through 1870s, what they label "initial proletarianization," saw little technological innovation or machine production outside the textile industry. Employers in this period transformed the labor process in various ways but seldom by technology. The second period, the 1870s through 1920s, what Gordon et al. call the era of "homogenization," saw technology thoroughly transform the manner in which work was done. The third period, from the 1930s through 1960s, which Gordon and his coauthors label as "segmentation," more closely resembled the first rather than the second era. Employers continued to transform work, but technology played a smaller role. In the third era, unlike the first, however, unions proved central to the reorganization of work and the discipline of labor. The final period, the 1960s to the present, lacks a rubric but is clearly a time, like the second era, in which technology is transforming totally, if not revolutionizing, work.

What remains constant throughout the four periods and what I will be examining in more detail below is the one inescapable reality of American labor history, the neverending struggle between workers and bosses for power. David Brody has put this point well. "The struggle of workers to retain a degree of job satisfaction, of managers to subordinate them to a rationalized system of production," he writes, "is a continuing story, and not one ending at any given stage of industrialism."[7]

For most of the nineteenth century, advanced technology scarcely impinged on the world of the worker and trade unions. Skilled workers, the vast majority of all union members, either themselves owned the tools of production or controlled the actual process of production using tools and machines provided by the boss. Skill was acquired neither through formal schooling nor management-initiated training programs. Instead, it was passed on through families—father to son or uncle to nephew—and union-controlled apprenticeship programs. The skilled workers who acquired the knowledge to puddle and mold iron, set type, cut garments, machine metal, blow glass, or brew beer, to name just a few of the multifarious skilled crafts in existence, were absolutely indispensable to production. Employers had no alternative source for the knowledge and skill possessed by craftsmen.

David Montgomery describes the work routine of skilled unionized iron-workers at a Columbus, Ohio, mill in the 1870s:

> The three twelve-man rolling teams, which constituted the union, negoti-
> ated a single tonnage rate with the company for each specific rolling job
> the company undertook. The workers then decided collectively, among
> themselves, what portion of that rate should go to each of them . . . , how
> work should be allocated among them; how many rounds on the rolls
> should be undertaken each day; what special arrangements should be made
> for the fiercely hot labors of the hookers during the summer; and how
> members should be hired and progress through the various ranks of the
> gang. To put it another way, all the boss did was to buy the equipment and
> raw materials and sell the finished product.[8]

Despite some of the hyperbole in Montgomery's words, they contain a large measure of truth. Prior to the machine age, coal miners, for example, worked with minimal supervision and at their own pace. They decided where and how to undercut a vein, how large an explosive charge to set, and how rapidly to load the coal. As befit an autonomous skilled worker, the miner provided his own tools (he even paid for the sharpening of his drills and the blasting powder he used), quit when he chose, and used his own judgment in working his room in the coal face. In the words of a third-generation miner, John Brophy, "that was one of the great satisfactions that a miner had—that he was his own boss within his workplace." He was also the living embodiment of an older tradition that would be passed on to his children.[9]

Other vignettes illustrate the pride and place of the nineteenth-century, skilled craftsmen. When Robert and Helen Lynd in *Middletown,* their classic study of Muncie, Indiana, during the 1920s, chose to suggest the impact of the modern factory on the city's workers, they compared the workers of the prosperity decade to their predecessors of the 1890s. Muncie's skilled glassblowers and building tradesmen of the 1890s, according to the Lynds, were among the town's most respected citizens, loyal union members, autodidacts, and community activists. They were truly full and equal citizens in a people's republic.[10] In the larger industrial city of Chicago, skilled iron molders proved their indispensability to the production process in the McCormick Harvester works when during a walkout they initiated in 1885, the company's determination to carry on production proved fruitless.[11]

Their indispensability to production determined the structure and behavior of the unions that skilled workers built. With few exceptions, the only unions that survived economic cycles in the nineteenth century consisted of highly skilled workers, those Benson Soffer has referred to as "autonomous workmen." Their power as individuals and as union members derived from their relative scarcity in the marketplace. As long as they monopolized the skills they possessed, and employers lacked an equally productive alternative, such workers wielded real power.[12] Some indeed felt powerful enough to do without unions and collective action, as the inability of most craft unions to organize a majority of workers in a trade proved. But those for whom collective action proved efficacious used trade unions to buttress their power in the marketplace. Most of the local craft unions in the nineteenth century, which subsequently evolved into the dominant national and international trade unions, based their constitutions, rituals, and practices on securing MBP. They limited membership, adopted stringent apprenticeship regulations, restricted the number of helpers a journeyman might employ, set daily production quotas (or "stints"), required all members to pledge never to work alongside a nonunionist, and often sought—and successfully at that—to make the union headquarters a hiring hall for employers. To the extent that they succeeded in achieving their goals, such unions became as indispensable to skilled workers as the latter were to employers.

At first, the threat to the MBP of such workers and unions did not come from innovations in the actual production process. Until the 1890s, most products continued to be made in traditional ways, and most of the skilled workers maintained their vital roles. But the market in which they sold their labor and in which the goods they manufactured circulated changed. The dual transport-communications revolution of the mid-nineteenth century created a national labor and products market. In response, as Lloyd Ulman describes so well in *The Rise of the National Union* (1955), local unions combined into national and international federations. Trades in which there was no national product competition (such as building and carting) developed national offices to coordinate the movement of tramping artisans (those nineteenth-century "knights of the road" who traveled from place to place seeking better jobs or the improvement of their skills as journeymen). As workers became more mobile, it was essential that craft unions develop policies to even the flow of labor to disparate markets and prevent local gluts from arising. The unions did so by issuing traveling cards, coordinating information on local labor-market conditions, and warning tramping artisans away from glutted localities. Those unions whose members manufactured goods that were increasingly competitive in a national marketplace had an equally strong motivation to transfer institutional authority from the local to national level. These unions sought to even the costs of production across space by establishing uniform wage, hour, and production standards, denying employers in one region or locality an advantage over their competitors elsewhere. The unions' ability to do so, of course, depended on their real MBP. As it turned out in practice in the late nineteenth and early twentieth centuries, the craft unions concentrated in local product markets had much more effective MBP than those in more nationally competitive product markets. Thus, unions of printers, carpenters, and teamsters, among others, grew and flourished over time, while the unions of iron molders, puddlers, and glassblowers, among others, dwindled into impotency.

All this is not to say that the actual organization of work scarcely changed in the nineteenth century. Such a statement would be far from accurate. The imperatives of more stringent competition in an ever-enlarging national marketplace impelled employers to seek cheaper methods of production. In the absence of substantial technological innovations, the simple division of labor became the most commonly used approach. American economic growth proved the acuity of Adam Smith's observation that the extent of the market governs the division of labor. As canals, railroads, and telegraph lines widened the American market, employers hired increasing numbers of green hands, women, and children, all of whom could be assigned extremely specialized production tasks that could be learned and mastered in a short time. Such cheap laborers spent their toiling hours performing a few simple, repetitive operations, which left them ignorant of the place of their job in the larger production process. In this system, in Karl Marx's terse comment, "it is not the workman that employs the instruments of labour, but the instruments of labour that employ the workman."[13]

Until the 1890s, however, the division of labor and specialization were not urgent concerns for most autonomous skilled craftsmen. Even in the shoemaking and garment trades, where specialization and the task system had been carried to extremes by the end of the 1870s, the most highly skilled workers, the cutters, retained their craft and its indispensability. As a consequence, they still possessed MBP and used it to keep their limited membership craft unions alive and well. But the last two decades of the nineteenth century were to change all that; they would usher in a great technological transformation that would leave few forms of work, laborers, or unions untouched.

Between the 1890s and the 1920s, employers totally transformed the world of work as it had existed. Not all traditional skills were eliminated, nor did all craft unions lose their power. But the main drift moved in precisely those directions. In the economy of the late nineteenth century, a time of falling prices, recurrent business slumps, and intensifying competition among firms, employers had little choice but to reduce their costs of production. This compulsion had an immediate impact on both workers and unions. In many trades and industries, the traditional ways of skilled workers and union practices posed an obstacle to the intensification of labor and reductions in the cost of production. As Andrew Carnegie noted concerning the policies of the Amalgamated Association of Iron, Steel, and Tin Workers, they placed a "tax" on production at his company's Homestead steelworks.

Employers responded to this situation in a variety of ways, all of which diluted skills and threatened union power. As Daniel Nelson has shown in his history of managerial reform between 1880 and 1920, employers slowly but steadily altered the actual factory environment and the flow of work in the plant, limited the arbitrary authority of plant foremen while increasing central office control of labor, and instituted new hiring policies and personnel practices to obtain a more docile and productive labor force. And what Nelson calls the "new factory system" successfully diluted the power of craftsmen and unions.[14] At the same time, employers rapidly innovated new production methods and introduced new machinery. The advanced technology of the steel industry did away with many of the skills possessed by ironworkers, and the whole thrust of technological innovation in the industry sought economy of labor, domesticating or eradicating the Amalgamated Association and severing the customary connection between productivity and wages. In the steel industry's future, the fruits of innovation would go to capital, not labor, and wages would be set in the marketplace, where technology and unrestricted immigration had reduced the power of the skilled and their unions.[15] Other industries followed a similar pattern. In the glass industry between 1890 and 1905, first semiautomatic and then fully automatic machines replaced the skilled hand glassblowers. In the printing trades, linotype machines and power presses displaced hand composition and printing. Granite and stonecutters watched nervously as mechanical planers eliminated customary hand skills.[16] Sometimes, employers introduced new machinery, even when it was less economical than the use of skilled workers, as was the case with the McCormick Harvester Company in 1886, when it used molding machines to break a strike among its unionized molders.[17]

These practices and tendencies reached their fullest expression in the policies associated with Frederick Winslow Taylor and his many disciples and imitators. Taylorism, or scientific management, sought to organize production systematically and induce workers to perform their assignments in the "one best way." The goal of scientific management, in the words of one associate of Taylor's, was "the establishment of standards everywhere, including standard instruction cards for standard methods, motion studies, time study, time cards . . . [and] records of individual output." The essential aim of Taylorism was to place the worker "at the bottom level of a highly stratified organization . . . [where] his established routines of work, his cultural traditions . . . [were all] at the mercy of technical specialists." And, as David Montgomery observes, scientific management "implied a conscious endeavor to uproot those work practices which had been the taproot of whatever strength organized labor enjoyed in the late nineteenth century."[18]

Absolute control of the production process and the elimination of worker autonomy reached their peaks in the meatpacking and automobile industries in the pre–World War I era. In both industries, moving production lines (a disassembly line in the slaughterhouses and the famous assembly line at Ford's Highland Park plant) determined the pace of work and could be intensified or moderated solely at the discretion of management. Packinghouse workers and car assemblers spent their whole work days engaged in the same simple, repetitive operations, which left them as devoid of skill as the day they entered the plant.[19]

Throughout the four decades of transformation, a continuous and simultaneous process of deskilling and reskilling of workers repeated itself. Certainly, skilled glassblowers, granite cutters, hand compositors, iron molders, coopers, and all-around machinists found their hard-acquired crafts obsolescent. At the same time, common laborers, who once merely fetched and hauled materials for the skilled production workers, found themselves located directly in production as machine operators or parts assemblers. The former common laborer, now redefined as a semiskilled operator, undoubtedly experienced a real improvement in status and perhaps even in skill. And the demand for common, casual day labor, which never entirely disappeared, could be readily satisfied by the ever-flowing stream of new immigrants, for whom any form of steady employment signified material betterment.[20] But new forms of skill also emerged; and, as Andrew Dawson writes: "The skilled stratum proved to be a highly adaptive social group in the face of innovation." All the basic industries—

including steel, automobiles, coal mining, and the railroads—needed highly skilled machine makers and maintenance people. In the maritime trades, skilled machinists, boilermakers, and stationary engineers replaced general seamen as steam substituted for sail. Even during the acme of technological innovation and scientific management, skilled workers were never, in Dawson's words, "a moribund excrescence upon the body of the labor force, but, for better or worse, a vital force within the working class."[21]

As a vital presence within the working class, skilled workers kept alive not only the traditions of craftsmanship but also the spirit of unionism. The craft unions sought, as best they could, to cope with the twin threats of technological innovation and scientific management. Generally, they tried to accommodate to technological change, not to resist it. They also attempted to adjust to the transformed market for their labor by widening their union jurisdictions, allying with competing craft unions, and diluting the eligibility requirements for union membership. In the end, however, their relative success or failure in accommodating to technological change depended more on their actual or residual MBP than on any concrete policies or practices they adopted.

Basically, as George E. Barnett and Sumner Slichter point out in their classic studies of labor and technological change, unions exhibited three primary ways of reacting to new production methods. They resisted change, chose to compete directly with new technology, or sought to obtain union control of machinery. Historically, unions, in fact, tried all three methods. Typically, before it became apparent that new technology would eliminate traditional skills, many craftsmen believed that their indispensability would enable them either to resist change or compete successfully with new machines by continuing to produce at a lower cost. As Slichter somewhat dyspeptically noted, "the history of the attempt of unions to adjust themselves to technological changes suggests that they have a strong tendency to do the right thing too late." By "the right thing," Slichter meant the choice to accommodate to technology and gain union control over machinery.[22]

By and large, most craft unions indeed tried to do the right thing. It was rare for a union in the late nineteenth century ever to oppose directly management's right to use new machines. At most, unions sought to contain the speed of change and preserve jobs by reducing the hours of work, despite the fact that most skilled workers probably agreed with a fellow worker who asserted that "labor saving machinery has made some men richer, most things cheaper, and the working classes poorer."[23] After studying carefully the response of printers', glassblowers', and stonecutters' unions to technological change between roughly 1900 and the 1920s, George Barnett concluded: "Not only is trade unionism officially committed to the view that resistance to machinery is futile, but it is almost unanimous in holding further that resistance to the introduction of machinery delays, or makes impossible, the adoption of measures which may mitigate the harmful effects of the introduction of machinery."[24]

Most craft-union leaders made quite clear their receptivity to technological change. George W. Perkins, the president of the Cigar Makers' International Union, an institution shaken by the introduction of the automatic cigar-making machine, said at his union's 1923 convention: "No power on earth can stop the at least gradual introduction and use of improved machinery and progressive methods of production. Any effort in that direction will react against those who attempt it. Our own condition proves that efforts at restriction were futile, and ineffective, and injurious. Without an exception, every organization, since the beginning of the factory system, that has attempted to restrict the use of improved methods of production has met with defeat."

At the end of the 1920s, William Green, president of the American Federation of Labor (AFL), and Matthew Woll, one of its more influential spokesmen, reiterated Perkins's position. "The American labor movement," asserted Green, "welcomes the installation and extension of the use of machinery in industry." Woll added: "it is not the function of the labor movement to resist the machine. It is the function of the labor movement to turn the installation of machinery to the good of the worker."[25]

How successful were the labor movement and the craft unions in turning technological change to the advantage of the worker? The answer is that they were not especially successful. Why? To begin with, technological change fundamentally transformed labor's MBP. In industry after industry, new or better machines eliminated the need for skilled workers. McCormick's mechanical molders, which in 1885 replaced skilled molders but at a higher cost, soon also turned out a superior product at a lower cost. In the steel industry, as Charles Schwab commented, an employer could hire an entirely green hand and within two weeks turn him into an efficient, productive worker. This trend repeated itself persistently. Hand glassblowers, practicing a highly skilled craft, first protected their jobs by competing directly with new machines and then by applying their skills to the control of semiautomatic machines, which were run more productively by craftsmen.[26] But then employers introduced fully automatic machines on which skilled workers produced no cost advantage.[27] When the

Lynds studied Muncie, a center of glass-bottle production, in the 1920s, they found unionism in the industry dead.[28]

Only in those cases in which skilled workers continued to possess MBP did their unions succeed in controlling the introduction of machinery or in growing. Printers and pressmen, whose skills proved as necessary and economical on the new linotypes and power presses as they had been for the old hand processes, retained much autonomy on the job and belonged to stable, flourishing unions. Less-skilled workers were simply noncompetitive in the labor market.[29] The same was true of many building-trades workers, whose skills were yet to be made obsolescent, who were much in demand in the 1920s, and who competed only in local labor and product markets. At a time (the 1920s) when the labor movement in general declined (between 1921 and 1929, total union membership fell from over 5 million to about 3.5 million), the printing and building trades unions actually grew in size. Elsewhere, however, workers and unions saw their MBP diminish; and, as it did, they suffered. Unions never penetrated the oligopolistic mass-production industries, in which technological innovation and scientific management had progressed furthest. In railroad shops and small machine shops, where new tools and managerial methods had been introduced, all-around machinists lost out to newly trained specialists who did not belong to the union. And in the coal mines, mechanical undercutting machines, plus competition from more productive nonunion mines, created an enormous labor surplus. The United Mine Workers of America (UMWA) was reduced from being the largest single union in the country, with more than a half million members in 1920, to a paralyzed union with fewer than a hundred thousand dues-paying members only ten years later.[30]

Throughout this long era of technological change and transformation of the labor process, trade unionists sought to grapple with the new order of production. From the mid-1880s on, labor leaders increasingly lamented the passing of the craftsman and demanded a labor movement that would organize workers regardless of skill. Part of the rationale for the Knights of Labor, the first labor federation in the United States to achieve mass membership (an estimated 700,000–800,000 members in 1886), lay in its effort to organize those workers lacking clearly defined skills. Declaring craft unions an anachronistic relic from the handicraft era of production, the Knights of Labor tried to function as a general union that opened membership to all, regardless of skill, gender, or race. They failed. Only the allegedly antiquarian craft unions, whose members still possessed MBP, survived the business cycles of the late nineteenth century and flourished during the economic expansion from 1897 through 1903.

In 1905, the Industrial Workers of the World (IWW) repeated part of the experience of the Knights of Labor. Its founding manifesto declared that "laborers are no longer classified by differences in trade skill, but the employer assorts them according to the machines to which they are attached. These divisions, far from representing differences in skill, or interests among laborers, are imposed by the employers that workers may be pitted against one another."[31] Thus, the IWW, like the Knights of Labor before it, tried to organize unskilled as well as skilled workers to make the American labor movement as "modern" as the corporations with which they contended. But the IWW also proved less than a success. It never developed an alternative to the MBP of the craft unions; and at a time when unrestricted immigration regularly replenished the market for machine operators and common laborers, its successes proved ephemeral.

Craft unionists, too, took cognizance of their new universe of work. "Every day our trade is becoming more and more specialized," remarked James O'Connell of the International Association of Machinists, "and if we hope to . . . protect our craft it is necessary that our qualifications for membership be radically changed." By 1900, leaders of the Butcher Workman's Union realized that "today it is impossible to draw the line where the skilled man leaves off and the unskilled man begins. . . . [This] makes it necessary to organize all working in the large plants under one head."[32] The United Mine Workers of America had always operated on that principle, organizing all who worked in and around mine pits, including carpenters, pumpmen, engineers, and machinists. And at its 1901 convention in Scranton, Pennsylvania, the AFL formally recognized the right of the coal miners to organize workers heretofore deemed within the exclusive jurisdiction of specified craft unions. To that degree, the AFL's "Scranton Declaration" sanctioned industrial or general unionism. But the AFL made other attempts to bring trade unionism structurally into a new technological era. Its leaders encouraged the formation of federated union departments—the mining, building, metal, and railway trades departments, among others—that would enable related craft unions to act as a unit against concentrated capital.[33] Individual craft unions also tried to make their own separate peace with the new technology. The Carpenters' Union, the largest and perhaps most successful of the building-trades unions, followed the principle of "once of wood, always of wood." It allowed its members to work with all sorts of new construction materials and recruited among people who had never worked with wood and belonged to or fell within the jurisdiction of other unions.[34]

Before and during World War I, many labor leaders also began to sense or act on the shift in labor's strength from MBP to WBP. That, after all, was at the root of the IWW's assertion that the real struggle between labor and capital occurred at the point of production and that the new capital-intensive technology made large firms especially vulnerable to conventional strikes, intermittent strikes, slowdowns, passive resistance, and even sabotage. It was also partially behind the militant strike wave of 1916–22, which involved mostly conventional AFL unions and that, as David Montgomery argues, was fought over control issues at the point of production. He also suggests that, even in the absence of strikes, conventional unionists fought a daily battle with management over control within the workplace.[35] But in this period, as Montgomery's research also demonstrates, workers' struggles remained closely associated with MBP, their intensity rising as unemployment fell and declining as unemployment rose.[36]

As we have already seen, until the end of the 1920s, industrial or general unionism had proved itself a failure. Not only had the IWW failed, but AFL attempts to organize steelworkers, meatpackers, and nonoperating railway employees all collapsed between 1919 and 1922, as did such previously successful industrial unions as the UMWA and the International Ladies' Garment Workers. The craft unionists, who had never really been eager to unionize the less skilled (many of the craft unions that made half-hearted efforts to organize the nonskilled offered them only subordinate, so-called "Class B" status in the union), had a ready explanation for the failure of industrial unionism. Union strength could not be built in the absence of MBP, alleged the craft unionists, and nonskilled machine operators were merely interchangeable bodies in a glutted labor market, people whom Dan Tobin, president of the Teamsters' Union, could readily dismiss as "the rubbish at labor's door." There was an element of truth in that belief. As David Brody has written of the American labor movement as it existed in the 1920s: "The bitter truth was clear: depending on their own economic strength, American workers could not defeat the massed power of open-shop industry."[37] But they could use their imperceptibly rising WBP, which craft unionists did not yet perceive, on the shop-floor level to limit partially management's efforts to increase labor productivity. Stanley Mathewson's 1931 study *Restriction of Output by Unorganized Workers* showed precisely how workers informally practiced the stint, the slowdown, and even sabotaged production in the most technologically advanced plants. Research sponsored directly by corporations and conducted by such social scientists as Elton Mayo, F. J. Roethlisberger, and W. J. Dickson also revealed how vulnerable capital-intensive industry was to worker resistance. But not until the Great Depression of the 1930s would it become evident how the informal WBP exposed by Mathewson and others would transform itself into the formal power exercised by institutionalized trade unions.

One of the great puzzles of American labor history is how and why trade unions for the first time breached the antiunion defenses of mass-production industry at a time of deep depression and mass unemployment. It should not be necessary here to describe the details of the history of the unionization of mass-production industry or the specifics of what has come to be known as the New Deal "revolution in labor law." Suffice it to say that, by the end of the 1930s, trade unions had organized the automobile, steel, and electrical goods industries, among others, and that the labor movement was three times as large as it had been in 1933. Except for Sweden, no other labor movement in the industrial world advanced as rapidly and successfully as that in the United States. The American labor success story during the Great Depression was closely associated with the concentrated character of American industry and its technological virtuosity.

Although continuous-flow production and the assembly line, characteristics of the American mass-production system, homogenized labor and subjected the mass of workers to the dictates of machine technology, it also increased the potential vulnerability of capital to direct action by workers at the point of production. If the size and scale of American corporate enterprises provided capital with enormous material resources with which to confront and defeat workers' resistance, this capital-intensive structure also intensified the damage that could be done to an entire corporation by a strike in only one of its key plants and the disruption that could be wrought in the national economy by a strike in an essential industry. As one steelworker quoted by David Montgomery observed, "bringing the workflow to a crunching halt is both easy and commonplace for those who are familiar with the intricacies of their machinery." The truth of this observation was established by the Goodyear rubber workers who sat down on the job in 1936, the Flint, Michigan, autoworkers who did the same in January–February 1937 and won recognition and a union contract from General Motors, and also the steelworkers who by threatening to strike at U.S. Steel won a contract in March 1937 without even walking off the job.[38]

These successes were all linked to the emergence of the Congress of

Industrial Organizations (CIO) as a direct competitor to the AFL and one that recognized the significance of capital intensity and WBP for trade unionism. But the AFL unions learned quickly from the example of the CIO. Craft unionists became more receptive to recruiting the nonskilled and used their superior resources to grow more rapidly after 1938 than their industrial-union competitors. By 1940, the AFL was far larger than the CIO, and its affiliates acted just as aggressively in the workplace.[39]

World War II further revealed the vulnerability of concentrated capital to the shop-floor power of its employees. As recent books by Nelson Lichtenstein and Howell John Harris have shown, corporations were deeply troubled by a lack of discipline among their workers, which they attributed to the rise of the CIO in the late 1930s and the labor scarcity caused by the war.[40] During the war itself, wildcat strikes, lax work habits, and absenteeism, especially among women workers, caused a great deal of trouble for plant managers. Because government policy during the war also favored unions to the extent that it guaranteed their security through federal administrative rulings, corporations sought a way to live with unions and yet regain shop-floor discipline. By 1945, they had no choice in a world in which almost 15 million workers (nearly 35 percent of the nonagricultural labor force) belonged to trade unions.

The postwar social contract between management and labor flowed directly from capital's vulnerability to direct action at the point of production. To reassert its authority at the workplace, management recruited the assistance of union officials. Corporations promised unions recognition, security, and peaceful relations; they offered their employees higher wages, annual productivity increases, protection against inflation, attractive fringe benefits, and stable jobs. In return, workers promised higher productivity, and unions agreed to police discipline on the shop floor. Unions also promised not to interfere with management's prerogatives, generally defined as the right to manage by allocating capital, introducing new technology, or reorganizing work routines. And unions guaranteed not to strike during the duration of contract, which was more and more often a multiyear agreement. In a sense, then, capital paid labor well to establish management's right to do what it wanted to do. "By so agreeing," David Brody has written, "companies and unions revealed what was, at rock bottom, the common intent of their encompassing contractual relationship—the containment of spontaneous and independent shop-floor activity." And, he adds, "company and union were drawn into unacknowledged collaboration against shop-floor militancy."[41]

For one-quarter of a century after World War II, that unacknowledged bargain between management and unions effectively contained worker resistance at the point of production while conceding capital the prerogatives it demanded. Management introduced new technology, reorganized the labor process, and greatly increased per capita productivity, all with minimal union resistance. As long as workers received higher wages for increased productivity, job security through seniority systems, and supplementary unemployment benefits to guarantee full earnings during momentary periods of cyclical unemployment, unions proved less resistant to technological change than ever. For corporations finally seemed to have accepted what had always been the union sine qua non for accepting new technology: that its impact on the worker be cushioned and the worker's fate not be left to the vagaries of the marketplace. Thus, technological change, which proceeded steadily in the 1950s and 1960s, caused many pessimists to worry about the impact of automation but produced few changes in union structure, behavior, or attitudes toward new methods of production.

By the 1970s, however, it became evident that workers and trade unions were caught up in a second "great transformation" in technology and the labor process comparable to that of the period from the 1890s through 1920s. Once again, corporations found themselves faced with increasingly competitive markets and shrinking profits. This time, the competition arose externally as well as internally and in some ways proved even more threatening to established corporate enterprises. And once again, firms responded by seeking to increase productivity and lower labor costs by reorganizing work routines and computerizing machinery. It goes without saying that this application of computer technology to industry has reduced total employment in the traditional mass-production industries and substantially lowered membership in the major industrial unions formed during the late 1930s and 1940s. Since the end of the 1960s, as we all know, union membership has grown less rapidly than the total labor force and in years of higher than normal unemployment has actually fallen absolutely.

Not only have corporate enterprises increased labor productivity through technological innovation; they have also moved those jobs still requiring a measure of labor intensity to low-wage areas overseas. That, too, has been made possible by the new technology of almost instantaneous international transmission of data and managerial decisions. Computerization and international mobility of capital have thus combined to imperil the American labor movement as it has functioned since the 1940s.

Overall, the trade-union response to this second great transformation seems quite in character with past forms of behavior. Unions, by and large, have sought to accommodate the new technology, not resist it. At most, they have tried to slow the pace of change to soften its potential negative impact on workers. Thus, the longshoremen's unions on both coasts accepted containerization in return for a combination of guaranteed jobs and annual wages. The International Typographical Union (ITU), with its long history of accommodating technological change through control of work, followed tradition. As computerized typesetting replaced the linotype machine and made ordinary typists as productive as skilled printers and also cheaper, the union continued to insist that "the better the operator [meaning a union person] the lower the cost of production."[42] For a time, the printers' union even sought to remain ahead of employers in technological change by operating an advanced school in technology for printers at ITU headquarters in Colorado Springs, Colorado. But printing technology had become so complex and capital intensive by the late 1960s that the union could not match the investments of private enterprise and had to close its training school.[43] Indeed, today, traditional printers, outside of a few specialty job shops, are a dying breed as their union has surrendered all control over technology to guarantee the income, if not the skills and jobs, of currently employed printers.

Even the sector of the labor force that benefited from the technological transformation of the 1890–1920 era, the highly skilled metal workers, now suffers as the electronics revolution and microprocessors bring numerically controlled machine tools to small shops as well as large firms.[44] As a U.S. Commerce Department official recently commented, "the problem is that there is nothing in between. If you are not a banker, you are in McDonald's."[45] Indeed, this is true. For today, McDonald's and Burger King employ more workers than the steel industry, and jobs grow most rapidly in the service and clerical sector of the economy, which has long been impervious to the penetration of unions.

Aside from unions' customary tactic of accommodating technological change, they have sought to cope with current realities through a series of mergers. For example, in 1980, the Amalgamated Meat Cutters and Butcher Workmen (who had earlier swallowed the Fur and Leather Workers' Union) merged with the Retail Clerks to form the United Food and Commercial Workers, now the largest single union in the AFL-CIO. Even earlier, the Steelworkers' Union had taken over the Mine, Mill, and Smelter Workers, and the Amalgamated Textile Workers had allied with the United

Textile Workers. These and other union mergers will likely reduce the total number of affiliated AFL-CIO unions and appear to be a logical response by the labor movement to the continued centralization and concentration of capital. But neither union accommodation to technological change nor union mergers have enabled the labor movement to make much headway among young employees in widely scattered service establishments, clerks in increasingly computerized work settings, or workers in the so-called high technology firms.

The future of the American labor movement remains highly problematic. In those industries in which unions exist and capital intensity renders firms vulnerable to worker resistance at the point of production, unions are probably here to stay. On the whole, as David Brody notes, where unions and collective bargaining were well rooted, their stabilizing effects for the employer exceeded the potential benefits of seeking to uproot unionism.[46] The big question concerns the future of the service and clerical sectors. As those sectors grow more capital intensive, as seems to be happening especially in office work, will they too become more vulnerable to worker resistance at the point of production (WBP) and hence more open to unionism? I prefer to close with a question, not an answer or a prophecy.

Notes

An earlier version of this essay appeared in *Technology, the Economy, and Society: The American Experience,* ed. Joel Colton and Stuart Bruchey (New York: Columbia University Press, 1987), 162–85. © 1987 by Columbia University Press. Reprinted with the permission of the publisher.

1. Cited in Laszlo Makkai, "Ars Historica: On Braudel," *Review* 6 (Spring 1983): 452.

2. David Landes, *Unbound Prometheus* (London: Cambridge University Press, 1969), 3.

3. Stephen A. Marglin, "What Do Bosses Do?," *Review of Radical Political Economics* 6 (Summer 1974): 60–112; Katherine Stone, "The Origins of Job Structures in the Steel Industry," in *Labor Market Segmentation,* ed. David M. Gordon et al. (Lexington, Mass.: Heath, 1975).

4. David Brody, *Steelworkers in America: The Nonunion Era* (1960; rpt., Urbana: University of Illinois Press, 1998), chaps. 2 and 3; Daniel Nelson, *Managers and Workers* (Madison: University of Wisconsin Press, 1975), chaps. 3–8.

5. Giovanni Arrighi, "The Labor Movement in Twentieth-Century Western Europe," in *Labor in the World Social Structure,* ed. Immanuel Wallerstein (Beverly Hills, Calif.: Sage, 1983), 55–56.

6. Ibid., 56.

7. David Brody, "The Old Labor History and the New," *Labor History* 20 (Winter 1979): 117.

8. David Montgomery, *Workers' Control in America* (New York: Cambridge University Press, 1979), 12–13.

9. Jerold S. Auerbach, *American Labor: The Twentieth Century* (Indianapolis: Bobbs-Merrill, 1969), 43–48; John Brophy, *A Miner's Life* (Madison: University of Wisconsin Press, 1964), chap. 4.

10. Robert and Helen Lynd, *Middletown: A Study in American Culture* (New York: Harcourt Brace, 1956), 76–79.

11. Robert Ozanne, *A Century of Labor-Management Relations at McCormick and International Harvester* (Madison: University of Wisconsin Press, 1967), 13–19.

12. Benson Soffer, "A Theory of Trade Union Development: The Role of the 'Autonomous' Workman," *Labor History* 1 (Spring 1960): 141–63.

13. Karl Marx, *Capital,* vol. 1 (New York: International Publishers, 1967), 423–24.

14. See Nelson, *Managers and Workers.*

15. Brody, *Steelworkers,* chap. 3.

16. On these developments, see George Barnett, *Chapters on Machinery* (Carbondale: Southern Illinois University Press, 1969), chaps. 1–4.

17. Ozanne, *Century of Labor-Management Relations,* 20–25.

18. The quotations are from Montgomery, *Workers' Control,* 26–27. For a more sober evaluation of Taylorism, see Daniel Nelson, *Frederick W. Taylor and the Rise of Scientific Management* (Madison: University of Wisconsin Press, 1980).

19. David Brody, *The Butcher Workmen: A Study of Unionization* (Cambridge, Mass.: Harvard University Press, 1964), chap. 1; Stephen Meyer III, *The Five-Dollar Day: Labor Management and Social Control at the Ford Motor Company, 1908–1921* (Albany: SUNY Press, 1981), chaps. 2 and 3.

20. Andreas Graziosi, "Common Laborers: Unskilled Workers, 1890–1915," *Labor History* 22 (Fall 1981): 512–44.

21. Andrew Dawson, "The Paradox of Dynamic Technological Change and the Labor Aristocracy in the United States, 1880–1914," *Labor History* 20 (Summer 1979): 325–51, esp. 338–39.

22. The quotation is from Sumner Slichter, *Union Policies and Industrial Management* (Washington, D.C.: Brookings Institution, 1941), 203. Cf. Barnett, *Chapters on Machinery,* chap. 6.

23. Irwin Yellowitz, *Industrialism and the American Labor Movement, 1850–1900* (Port Washington, N.Y.: Kennikat Press, 1977), 93.

24. Barnett, *Chapters on Machinery,* 141.

25. The statements by Perkins and Green are both quoted in Slichter, *Union Policies,* 205–6.

26. Barnett, *Chapters on Machinery,* chap. 3.

27. Ibid., chap. 4.

28. R. and H. Lynd, *Middletown,* 76–80.

29. Barnett, *Chapters on Machinery,* chap. 1; Elizabeth F. Baker, *Printers and Technology* (New York: Greenwood Press, 1957).

30. Melvyn Dubofsky and Warren Van Tine, *John L. Lewis: A Biography* (New York: Times Books, 1977), chaps. 4, 7, 8.

31. Melvyn Dubofsky, *We Shall Be All: A History of the IWW* (Chicago: Quadrangle Books, 1969), 79.

32. David Brody, *Workers in Industrial America* (New York: Oxford University Press, 1980), 29–30.

33. Philip Taft, *The A. F. of L. in the Time of Gompers* (New York: Octagon Press, 1957), chap. 13.

34. Robert Christie, *Empire in Wood* (Ithaca, N.Y.: Cornell University Press, 1956).

35. Montgomery, *Workers' Control,* 82, 91–112.

36. Ibid., 94–95.

37. Brody, *Workers in Industrial America,* 45.

38. Montgomery, *Workers' Control,* 156; Giovanni Arrighi and Beverly Silver, "Labor Movements and Capital Migration: The U.S. and Western Europe in World-Historical Perspective," in *Labor in the Capitalist World-Economy,* ed. Charles Bergquist (Beverly Hills, Calif.: Sage Publishers, 1984), 183–216, esp. 191–200.

39. Christopher Tomlins, "AFL Unions in the 1930s: Their Performance in Historical Perspective," *Journal of American History* 65 (Mar. 1979): 1021–42.

40. Nelson Lichtenstein, *Labor's War at Home: The CIO in World War II* (New York: Cambridge University Press, 1982); Howell John Harris, *The Right to Manage* (Madison: University of Wisconsin Press, 1982).

41. Brody, *Workers in Industrial America,* 204–7.

42. Elizabeth F. Baker, *Technology and Women's Work* (New York: Columbia University Press, 1964), 175.

43. Conversations with Secretary Treasurer Thomas Kopeck, International Typographical Union, July 1981.

44. Robert Asher, "Connecticut Workers and Technological Change, 1950–1980," *Connecticut History* 24 (Mar. 1983): 47–60.

45. Ibid., 59.

46. Brody, *Workers in Industrial America,* 250.

9

A New Look at the Original Case:
To What Extent Was the United States Fordist?

A S a theory, model, or ideal type, "Fordism" appears to serve as an elegant explanation of the historical factors that combined to create in the United States the world's first mass-consumer society. It also suggests powerfully how and why capital and labor perceived their respective interests as harmonious rather than conflictual and thus joined to build a stable social order in the United States. Yet the promulgators of the concept of Fordism disagree about its characteristics and the timing of its introduction as an actual practice in the United States. Charles Maier, who first applied Fordism in his scholarly studies of the post–World War I reestablishment of conservative hegemony in Europe, saw it as a system of political economy initially introduced in the United States in the years before World War I that flowed from the principles of scientific management as elaborated by Frederick Winslow Taylor and practiced in the automobile industry through Henry Ford's use of the moving assembly line. According to Maier, Taylor, Ford, and their epigones used scientific managerial and production techniques to eliminate discord between managers and workers and establish the foundation for a mass-production, high-wage, mass-consumption society. Such a political economy appeared to reach fruition during the 1920s.[1] For Michel Aglietta, on the other hand, Fordism refers more to the political economy created in the United States in the two decades after World War II, a system in which trade unions and the national state allied with corporate enterprises to establish a "real" mass-consumption society.[2]

Let me clarify matters by stating baldly what Fordism means to me as a historian and precisely when I see it introduced into the production of goods and the practice of industrial relations in the United States. Simply put, Fordism was primarily an extension of Taylorism from the producer-goods sector of the economy, in which Taylor applied his managerial innovations, to the consumer-goods sector, in which Henry Ford introduced the first moving assembly line. Both Taylor and Ford shared a common desire to strip the worker of all responsibility for the conception and regulation of production, in return for which the direct producer would be amply rewarded materially. Managerial control of production would result in low-cost, standardized mass production; high wages for labor would enable workers to consume what they produced. Finally, a political economy based on mass production and mass consumption required the services of a noncoercive state (what Herbert Hoover called the "associational state") to encourage employers and workers, capital and labor, to practice the new cooperative capitalism of the 1920s, in which Taylorism and Fordism created a stable political economy. In the remainder of this paper, I propose to examine the theory, practice, and reality of that new political economy.

Theoretical Foundations of Fordism

The principles and practices of Fordism were first applied in the United States in the years between 1895 and 1915. As elaborated by Frederick Winslow Taylor and used by Henry Ford, scientific management (I will use that term interchangeably with Fordism, as I see no essential differences between the two) had one clear—indeed, predominant—aim: the cheapening of the cost of production by increasing substantially the output of individual workers (hence lowering unit costs). Let me be absolutely clear about one controversial aspect of this process. I see no evidence that the early practitioners of Fordism sought consciously to eliminate or dilute the skills of strategically situated, skilled workers. Indeed, as we will see later in this paper, skilled workers remained numerous, vital, and indispensable to the production process right through the 1920s. We must begin our understanding of what scientific management actually meant by distinguishing between Taylor's rhetoric and shop-floor practices. No doubt, Taylor actually wrote that the "inability of the man who is fit to do the work to understand the science of doing his work becomes more and more evident as the work becomes more complicated, all the way up the scale. I assert, without the slightest hesitation, that the high-class mechanic has a far smaller chance of ever thoroughly understanding the science of his work than the pig-iron handler has of understanding the science of his work . . . that the man who is fit to work at any particular trade is unable to understand the science of that trade without the kindly help and co-operation of men of a totally different kind of education." Thus, Taylor suggested that managers deliberately gather "all the great mass of tradi-tional knowledge, which in the past has been in the hands of the work-man, and in the physical skill and knack of the workman, which he has acquired through years of experience."[3] In practice, however, what Taylor and his disciples among the growing school of American industrial engi-neers actually tried to achieve was far more limited. Most often, they pro-posed to show both unskilled common laborers and skilled craftsmen how to increase their productivity through improved methods, and, more often than not, such improvements were built on the old system of driving la-bor. Where traditional foremen and managers had driven workers largely on the basis of tradition and intuition, Taylor-style engineers asserted that the stopwatch, the camera, and the right tools would enable workers to attain peak efficiency in productivity. It should also be noted that most of Taylor's innovations occurred in sectors of the economy that manufactured capital goods and that were not suited to mass production.

It was Henry Ford and his corps of engineers and managers who first applied Taylor's principles of scientific management to the mass produc-tion of a consumer good. Between 1908 and 1914, when he introduced the famous five-dollar daily wage at his Highland Park, Michigan, plant, Ford steadily Taylorized the labor process in his automobile plants, beginning first with the manufacture of mass-produced interchangeable parts and culminating with their fitting to the car chassis on the moving assembly line. By mass-producing parts and assembling them through the labor of an army of highly specialized workers who performed minutely subdivided tasks, the Ford Motor Company reduced labor costs in two ways: "first by making the workman extremely skilled, so that he does his part with no needless motions, and secondly by training him to perform his operation with the least expenditure of will-power, and hence with the least brain fatigue."[4] By designing skills into special-purpose machines and tools that could be operated efficiently by nonskilled workers, Ford, in the words of the historian of the company's transformed labor process, "Taylorized work processes and eliminated wasteful moments and motions in the per-formance of work." In following the principles formulated by Taylor and extending them to the mass production of a consumer good, the Ford managers created an integrated industrial system with a new division of labor, an altered occupational structure, and a system of driving labor built into the technology itself.[5]

Although Taylor, Ford, and other managers who followed similar production practices were primarily concerned with lowering unit costs, they expected as a side-effect of their managerial innovations to eliminate both generic labor-capital conflict and the specific threat posed by trade unions. Taylor, Ford, and their ilk viewed workers as "economic men," people driven by purely rational and instrumental material needs. Taylor, for example, promised skilled mechanics and common laborers that, in return for surrendering complete control of the labor process to their superiors, they would receive a fair share of the rewards of increased productivity through scientifically set, differential piece rates and premium bonuses. By contrast, Taylor asserted, informal work-group production norms and formal union production standards only served to reduce the earnings and income of most workers, who sacrificed their material betterment to protect the jobs of a minority of inefficient, nonproductive workers. Both Taylor and Ford, moreover, in the words of the latter, believed fervidly that "no man wants to be burdened with the care and responsibility of deciding things." Let managers and engineers make the decisions, reasoned Ford and Taylor, and workers would enjoy superior material and moral circumstances. Where Taylor promised workers in the specialized metal trades differential piece rates and premium bonuses, Ford in 1914 offered his mass-production workers, whose pace of work was set by the assembly line, the five-dollar day. The institution of such a new order based on scientific management and higher wages, one in which managers treated "men like men in man fashion," promised Ford, would prove "that barriers between employers and employees thought to exist and that often do exist can be largely removed."[6]

Promises and rhetoric notwithstanding, scientific management and Fordism were scarcely concerned with the material or moral improvement of workers. For engineers such as Taylor and entrepreneurs such as Ford, the bottom line remained always per capita productivity, unit cost reduction, and greater efficiency (in Ford's case, moreover, the profit rate remained the real bottom line). Ford's five-dollar wage, the company's welfare program, and its transformed occupational structure all, at bottom, rested on the productive efficiency of labor. The goal of the Ford system, said a senior manager, was "to grade the men in our employ according to their efficiency and to see that every man gets a square deal and receives the wage he is entitled to as soon as he reaches our different standards of proficiency progressively arranged." For the nonproficient and inefficient, there was no five-dollar wage and usually no job.[7]

The principles elaborated by Taylor between 1895 and 1914 and perfected in practice by Ford between 1908 and 1914 were not really put to the test until the decade of the 1920s. The eruption of World War I in the summer of 1914 and the entrance of the United States in the Great War in April 1917 created a scarcity of labor, diminished employers' concern with lowering unit costs of production (war orders and contracts guaranteed profits regardless of the cost of production), and heightened the power of workers to resist managerial control of the labor process either through informal work practices or union power, which waxed considerably during the war years. Scientific management and Fordism would have to await the return of peace, stability, and what Warren G. Harding called "normalcy" to determine if it could deliver what its promoters promised.

The Testing Time of Fordism

Before capitalists and their allies in the apparatus of the national state could practice the "new capitalism" based on mass consumption, they first had to purge the economy of war-induced price and wage inflation. A short, sharp depression in 1920–21 accomplished that. As a result of high unemployment (above 12 percent in 1921) and a wave of massive strikes (1919–22) that ended mostly in defeat for workers seeking to defend wartime wage standards, prices and wages declined substantially. For the remainder of the 1920s, price stability prevailed and real earnings actually rose on average because most workers toiled for a greater number of hours.

Stable prices and relatively full employment provided the foundation for the takeoff of a second industrial revolution generated largely by the mass-production, consumer-goods sector, especially automobiles, petrochemicals, and electrical appliances. The United States seemed awash in an ocean of private automobiles, service stations, synthetics, and household appliances. Lincoln Steffens, who had glimpsed a future that worked in the Soviet Union in 1920, said of the United States in 1928: "Big business is producing what the socialists held up as their goal. Food, shelter, and clothing for all." The cornucopia of consumer goods, many observers noted, diluted class distinctions. Low-priced, mass-production goods, including major consumer durables purchased on credit, enabled all Americans to dress alike, eat alike, drive alike, and, according to Robert and Helen Lynd's study of a midsized industrial city, think alike. As Calvin Coolidge, the departing president of the United States, phrased it in 1928: "We are reaching and maintaining the position where the propertied class and the employed class are not separate, but identical."[8]

Corporate leaders especially sang hymns to the new capitalism. "We are acquiring a new industrial philosophy," trilled a leader of the U.S. Chamber of Commerce in 1929, "that the fundamentals of decent and right conduct laid down by Jesus of Nazareth constitute the soundest, most sensible, and workable economic system to devise." "It is a great joy to me to realize," chorused the hard-driving steelmaster Charles Schwab, "that humanity rules American industrial life today." Corporate America, wrote the economist Herbert Feis, "has worked out simple means and policies for insuring steady and peaceful advancement of industrial life." Those means included, according to Schwab, steady employment, a voice for workers in determining the conditions of labor, the opportunity to acquire capital (stock), and security in old age. Or, as Coolidge put it in his more hyperbolic language: "Brains are wealth and wealth is the chief end of man. . . . The man who builds a factory builds a temple; the man who works there worships there."[9]

Scientific management and Fordism also altered their visages during the 1920s. Taylorism originally perceived workers as little more than extensions of the tools and machines that they manipulated. Just as engineers designed machines for optimum efficiency, they could also fashion workers into perfect automatons of production. By the 1920s, however, industrial engineers had learned that while workers might be manageable, they were not malleable. Managerial innovations at the workplace repeatedly caused friction or conflict among workers who exercised their wills and refused to act as automatons. It was time, said industrial engineers and corporate managers during the 1920s, to realize that men were not synonymous with machinery. Once more, Charles Schwab put that new consciousness into clear language. Effective management, he observed, "is going to depend more and more upon the management of men than upon the organization of machines and other problems of practical engineering. . . . Industry's most important task in this day of large-scale production is management of men on a human basis."[10]

The new generation of scientific managers, who had learned industrial psychology in colleges and professional schools, sought to practice human relations in the workplace. Whether as engineers, personnel officials, or plant supervisors, they strove to transform their subordinates into men and women who identified their own interests as synonymous with those of the enterprise. The more fully workers identified with the goals of the enterprise, the less likely they would quit (labor turnover was first identified as a major problem during the World War I years, and thereafter employers concentrated on reducing its incidence), the less likely they would resist managerial orders, and the more likely they would labor efficiently.

Industrial relations as human relations in its 1920s version suggested that firms eliminate all those aspects of the employment relation that caused anxieties among workers. And that was precisely the aim of the welfare programs implemented by many of the most profitable large enterprises. Informal forms of plantwide seniority insured long-term employees against unexpected layoffs; company health plans protected workers against sudden illness; and company-funded pensions promised loyal employees a measure of security in old age.[11] To increase employee loyalty to the firm, managers defined their subordinates as citizens of the enterprise, as participants in a model industrial democracy. Building on the Employee Representation Plans (ERP) that had come into vogue as an alternative to the upsurge of unionism during the war years, managers proclaimed that workers have "a fundamental right, namely, the right to representation in the determination of those matters which affect their own interests." To the extent that workers elected representatives of their own choice to voice shop-floor sentiments directly to management, the two parties would understand each other better and cooperate to eliminate waste, improve product quality, and heighten efficiency. In the words of a study made by the National Industrial Conference Board concerning ERPs: "Beyond the settlement of grievances . . . is the broader and more constructive accomplishment of employee representation in welding together management and working force into a single, cohesive productive unit."[12]

The humanizing of scientific management prompted many sectors of the labor movement to alter their attitude toward Taylorism. Before World War I, the unions, especially those concentrated in the metal trades, which bore the brunt of managerial innovations in the labor process, rejected scientific management outright.[13] In the 1920s, the American Federation of Labor (AFL) and its Metal Trades Department offered management labor's cooperation in eliminating waste from industry and promoting more efficient standards of quality production.[14] The two most notable, and perhaps outspoken, advocates of scientific management among trade unionists represented workers in sectors of the economy in which employers seldom had the resources or ability to practice Fordism. Sidney Hillman of the Amalgamated Clothing Workers of America (ACWA) spoke for workers who toiled in the extremely competitive men's clothing industry, in which tiny producers, including a myriad of subcontractors (or sweaters) with barely any capital, far outnumbered the owners of large, modernized factories. Hillman's union promoted industrial engineering (indeed, the ACWA hired its own engineers and made their services available to employers), the scientific setting of piece rates, the elimination of waste in industry, and the rationalization of a chaotic trade. In fact, the union offered to do for clothing firms what they could not achieve for themselves.[15] Hillman's policies and practices prompted the *New York Times* in 1925 to characterize him as a labor statesman who pioneered joint planning with men's clothing manufacturers. Interestingly, the *New York Times* contrasted Hillman with John L. Lewis of the United Mine Workers of America and described the latter as "the older type of labor executive . . . unreceptive to newer principles." Yet no labor leader of the time more forcefully expounded the principles of Fordism than did Lewis in a book published in 1925, *The Miner's Fight for American Standards*. The American system, he stressed, was based on expensive labor, not cheap labor—labor that earned enough to purchase the products of American industry and provide the economy with an adequate, stable domestic market. "Those who seek to cheapen coal by cheapening men [through lower wages]," Lewis stressed, "seek to reverse the evolution of American industry." He promised to promote efficiency and to ally with the engineer in eliminating waste. Modern science and engineering could be used by managers, trade unionists, and public officials to establish a corporate society based on high wages, mass consumption, and reasonable profits.[16] That, in a nutshell, was the essence of Fordism; yet, as Lewis realized, its achievement in practice depended on the cooperation of the state.

Lewis thought that he had precisely the sort of public official the achievement of Fordism needed in the person of the secretary of commerce, Herbert C. Hoover. Himself a mining engineer and an advocate of efficiency in industry by training and business experience, Hoover brought the principles of scientific management to the highest levels of the state. He used the same language as the corporate proponents of welfare capitalism and the advocates of human relations in industry. Hoover suggested that joint private-public planning could smooth the business cycle and promote full employment. He insisted that a mass-production economy required mass consumption based on higher wages. He proposed that labor and management cooperate to eliminate waste in industry and offer workers a voice in the enterprise. Voluntary associational activities between capital and labor that would be sanctioned, but not coerced, by the state could ensure safe and healthful standards of work; establish the proper balance between profits and wages; and create a harmonious society in which order and liberty reached equilibrium. The final capstone to the principles of Fordism, Hoover's public policies, which the historian Ellis Hawley has defined as the "associational state," personified the uniquely American practice of voluntarism.[17]

That the associational state and the principle of voluntarism worked was proved by the history of labor in the United States between 1923 and 1929. Wherever managers practiced welfare capitalism, implemented scientific management with a human face, and provided workers a "voice" in the enterprise, unionism either disappeared or never visited. By 1929, the labor movement had lost almost half its membership from its 1920 peak. Unions survived securely only in those sectors of the economy outside the mass-production core; or where markets were locally based; or in firms that were relatively impervious to the innovations of Taylorism—such as the building and trucking trades. In 1928–29, industrial conflict fell to its lowest level since records of its incidence first began to be compiled in the 1880s, and labor turnover dropped to levels not seen since economists first began to study the phenomenon carefully during the war years.

Fordism had achieved its dearest aim indeed, the worker's voluntary consent to subordination. As one railroad executive reported: "The employee is much happier than under the old regime. . . . He is a peaceful worker and a peaceful citizen and he wants to be let alone in that state." Class consciousness and the trade-union mentality it generated seemed relics of a distant past. "The desire for steady employment and higher earnings," noted the economist Sumner Slichter, "became more dominant in the minds of the workers than the feeling for industrial freedom and independence." To which the French visitor and observer Andre Siegfried added: "The American workman, when he realizes that society assures him a comfortable income, is ready to accept the existing order of industry."[18]

Fordism in Practice

At the level of theory, rhetoric, and also in retarding union growth and diluting labor-capital conflict, Fordism worked during the 1920s. In terms of substantially transforming shop-floor practices; providing rising incomes and job security for most workers; and establishing a basis for a real mass-consumption society, Fordism proved less than a complete success.

Two aspects of the application of scientific management to the shop floor during the 1920s seem most evident. First, never did the new managerial techniques affect the vast majority of workers. For example, Taylor's favored premium and bonus piece-rate wage plans at most affected 37 percent of all employees in industry and may have, in fact, covered as few as 7 percent. Second, the innovations rarely diluted the skills of the most strategically placed craftsmen. Across industries, managers rejected scientific management as inappropriate for the sort of work done by their more skilled employees. In 1928, the National Industrial Conference Board concluded in its survey of actual work practices that piece rates have "been found unsuited in the manufacture of custom made articles, specialities and small quantities, experimental work and articles where quality is of the first importance."[19] Even at the Ford Motor Company, there is no clear statistical evidence that the actual, absolute numbers of highly skilled workers decreased during the 1920s or subsequently.[20] What most troubled skilled workers about scientific management was not its threat to their skills or autonomy on the shop floor but its impact on their wage rates (felt to be negative) and job security.[21] Scientific management instead had its greatest impact on hitherto unskilled workers who could now work as other than unskilled, day laborers and found themselves upgraded to the category of semiskilled machine operators. For them, direct participation in the process of production did not mean toil as degraded automatons or threats to wage rates and job security. More often, such work, which was overwhelmingly concentrated in the newer, mass-production consumer industries, brought more interesting jobs, greater security, and higher wages.[22]

Even where managers most assiduously tried to apply Taylorism, workers escaped its clutches. Machine operators as well as skilled workers practiced and perfected informal restrictions on output. Moreover, time- and motion-study specialists rarely had any truly efficient or consistent way to measure productivity. Typically, they operated more through intuition than science. As Stanley Mathewson reported in his justly famous book about restriction of output among workers: "For every worker . . . who appeared overtaxed, we encountered dozens who were successfully matching wits with management in self-protective resistance against wage-incentive plans, piece-rate cuts and prospective layoffs."[23]

Even harder to read clearly than the impact of scientific management on the shop floor was the effect of Fordism on the material standards and consumption habits of workers. And that is most true of the workers at Ford itself, where, during the 1920s, first the six-dollar day and then the seven-dollar wage superseded the famous five-dollar day. To begin with, not all Ford employees qualified for the high minimum wage. Only married men with suitable family arrangements automatically qualified, and even they had to work for the firm for a minimum of six months. Second, no Ford workers had guaranteed employment or the assurance of daily, weekly, and monthly—let alone annual—incomes. Finally, one must struggle to interpret the meaning of a U.S. Bureau of Labor Statistics (BLS) survey in 1929 of the living standards of 100 Ford families, probably chosen from among a group of more advantaged workers. The sample took home earnings of $1,694 a year (little more than the BLS's recommended minimum health and decency budget of $1,500). Fewer than one-half had central heating in their homes, and not quite one-third owned their homes. Perhaps more remarkable given Ford's commitment to low-cost production, high wages, and mass consumption, fewer than one-half the sample of his workers owned their own cars. More of the families ran a deficit in their budget than saved money, and most financed their purchase of appliances on credit. Was their glass half full or half empty, and what can be said of their less fortunate brothers and sisters in the automobile-industry labor force?[24]

The source most often cited to prove that workers had become consumers during the 1920s and that they had bought the culture of the "business class" lock, stock, and barrel, Robert and Helen Lynd's *Middletown*, can also be read another way. Clearly, they found no hint of class consciousness among the working people of Muncie, Indiana, nor any dissent among them to the city's bourgeois culture. Surely, the Lynds also discovered a working class eager to participate in the joys of consumption. Yet the extent to which Muncie's workers shared the pleasures of consumption and the rewards of bourgeois culture was more ambiguous. Wherever the Lynds moved among working-class families, they discovered a deep sense of insecurity mixed with anxiety, fear among husbands and especially wives concerning the stability of the former's employment; knowledge that illness, injury, or unemployment for the primary wage earner meant family deprivation; concern that their children could not afford the clothes worn by business-class children and hence participate to the fullest in school and community social activities. They noted pointedly that some laboring-class families who achieved the ultimate consumer posses-

sion, ownership of an automobile, did so at the expense of installing in-
door plumbing in their homes. Obviously, Muncie's working class (80
percent of the population by the Lynds' calculations) shared only partially,
if at all, in the joys of a mass-consumption culture. Where Muncie's business class reveled in a sense of mastery, according to the Lynds, its laboring class found only impotency.[25]

The Lynds' portrait of working-class existence in Muncie in the mid-
1920s may be criticized for its impressionistic and anecdotal character. Yet
the most recent scholar to examine the material standard of living among
workers during the 1920s reaches similar conclusions. Frank Stricker
agrees that most workers undoubtedly earned more and lived better in 1929
than they had in 1914. Nevertheless, he suggests that the bulk of the gains
came between 1916 and 1919, a result of war-induced labor scarcity, and
not between 1923 and 1929, a product of Fordism. Stricker, moreover, finds
that such improvements in working-class standards were extremely un-
evenly distributed. White-collar workers, the most rapidly growing sector
of the labor force, benefited much more substantially than blue-collar
workers. And among blue-collar workers, the more highly skilled (once
again, those least affected in practice by Fordism) enjoyed the greatest
gains.[26] Stricker also suggests that, owing to irregularity of employment,
illness, injury, and other factors, as well as low wages, between 42 and 50
percent of all working-class families in the year 1929 lived at or below the
poverty level. Instead of sharing in the splendors of a high-mass-consump-
tion culture, most workers, in Stricker's words, participated in "the struggle
for economic security, not the struggle to keep up with the Joneses."[27]

What made that struggle for security most perilous was the common-
ality of irregularity of employment. As the Lynds found repeatedly in their
interviews with working-class families in Muncie, the loss of jobs and the
term "deadline" (the age at which people became too old for steady employment) filled the conversations, especially among working-class wives.
Alex Keyssar's recent prizewinning study of unemployment in the state
of Massachusetts between 1870 and 1920 lends statistical validation to the
Lynds' more impressionistic observations. Examining not just total unemployment rates for any particular moment in time but also the frequency
of unemployment for different groups of workers, Keyssar concludes that
the actual loss of jobs (or the fear of such an event) was perhaps the single
most dominant reality in the lives of workers. Even during the 1920s, after reforms had brought some stability to the hitherto chaotic labor markets in Massachusetts (mostly in the form of informal seniority arrange-

ments and internal job ladders), unemployment remained a persistent threat to almost all blue-collar workers.[28]

The perilousness of working-class life and the slim margin that kept many working-class families above the poverty level were exposed graphically when the Great Depression hit. As the scythe of unemployment cut across working-class America, millions of families fell through the floor of comfort into poverty. The prosperity of the 1920s had not enabled them to accumulate the resources or savings to carry them safely through a deep economic contraction. Many lost the homes, automobiles, and other consumer durables that they had purchased on the installment plan in better times. Though corporate managers and state managers tried once again to use Fordist principles to combat depression—cartel-like arrangements to stabilize production, employment, wages, and prices, as well as investment—such principles now worked even less well than they had during the more prosperous 1920s.[29] Fordism had been more promise than performance, more myth than reality during the "new era." The Depression exposed the base metals beneath the gilded surface of Fordism.

The New Deal and the Coming of Keynesianism

Despite Fordism's failure to bring production and consumption into equilibrium or to distribute prosperity equitably across society during the 1920s, the early New Deal quite consciously sought to implement Fordist techniques of macroeconomic management. The National Industrial Recovery Act (NIRA) of June 1933 drew directly on concepts for national economic planning that had been germinating since the World War I years and earlier. It also relied for its successful implementation on the sort of private associational business planning that Hoover had conceptualized during the 1920s. The National Recovery Administration (NRA), the agency established to implement the program, encouraged businesses to form associations that would adopt codes of fair competition, codes that would sanction the elimination of price competition in previously competitive markets and guarantee workers minimum wages and improved working conditions. NRA administrators expected that the elimination of competition would enable manufacturers to raise prices and hence increase investment, employment, and wages. Fuller employment and higher wages, in turn, would supply the mass demand to consume the output of mass production. Although Section 7a of the NIRA legitimated the right of workers to unionize and bargain collectively—another stratagem to distribute more of the product from profits to wages—the NRA tolerated the efforts of employers to create company unions, ERPs, and other union-avoidance measures. From July 1933 on, such antiunion devices proliferated, just as they had during World War I and its immediate aftermath. In only one way did early New Deal economic policy appear to diverge fundamentally from the policies of Harding, Coolidge, and Hoover: the New Deal placed the coercive power of the state behind associational planning by business cartels. The federal government could punish firms that violated NRA codes of fair competition. More often than not, however, the NRA merely ceded to private business associations the right to plan in their own interests.[30]

In practice, Fordism, buttressed by the coercive power of the state, failed as abysmally as Hoover's voluntary associational approach. Larger firms used the cover of the NRA codes to eliminate competition from smaller firms. Some of the largest firms, like the Ford Motor Company, even refused to cooperate with the NRA. Outside of the soft-coal and clothing industries, where the singular structure of competition and a history of union strength saw the reemergence of union power, employers successfully resisted the growth of unionism, collective bargaining, and the need to redistribute more of the economy's product to wages. In short, Fordism, as practiced by the early New Deal, failed to create consumer demand adequate to stimulate stable and greater production, higher investment, and fuller employment.[31]

The failures of their initial reforms prompted New Dealers to scrap Fordism as a solution to the Depression and to resort instead to Keynesian measures of economic stimulation. As part of the attempt to generate greater consumer demand, some of the New Dealers planned to place the full power of the federal government behind the struggle of workers to unionize and bargain collectively. The National Labor Relations Act (NLRA) of 1935 (the Wagner Act) accomplished precisely that. Its sponsors and drafters based their labor policies on an underconsumptionist analysis of the causes of the Great Depression. Convinced by the history of the 1920s and the experience of the NRA that employers would not voluntarily share profits equitably with employees, the advocates of the Wagner Act saw trade unions as an instrument through which workers acting collectively could wrest for themselves a larger share of the national product. Thus, the NLRA stripped from employers every device that they had used successfully during the 1920s and 1933–34 to avoid dealing with independent trade unions. Employers, of course, proved as loath to recognize unions under the Wagner Act as they had been under the NRA. Only overt struggle by workers wrested union recognition and collective bargaining from recalcitrant firms; and even then, labor's triumphs remained limited and vulnerable.[32]

The Wagner Act, however, was only one part of the New Deal's effort in 1935 to stimulate demand by increasing mass purchasing power. The Revenue Act of 1935, through more steeply graduated income- and corporate-tax rates, sought to use fiscal power to redistribute excess income from the rich to the poor, who would spend money immediately. The Social Security Act of 1935, by guaranteeing income to the unemployed, the elderly, and the dependent, generated additional buying power. In practice, however, congressional conservatives diluted the most progressive features of the Revenue Act and insured that Social Security would have a short-term regressive fiscal impact (social security payroll taxes were to be levied for five years prior to the first old-age benefit payments).[33]

Overall, the shift from Fordism to Keynesianism seemed to work. The unionization of the mass-production industries, epitomized by the Congress of Industrial Organizations' triumph over General Motors and U.S. Steel within three weeks in February and March 1937, coincided with a vigorous wave of economic expansion from the summer of 1936 through the spring of 1937. For the first time since the onset of the Great Depression, production, employment, and wage levels began to approach precrisis levels. Unfortunately, however, Roosevelt celebrated the success of Keynesianism by ending his experiment with the new macroeconomics. Economic expansion prompted the president to cut federal spending. The result was an economic contraction in 1937–38 even sharper than that of 1929–32. Production, employment, investment, and union growth all declined substantially, proving in perverse fashion the validity of the Keynesian prescription for economic illness.[34]

Further proof came with the experience of the United States during World War II. The war saw the total application of Keynesian economic principles. State fiscal management and unlimited spending on the war effort generated levels of employment and prosperity not experienced since the heady days of World War I. The National War Labor Board defended unions against employer attack, in the process insuring the new unions in the mass-production industries against the loss of membership and influence at the bargaining table. During the war, tripartite negotiations among employers, labor leaders, and public officials created the foundation for what became the postwar regime of full employment, rising real wages, macroeconomic management by the state, and a truly mass-consumption society. That achievement, unlike the Fordism of 1909–29, produced almost thirty years of economic equilibrium, material prosperity, and social harmony. Unlike Fordism, the Keynesian regime offered a place, albeit subordinate, to organized labor; required the state to manage the economy; and reserved seats for ordinary consumers at an American feast. All that, to be sure, represented no small accomplishment, one that its creators might well take pride in.[35]

Conclusion

Today, the system put together by the New Deal, the World War II planners, and the postwar Keynesians stands in shambles. History has played its customary tricks on the actors. Once again, we live in an age in which capitalists and their allies prescribe a new Fordism as the cure for what ails us. Workers are told to work harder for less compensation. Computerization and robotization, the current applications of science to production, are sold as the means to future prosperity. Managers demand the right to manage without union restraint, and alternative industrial relations are promoted as a substitute for collective bargaining. Put another way, the new Fordism insists that cooperative industrial relations replace adversarial relations between labor and capital, that workers ally with their employers without the intervention of third parties to increase production, improve the quality of products, and lower unit costs. Such practices, it is claimed, would make the American economy once again competitive on the domestic and world markets.[36] Thatcherism and Reaganism are simply manifestations of the new Fordism at the level of the state.

Notes

An earlier version of this essay appeared in *Le Processus de Salarisation dans l'Économie Mondiale,* no. 12 (Contributions to a colloquium on June 9–10, 1988, organized by GIS Économie Mondiale Tiers-Monde Développement, the Fernand Braudel Center at Binghamton University, SUNY, and Maison des Sciences de l'Homme, Paris), 9–42.

1. Charles Maier, *In Search of Stability: Explorations in Historical Political Economy* (Cambridge: Cambridge University Press, 1987), 19–53. Actually, the concept of Fordism originated outside the academic arena and was initially suggested as an explanation for American exceptionalism by Antonio Gramsci in the

1920s. See Gramsci's *Selections from the Prison Notebooks* (New York: International Publishers, 1971), 279–318.

2. Michel Aglietta, *A Theory of Capitalist Regulation* (London: Verso, 1979); cf. Mike Davis, "'Fordism' in Crisis: a Review of Michel Aglietta's *Regulation et Crises: L'experience des Etats-Unis*," *Review* 2 (Fall 1978): 207–69. For a recent suggestive critique of Fordism that appeared just as I finished a draft of this paper, see John Bellamy Foster, "The Fetish of Fordism," *Monthly Review* 39 (Mar. 1988): 14–33.

3. Frederick Winslow Taylor, *The Principles of Scientific Management* (New York: W. W. Norton, 1967), 25–26, 40–41, 59, 74, 130, 140; David Montgomery, *The Fall of the House of Labor* (New York: Cambridge University Press, 1987), esp. chaps. 1 and 5; cf. Daniel Nelson, *Frederick W. Taylor and the Rise of Scientific Management* (Madison: University of Wisconsin Press, 1980), 101–3, 168–74. Nelson also observes that "scientific management in practice had relatively little direct impact on the character of work or the activities of production workers" (137).

4. Stephen Meyer III, *The Five-Dollar Day: Labor Management and Social Control in the Ford Motor Company, 1908–1921* (Albany: State University of New York Press, 1981), 22.

5. Ibid., 11, 51–52.

6. For Taylor's ideas on the setting of wage rates, see his *Principles of Scientific Management;* for Ford's words and beliefs, see his testimony in 1915 before the United States Commission on Industrial Relations, *Final Report and Testimony* (Washington, D.C.: Government Printing Office, 1915), 8:7627–29.

7. Meyer, *Five-Dollar Day,* 106; cf. Martha May, "The Historical Case of the Family Wage: The Ford Motor Company and the Five-Dollar Day," *Feminist Studies* 8 (1982): 399–424; on Taylor's lack of concern for the impact of his policies on workers, see Nelson, *Frederick W. Taylor,* passim.

8. William E. Leuchtenberg, *The Perils of Prosperity, 1914–1932* (Chicago: University of Chicago Press, 1958), 202–3 (for the quotations), 186–88; Robert S. and Helen Lynd, *Middletown: A Study in American Culture* (New York: Harcourt Brace, 1956).

9. For all the quotations (save the last), see David Brody, *Workers in Industrial America* (New York: Oxford University Press, 1980), 48–52. The last quotation is from Leuchtenberg, *Perils of Prosperity,* 188.

10. Brody, *Workers,* 52–53.

11. On the creation of job ladders as a part of internal labor markets and the introduction of forms of seniority, see Sanford Jacoby, *Employing Bureaucracies* (New York: Columbia University Press, 1985), chap. 6; Ronald Schatz, *The Electrical Workers* (Urbana: University of Illinois Press, 1983), chap. 1.

12. Brody, *Workers,* 55–56.

13. Montgomery, *Fall of the House of Labor,* chap. 5.

14. On this development, see Milton Nadworny, *Scientific Management and the Unions, 1900–1932* (Cambridge, Mass.: Harvard University Press, 1955).

15. Steven Fraser, "From the 'New Unionism' to the New Deal," *Labor History* 25 (Summer 1984): 405–30; idem, "Dress Rehearsal for the New Deal: Shop-Floor Insurgents, Political Elites, and Industrial Democracy in the Amalgamated Cloth-

ing Workers," in *Working-Class America,* ed. Michael Frisch and Daniel Walkowitz (Urbana: University of Illinois Press, 1983), 212–55.

16. Melvyn Dubofsky and Warren Van Tine, *John L. Lewis: A Biography* (New York: Times Books, 1977), 137–38.

17. Ellis Hawley, "Herbert Hoover, the Commerce Secretariat, and the Vision of an 'Associative State'," *Journal of American History* 61 (June 1974): 116–40; idem, "Secretary Hoover and the Bituminous Coal Problem, 1921–1928," *Business History Review* 42 (Autumn 1968): 247–70; idem, "The Discovery and Study of 'Corporate Liberalism'," *Business History Review* 52 (Autumn 1978): 309–20.

18. The quotations can be found in Brody, *Workers,* 66.

19. Daniel Nelson, "Scientific Management and the Workplace, 1920–1930," paper read at the Harvard Business School Seminar on the History of Business, April 11, 1988, 6–9.

20. Meyer, *Five-Dollar Day,* 50–51, includes two tables that indicate that between 1913 and 1917, when scientific management and mass production were introduced most fully at the company, the number of skilled workers (including foremen and others not directly involved in production) held at about 28 percent of the total labor force. In the mid-1920s, at the giant Ford River Rouge complex, Nelson Lichtenstein reports that more than seven thousand workers were defined as highly skilled craftsmen. Lichtenstein, "Walter Reuther and the Rise of Labor-Liberalism," in *Labor Leaders in America,* ed. Melvyn Dubofsky and Warren Van Tine (Urbana: University of Illinois Press, 1987), 281.

21. Nelson, "Scientific Management," 20.

22. Ibid., 21–22. For the origins of these changes, see Montgomery, *Fall of the House of Labor,* chaps. 2 and 3.

23. Stanley Mathewson, *Restrictions of Output among Unorganized Workers* (New York: Viking Press, 1931), esp. 146, 151, 153; Nelson, "Scientific Management," 11–14.

24. Brody, *Workers,* 63–64.

25. For a different and more common reading of the Lynds' *Middletown,* one that stresses the spread of a culture of consumption among workers and the rising real standards of living, see Brody, *Workers,* 64–65.

26. Frank Stricker, "Affluence for Whom?—Another Look at Prosperity and the Working Classes in the 1920s," *Labor History* 24 (Winter 1983): 5–33. Stricker's findings concerning the enormous earnings gap separating less skilled from more skilled workers recalls Peter Shergold's conclusions after comparing wages and earnings among workers in the Pittsburgh area of the United States and the Birmingham area in England in the early twentieth century. Shergold found that unskilled workers in both countries earned roughly comparable real wages, but skilled workers in the United States earned far more than their English counterparts. See Shergold's *Working-Class Life: The "American Standard" in Comparative Perspective, 1899–1913* (Pittsburgh, Pa.: University of Pittsburgh Press, 1982).

27. Stricker, "Affluence," 33.

28. Alexander Keyssar, *Out of Work: The First Century of Unemployment in Massachusetts* (Cambridge: Cambridge University Press, 1986), 286–89.

29. Brody, *Workers,* 73–77.

30. Bernard Bellush, *The Failure of the NRA* (New York: W. W. Norton, 1975), chaps. 1–4; Ellis Hawley, *The New Deal and the Problem of Monopoly* (Princeton, N.J.: Princeton University Press, 1966), chaps. 1–7; Sidney Fine, *The Automobile Industry under the Blue Eagle: Labor, Management and the Automobile Manufacturing Code* (Ann Arbor: University of Michigan Press, 1963); Louis Galambos, *Competition and Cooperation: The Emergence of a National Trade Association* (Baltimore, Md.: Johns Hopkins University Press, 1966); Stanley Vittoz, *New Deal Labor Policy and the American Industrial Economy* (Chapel Hill: University of North Carolina Press, 1987), chaps. 4–6.

31. See the sources cited in note 30 as well as James Hodges, *New Deal Labor Policy and the Southern Cotton Textile Industry, 1933–1941* (Knoxville: University of Tennessee Press, 1986), chaps. 4–8; Irving Bernstein, *Turbulent Years: A History of the American Worker, 1933–1941* (Boston: Houghton Mifflin, 1970), 30–36, 172–216; Daniel Nelson, *The Rubber Workers* (Princeton, N.J.: Princeton University Press, 1988); idem, "Managers and Nonunion Workers in the Rubber Industry: Union Avoidance Strategies in the 1930s," paper read at "Historical Perspectives on American Labor: An Interdisciplinary Approach," New York State School on Industrial and Labor Relations, Ithaca, N.Y., April 21–23, 1988; Sanford M. Jacoby, "Reckoning with Company Unions: The Case of Thompson Products, 1934–1964," paper read at "Perspectives on American Labor."

32. Steven Fraser, "Sidney Hillman: Labor's Machiavelli," in Dubofsky and Van Tine, *Labor Leaders*, 207–33; idem, "From the 'New Unionism' to the New Deal"; Christopher L. Tomlins, *The State and the Unions: Labor Relations, Law, and the Organized Labor Movement in America, 1880–1960* (New York: Cambridge University Press, 1985), chaps. 4–5; Brody, *Workers,* chaps. 3–4; Bernstein, *Turbulent Years,* chaps. 7, 10–13; Sidney Fine, *Sit-Down: The General Motors Strike of 1936–37* (Ann Arbor: University of Michigan Press, 1969); Dubofsky and Van Tine, *John L. Lewis,* chaps. 11–12, 14.

33. Arthur M. Schlesinger Jr., *The Politics of Upheaval* (Boston: Houghton Mifflin, 1960), 325–44; Mark H. Leff, *Limits of Symbolic Reform: The New Deal and Taxation, 1933–1939* (Cambridge: Cambridge University Press, 1984).

34. William E. Leuchtenberg, *Franklin D Roosevelt and the New Deal, 1932–1940* (New York: Harper and Row, 1963), 244–50.

35. John Morton Blum, *V Was for Victory: Politics and American Culture during World War II* (New York: Harcourt Brace Jovanovich, 1976), chap. 3; Nelson Lichtenstein, *Labor's War at Home: The CIO in World War II* (New York: Cambridge University Press, 1982), chaps. 4–5, 8–11; idem, "From Corporatism to Collective Bargaining: Organized Labor and the Eclipse of Social Democracy in the Postwar Era," paper read at "Historical Perspectives on American Labor"; Patrick Renshaw, "Organized Labour and the United States War Economy, 1939–1945," *Journal of Contemporary History* 21 (1986): 3–22.

36. Thomas A. Kochan, Harry C. Katz, and Robert B. McKersie, *The Transformation of American Industrial Relations* (New York: Basic Books, 1986). See also Charles Sabel, *Work and Politics: The Division of Labor in Industry* (New York: Cambridge University Press, 1982), 209–19, for a brief analysis of contemporary Neo-Fordism.

· 10 ·

If All the World Were Paterson: Herbert Gutman, the American Working Class, and the Future of Labor History

SOME years ago, Sam Bass Warner titled an essay that he wrote (and later published in the *Journal of American History*) "If All the World Were Philadelphia," suggesting that the history of Philadelphia over two centuries could be used as a model for understanding the development of all of urban America and, indeed, much of U.S. history. In this essay, I also want to do something much like that, taking the city of Paterson, New Jersey, and using it and its history as a way to understand better the contributions of Herbert Gutman to the profession of history (in the dual sense: as a career and also as professing beliefs or a faith to a broader audience) and to consider what Paterson can teach us about the larger themes of U.S. and even world history. In addition, I want to suggest several new directions toward which labor historians should direct their attention today and in the future.

Like me, Gutman came to write labor history and to become a labor historian by a circuitous path.[1] By the time the two of us (as well as David Brody and David Montgomery) began seriously to do history in a different vein, the field of labor history, as a subdiscipline of a new and broader approach to the past that would be labeled "social history," had been born. The impulse, to be sure, was not exclusively indigenous. E. P. Thompson's pathbreaking *The Making of the English Working Class* defined the field of labor history for a new generation in Britain and many of its peers on the Continent and in the United States. Gutman, Brody, Montgomery, and I were already researching, teaching, or writing labor history before Thompson burst on the scene, but his book helped legitimate our "history" as a valid scholarly enterprise.

As labor history became accepted and established in departments of history, its first-generation practitioners, Gutman most notably, sought to revise the approach to the field pioneered by the Wisconsin school associated most closely with John R. Commons and Selig Perlman. In his famous article on "Work, Culture, and Society in Industrializing America," published in the *American Historical Review* in 1973, Gutman, for example, directly challenged Commons and Perlman, and he condemned their scholarship for its narrow focus on formal institutions and unionized workers. (Brody had done the same even earlier in his 1960 book *Steelworkers in the Nonunion Era* and, in the process, provoked considerable criticism of his new history). The critique of the Wisconsin school in which I shared was probably part of a generational process in which younger scholars systematically revise the scholarship of their intellectual parents. As we aged and matured, however, and those we might today characterize as the academic grandchildren, the third generation of labor historians, came of age, we developed a new and firmer appreciation of the debt that we owed collectively to our pioneering parents in Madison: Commons, Perlman, and Philip Taft. And I must include the women in the group (which is why I used "parents" in preference to "fathers"): Helen Sumner and Elizabeth Brandeis.[2]

During the quarter of a century in which Herbert Gutman led the way in refashioning both our understanding of the American past and how we actually write history, his interests, approaches, and beliefs caused him to weave the American past into an increasingly complex fabric, one in which the different colors and patterns imperceptibly shaded into each other.[3] Yet several strands in Gutman's fabric of history remained distinct, clearly shaped the larger pattern, and were woven from raw materials provided by the history of Paterson, New Jersey.

What were the aspects of Gutman's history that remained constant over time? And what part did Paterson play in their formulation? First, Gutman's commitment to restoring ordinary people—working men and women, enslaved and emancipated African Americans, and immigrants from around the globe—to their rightful place in the narrative of the American past never flagged. Not only did he write such common people into his history, but he also endowed them with agency. Toward the end of his life, Gutman cited Jean-Paul Sartre to insist that the central historical narrative must be "not what 'one' has done to man, but what man does with what 'one' has done to him." Or, in Gutman's own words: "Studying the choices working men and women made and how their behavior affected important historical processes enlarges our understanding of 'the condition of being human.'"[4] Second, Gutman sought to reconceptualize how we periodized the past, to shift the focus of the historian's lens away from presidential elections and administrations, foreign and civil wars, away from such periods as the Age of Jackson, the American Civil War and Reconstruction, the Age of Roosevelt I and II. Instead, he pushed us toward longer-term trends and processes, toward a long nineteenth century that ran from 1815 to 1919, a period in which the American working class periodically refashioned itself and its culture. If Gutman never succeeded, if he never even tried to write a Braudelian history of the *longue durée*—one that focused on structures and conjunctures rather than events—he did create an American history of what might be called the *demi-longue durée,* a history that banished such staples of the traditional narrative as presidential elections and wars from the text and replaced them with descriptions of how longer-term historical processes composed and recomposed the working classes. He also wrote a different sort of history of events, again turning away from such staples of labor history as the Haymarket Riot, the Homestead Lockout, or the Pullman Boycott. He examined instead theretofore obscure conflicts in isolated mining communities and smaller industrial cities, neglected historical events that, in Gutman's skilled hands, illuminated the most salient features of American society and culture in the late nineteenth century. Third, Gutman sensitized us to the remarkable variety and variability of American working-class history, observing in one of his last published essays, written jointly with Ira Berlin, how in only one generation, between 1850 and the 1880s, the descendants of the original American proletariat had nearly vanished from the working class, replaced by immigrants and their children.[5]

The history of Paterson provided Gutman with much of the materials and evidence that he needed to write a revised history of the United States; and, at one time, he even planned to write a history of that industrial city that would encapsulate all the central themes alluded to above.[6] For in Paterson, historians could clearly see, as Gutman demonstrated in a number of essays and articles, the persistent recomposition of the working classes over the *longue durée.*

The long nineteenth century begins with Alexander Hamilton's eighteenth-century conception of the site at the falls of the Passaic River as a place that would provide the power for textile mills that would employ the surplus labor of redundant and dependent American-born women and children, plus a handful of skilled men. It then moves to mid-nineteenth-century Paterson, a major site for the production of steam locomotives and small machine tools built by a labor force consisting largely of skilled, American-born, German-born, and British-born mechanics.[7] There is a jump ahead another couple of decades to a Paterson fast becoming the silk capital of the United States and using the labor of newer immigrant German and English workers as well as others from France and Switzerland.[8] One can then examine the silk capital that Paterson became at the turn of the twentieth century, its labor force composed increasingly of new immigrants from Italy, Poland, and other peripheral regions of the world economy.[9] Finally, the *longue durée* would conclude with an examination of Paterson today, a city whose old mills and machine shops have been razed, shuttered, or converted to museums, a city whose working classes have become increasingly nonwhite and composed in the main of yet another contingent of new immigrants and their children.[10]

The fact that the development of Paterson encapsulated for Gutman all the primary structures, processes, and tendencies at work in the creation of an industrial society in the United States led him to draw on his studies of peoples and events in that city to create a revisionary narrative of the Gilded Age. In one of three essays on Paterson history that form the keystone middle section of his collection *Work, Culture, and Society,* Gutman laid out clearly what became his singular view of the late nineteenth century: (1) the values of the new industrialists did *not* easily and quickly replace "older patterns of thought and social ties" that drew Patersonians together across the boundaries of class, status, and wealth; (2) the city's American-born and immigrant working people, skilled and unskilled alike, maintained thriving "vital subcultures" that placed them at odds with the culture of the new industrialism; (3) such working-class subcultures endowed cities like Paterson with a particular social structure and a special quality of life; (4) urban politics throbbed to the beat of these vital subcultures, and the working-class presence made itself felt through the mediation of political machines whose leaders were sensitive to the values and needs of their constituents.[11]

If Gutman revised our perceptions of the past, he nevertheless did so in the most traditional of historical manners. In our current postmodernist age—in which texts transform themselves miraculously before our eyes and in the minds of readers as well as authors, where meanings dissolve as rapidly as they form, where the signified and the signifier merge, and history appears as much fiction as fact—Gutman's texts seem remarkably traditional, even conventional. Some of his earlier essays, which remained unpublished until Berlin brought them together in print for the first time in *Power and Culture,* overwhelm the reader with details, piling fact on fact in an almost monomaniacal effort to recreate "the past as it actually was." How many historians would devote nearly 100 pages of text to the story of coal miners in the village of Braidwood, Illinois, suggesting implicitly, if not explicitly, that through such methods the facts (if one amasses enough of them) speak for themselves?[12]

However traditional or conventional Gutman's historical methods, he examined neglected aspects of the past and cast his findings in fresh ways. Not only was the study of working people rare among academic historians (in the 1950s, labor history remained a subject taught mostly in economics departments and industrial relations schools), but research into the lives of nonunion workers, the vast majority of all American workers, was rarer still. But Gutman scorned the conventional topics of labor history: trade unions, labor leaders, and great strikes. Instead, he sought to study the experiences of "forgotten people" and to demonstrate that they too had a past worth knowing and respecting.

As Gutman studied the past through assiduous reading in local newspapers, state labor reports, and labor journals, he recreated a world of quotidian experience. He proved that the history of ordinary people and everyday life (*alltagsgeschichte*) could be written, that the common people were not inarticulate, and that some of them could indeed be grandiloquent in their expressions. His early essays, through their fine-grained detail, restored hitherto invisible people to the stage of history. It is quite remarkable how in reading Gutman's essays, originally conceived in the late 1950s and written in the early and mid-1960s, today's reader sees women, nonwhites, and "new" immigrants as key participants in American history. Gutman wrote multicultural history before multiculturalism became for some a slogan or a cliché and for others fighting words. Well before he condemned the balkanization of labor and social history in the introduction to his first collection of essays published in 1976 and in an essay published five years later in the *Nation* called for a new synthesis in American history, Gutman proved that the history of women, of African Americans, and of immigrants could not be divorced from the history of labor; nor could the latter be separated from the national narrative. Just as he demonstrated how free workers partly made their own history, Gutman also disclosed in sometimes excruciating detail how black slaves made something of *their own* out of what their masters did to them. Gutman never ceased to give people, however subordinated or unfree, a voice and life of their own. And it was his piling up of detail on detail, his amassing of evidence, that convinced readers that the past was fact, not fiction, and that ordinary people were a vital part of that real past. That, in a nutshell, was Gutman's greatest contribution to scholarship.

When he tried to fit his data into a frame built from the theories of sociologists and anthropologists, especially Sidney Mintz and Eric Wolfe, Gutman proved less sure and subtle in his recreation of the past. In his most famous single essay on the working class, "Work, Culture, and Society," and also in more obscure ones, including several on Paterson, Gutman adopted a crude modernization model to explain how the (sub)culture (the resource) of workers enabled them either to adapt to or resist the demands of industrial society (the arena).[13] In that essay and elsewhere, Gutman suggested that the most decisive and violent moments in American labor history occurred when people new to industrial society first experienced the discipline of waged labor. People with traditional ways of life, drawn first from the farms of the New World—as was the case, for example, of the Lowell mill girls—later from the depopulated countrysides of Ireland and Germany, afterward from the southern and eastern periphery of Europe, and finally from the American "black belt," the Caribbean, and Mexico, recurrently rebelled, in Gutman's telling of the narrative, against the demands of an industrial society. In his narrative, the United States, unlike other industrial societies, remained irremediably violent because in every generation a new group of traditional, "preindustrial" people struggled to acculturate themselves to a society that valued timed activity, disciplined labor, and individual acquisitiveness. By implication, as such people grew more accustomed to the values and routines of a new regime, they adapted, modernized, and behaved in a more orderly fashion.

Although Gutman himself never explicitly drew such a conclusion, readers of his essays might easily have concluded that labor-capital conflict, rather than being intrinsic to industrial society, was merely a passing phase in the process of initial proletarianization. Gutman's unspoken debt to modernization theory and his tendency to polarize, or dichotomize, his subjects' subcultures and cultures into preindustrial and industrial varieties lent itself to just such an interpretation.[14]

In his eagerness to revise the past, Gutman went astray in other directions as well, especially in one of his early essays on the "rags to riches" myth as it revealed itself in the history of Paterson. Himself an astute critic of econometricians and quantifiers who misused their data or carelessly interpreted hard numbers, Gutman fell prey to a similar tendency in asserting that, in mid-nineteenth-century Paterson, "so many successful manufacturers who had begun as workers walked the streets of the city that it is not hard to believe that others less successful or just starting out on the lower rungs of the occupational mobility ladder could be convinced by personal knowledge that 'hard work' resulted in spectacular material and social improvement."[15]

Gutman may be correct about the social and economic origins of his Paterson metal trades' entrepreneurs—though it must be stressed that, as a group, they were overwhelmingly English-speaking, Protestant, and highly skilled sorts, men who scarcely experienced ragged lives—but he chose his sample from the wrong population universe. Instead of examining the whole population of skilled workers, or a random sample, or a scientific sample at one point in time and then estimating what proportion of them rose from respectability to riches, Gutman selected a small group of successful Paterson manufacturers and analyzed their origins. Although a solid majority of his industrialists may have risen from the machinist's bench to manage their own firms, the vast majority of their cohort of skilled mechanics and the even larger number of their less skilled contemporaries probably led obscure, unsuccessful, and penurious lives. If, as Gutman suggests, Paterson's industrialists "served as model, day-to-day evidence" about the reality of the rags-to-riches aspirations, readers of his other essays perforce must ask themselves why working people and their community allies should question the culture and the values of the new industrialists (their own kind) or, as Joseph P. McDonnell did in Paterson, build a movement based on collective action and class solidarity.[16]

Instead of using the evidence he drew from Paterson and other mid-sized industrial cities to write a history of the United States in the late nineteenth century as a narrative of the clash between two cultures, between two ways of life—one traditional, collective, and sharing; the other modern, individualistic, and acquisitive—Gutman might have used his own data to tell a slightly different and more complex story. (The brief think pieces and later essays collected in *Power and Culture* suggest that Gutman was in the process of doing precisely that.) Take, for example, his skilled mechanics, who rose from respectability to riches in Paterson, or McDonnell, who built an oppositional working-class movement in the city. Their respective values and behavioral patterns, individualistic and acquisitive in one case, collective and solidaristic in the other, did not simply arise from a clash in the New World between the traditional and the modern, between the preindustrial and the industrial. Gutman's English-speaking, immigrant entrepreneurs and radicals carried their cultures across the Atlantic, bringing with them British traditions of individual self-improvement (if America had Horatio Alger, the British had Samuel Smiles), Owenite socialism, and Chartism.

Subsequent generations of immigrants to Paterson and industrial America also brought with them experiences and cultures that were as much modern as traditional, as industrial as they were preindustrial. The history of Paterson in the late nineteenth century in particular shows a city whose economy and development were thoroughly embedded in what Immanuel Wallerstein and his colleagues at the Fernand Braudel Center have characterized as the "capitalist world-system." When Paterson became the silk center of the United States, much of the industry's investment capital came from Europe, from industrialists in France, Germany, Switzerland, and northern Italy, who were fleeing labor protest, rising production costs, and intensely competitive markets at home for cheaper labor and expanding markets abroad. And with capital came labor, as first British and then German, French, Swiss, and Italian silk and textile workers crossed the Atlantic to work in Paterson's silk mills.

A world economy created a global labor market and an international working class. The immigrants who came to Paterson at the end of the nineteenth century and the beginning of the twentieth century already had experienced in their lands of origin much that was new and carried with them modern as well as traditional cultural baggage.[17]

We cannot fault Gutman unfairly for insufficient awareness of the complex cultures that immigrants carried with them to the New World. At the time that Gutman published his pioneering essays, the dominant scholarly tradition in the United States treated the so-called "new" immigrants of the era 1881–1921, as well as their Irish predecessors, as uprooted peasants unfamiliar with disciplined waged labor and urban life. Thrust into an alien world of industry and cities, the newcomers grew disoriented, lacked the cultural resources to adapt successfully to new societies, and suffered from family, personal, and generational breakdowns, resulting in what the dominant Chicago school of urban sociology characterized as anomie. Oscar Handlin turned this portrait of first-generation immigrant life into his Pulitzer Prize–winning narrative *The Uprooted*.

Dissatisfied with the conventional portrait of immigrant life in industrial America, Gutman revised it with a vengeance. His immigrants, like Handlin's, remained primarily a rural peasantry, but they were not uprooted, anomic individuals unable to adapt to urban industrialism. Instead, Gutman's immigrants used traditional preindustrial cultures to sustain strong families and to nourish effective resistance to their exploiters.[18] A slew of young scholars, some themselves trained by Gutman, added to his portrait of immigrant workers in the United States as builders of strong families that sustained traditional values across generations.

Perhaps we might even claim that Gutman's stress on the immigrants' ability to act in their own right and on their own behalf, to be subjects as well as objects of history, to serve as agents of change rather than as victims of industrialism, cleared away enough intellectual detritus to enable other scholars to paint fuller portraits of immigrant workers as historical actors. Today, we know, as Gutman was just beginning to recognize, that the Europe the immigrants departed from, whether the south of Italy, the Austro-Hungarian Empire, or the czarist Empire, was not a world in stasis. Everywhere, starting first in the west and north of Europe as early as the fifteenth century and then moving steadily south and east, what is today known as "protoindustrialization" transformed rural societies. Waged labor was not an unknown condition among peasants, who often sold their labor power (usually by the piece) to capitalist masters to sustain a traditional way of life. Not only did peasants sell their labor, through the putting-out or domestic system, by working in their own cottages; many adult male peasants and their children migrated, seasonally and permanently, to cities to work for wages. Warsaw and Lodz in Poland; Vienna, Budapest, Prague, and Linz in Austria-Hungary; and Moscow, St. Petersburg, Vilna, and Kiev in czarist Russia were as much immigrant/migrant cities as Paterson, Pittsburgh, or Cleveland (for example, at the end of the nineteenth century, Vienna was overwhelmingly non-German-Austrian in its population, especially at the bottom of the economic ladder).

Whether at home in their rural cottages or at work in the mills of Lodz—or those of Paterson—these people were part-peasants and part-proletarians, one foot deeply embedded in a new world of waged labor in which the more intensive (both in time and speed) the work, the greater the reward, which provided the material resources for the other foot to embed itself as thoroughly in the old milieu of subsistence agriculture that was increasingly linked to local, regional, and world markets. Today we also realize, as Gutman perhaps did not, that immigrant workers had no quarrel with industrialism and disciplined waged labor when jobs were plentiful, the hours of work abundant, and wages relatively high; to labor productively and steadily was why they crossed the Atlantic to the New

World, where they could earn the wages needed to sustain the families many left behind in a more customary way of life in the Old World.[19]

Today, when we picture migrant workers, we may think of Chicanos, Mexicans, or Haitians following crop harvesting cycles up and down our eastern and western coasts. Their predecessors of a century and less ago we deem immigrants. In their own time, however, those we portray as immigrants followed lives of migrant labor. They crossed European frontiers or deserted the countryside for the city as employment opportunities rose and fell in harmony with shifts in the economic geography of the labor market. Migration across an ocean to the United States—or Argentina, Brazil, or Chile—was merely a larger step in an otherwise common journey around international labor markets.

Perhaps we should reconsider the meaning of this essay's title, "If All the World Were Paterson." Once upon a time some two centuries ago, Alexander Hamilton planned for Paterson to be a seed from which the United States would blossom into a mighty industrial nation; and a century later, entrepreneurs first in the metal trades and later in the silk industry transformed the city into a beehive of industrial productivity, a place that drew to it workers from around the world. As Paterson grew and prospered in an earlier version of the capitalist world economy, it celebrated its own multinational textile enterprises made productive and profitable by a working class that was international in its origins and beliefs. Yet, as we look at Paterson today and recall its more recent history (say, since the 1920s), we necessarily must reflect that the capitalist world economy destroyed as it created, provided work for hungry job seekers yesterday only to reject their descendants today, and established prosperity in some places only to remove it in others. What the economist Joseph Schumpeter characterized as capitalism's gale of "creative destruction" left behind in Paterson, and in many of the other nineteenth-century industrial cities that Gutman studied, a wake of destruction.

Despite the acuity and accuracy of many of the charges that Nick Salvatore has leveled against Gutman's scholarship—especially the assertion that Gutman allowed politics and ideology to shape his findings—it remains proper to commemorate Gutman's contributions to revising our national historical narrative by his placing at its center ordinary men and women in all their "multicultural" diversity. Gutman engaged in a masterful deconstruction of the dominant narrative our generation of historians had inherited. If our generation and its successors have not yet succeeded in constructing a new core narrative as powerful as the one Gutman demolished, he and we have nevertheless bequeathed to future generations a history that is far fuller, fairer, and truer to the past than the version it replaced. And when that new narrative is written, the history of Paterson can serve as a wonderful example of how over two centuries a modern world economy linked the fate of Paterson and its residents to structures, forces, peoples, and events elsewhere on the globe. From the middle of the nineteenth century to the present, Paterson has mixed the national and the international, the traditional and the modern, industrialization and deindustrialization into an ever-changing historical kaleidoscope. In truth, Gutman found in Paterson a perfect laboratory in which to test his theories of history.

What does that laboratory suggest about the way in which labor historians in the United States should approach their subject in the future? First, it demands that we embed the story of American workers in a larger world economy that set both capital and workers in motion. The immigrants who became the dominant core of the working class in the United States by early in the twentieth century did not arrive on North American shores as innocent babes in an unfamiliar capitalist or industrial economy. Industrial capitalism had already unloosed the forces that impelled millions of ordinary people in Europe and Asia, and later in Latin America and Africa, to migrate first within the lands of their birth and then to cross national borders and oceans in search of work, wages, and opportunities. We need to know much more about the lives of these people before they landed on the shores of the United States, to carry on the sort of research that Josef Barton did many years ago, that Rudolph Vecoli, Patrizia Sione and Donna Gabaccia, among others, are doing more recently, and that Dirk Hoerder is attempting on a global scale.[20] It is no longer adequate to view working-class activity in the nineteenth-century United States, and sometimes even later, through the lens of an artisanal radical republicanism that had its roots in the revolutionary generation and language of Tom Paine. Not when so large a proportion of the working class in the United States, artisans and journeymen included, shared at best an attenuated relationship to the republicanism of the "American Revolution." Not when the ideas and organizations promoted by artisans in the United States bore such a striking resemblance to that of their counterparts in Britain, France, and Germany.[21] And especially not when republicanism could and did lead many working people to extol values and forms of behavior more associated with individualism, acquisitiveness, and a desire to rise above one's class rather than collectivism, altruism, and class solidarity. Gutman taught us that we must pay heed to the vast majority of working people who never belonged to trade unions or other formal institutions built by the militant minority of workers.

In equal measure, however, and unlike Gutman, it is past time to give serious attention to those working people who neither joined unions, nor radical political organizations, nor resisted their employers but instead shared a belief in an "American way of life" that promised all the chance to rise in a land of opportunity. We need labor historians who are as sensitive to the minds and values of the working people who labored in Sandy Jacoby's "Modern Manors" as Jacoby is to the employers and corporate managers who created what the socialist William J. Ghent once characterized as a "benevolent feudalism."[22] Even more, we need scholars who are as attentive to the mass of workers, male and female, who proved more loyal to their churches or religious faiths than to their unions or class. Labor history needs its own Robert Orsis and John McGreevys.[23] Blue-collar Nixon, Reagan, or even Gingrich Republicans are no recent phenomenon, nor are such people the victims of a false consciousness. To express what I am saying another way, we need historians who are sensitive not only to the diversity—ethnic, racial, gender, and sexual—of working people in the United States but also to their multiple forms of belief and behavior, religious, cultural, and political. After all, Merle Haggard, Patsy Cline, and Bob Dylan sing to working people in a different voice than Pete Seeger, Woody Guthrie, and Billy Bragg—or, for that matter, Robert Johnson, Howlin' Wolf, and Bessie Smith.

An even more formidable subject awaits future historians of labor in the United States, and that is how to imbricate the story of American workers in all its diversity within the development of the modern world economy, how to turn what Aristide Zolberg has called a tale of "many exceptionalisms" into a narrative of shared experiences that link working people across national borders and regions of the globe.[24] More than ever, we need a labor history that is common as well as diverse, global as well as national. Such an agenda should keep historians busy for far longer than the field of labor history has existed as a subfield within our larger academic discipline.

Notes

1. In reading all the memorials to Gutman that appeared in scholarly journals after his death, I find no clear sense or decisive turning point when Gutman defined

himself as a labor historian (as distinct from being a more traditional sort of scholar of the American past). True, he chose what were then nontraditional or unconventional subjects for his attention, as did I; yet, as his entire scholarly career attests, he intended to use such subjects to illuminate the broader themes of U.S history, and he persistently objected to what he defined as the balkanization or microspecialization of scholarly fields. See especially *Labor History* 29 (Summer 1988), a special volume devoted solely to Gutman and his scholarship, and *Radical History Review* 34 (1986): 107–12.

2. For Gutman's shifting and more positive estimation of the contributions of the Wisconsin school, see Ira Berlin, "Introduction: Herbert G. Gutman and the American Working Class," in Herbert G. Gutman, *Power and Culture: Essays on the American Working Class,* ed. Ira Berlin (New York: Pantheon, 1987), 3–69. Cf. Leon Fink, "John R. Commons, Herbert Gutman, and the Burden of Labor History," *Labor History* 29 (Summer 1988): 313–22; idem, "A Memoir of Selig Perlman and his Life at the University of Wisconsin: Based on an Interview of Mark Perlman," *Labor History* 32 (Fall 1991): 503–25; idem, "'Intellectuals' versus 'Workers': Academic Requirements and the Creation of Labor History," *American Historical Review* 96 (Apr. 1991): 395–421. Cf. also Melvyn Dubofsky, "Give Us That Old-Time Labor History: Philip S. Foner and the American Worker," *Labor History* 26 (Winter 1985): 118–37, and David Brody's 1992 presidential address to the Pacific Coast Branch of the American Historical Association, "Reconciling the Old Labor History and the New," *Pacific Historical Review* 62 (Feb. 1993): 1–18.

3. For how Gutman changed as a scholar and how he steadily revised his early, less mature forays into the writing of history, see Ira Berlin, "Introduction: Herbert G. Gutman and the American Working Class"; more especially, see Michael Merrill, "Interview with Gutman," in Gutman, *Power and Culture,* 329–56.

4. Gutman, *Power and Culture,* 326.

5. Ibid., chap. 11. For a more critical perspective on Gutman's work, one that suggests that his early essays lacked historical dimension, misinterpreted the events that they described, and lacked a solid basis in the sources, see Nick Salvatore, "Herbert Gutman's Narrative of the American Working Class: A Reevaluation," *International Journal of Politics, Culture and Society* 12 (1998): 43–80.

6. Gutman, *Power and Culture,* 32–33.

7. This Paterson is described in Herbert Gutman, *Work, Culture, and Society in Industrializing America* (New York: Knopf, 1976), chap. 4.

8. Gutman, *Power and Culture,* 256–57.

9. Patrizia Sione, "Industrial Work, Militancy, and Migrations of Northern Italian Textile Workers in Europe and in the United States, 1880–1902" (Ph.D. diss., State University of New York at Binghamton, 1992).

10. Christopher Norwood, *About Paterson: The Making and Unmaking of an American City* (New York: Harper and Row, 1975).

11. Herbert Gutman, "A Brief Postscript: Class, Status, and the Gilded Age Radical—A Reconsideration," in *Work, Culture, and Society,* 272. A slightly revised version of this essay, one that does not alter its original interpretation, is "Joseph P. McDonnell and the Workers' Struggle in Paterson, New Jersey," in Gutman, *Power and Culture,* 93–116. Gutman's work on Paterson (though not yet in print)

and the interpretations he drew from it concerning the character and content of life in the Gilded Age preceded the publication of the essay that first brought his reinterpretation of the history of the late nineteenth century to wide attention. See Gutman, "The Workers' Search for Power: Labor in the Gilded Age," in *The Gilded Age: A Reappraisal,* ed. H. Wayne Morgan (Syracuse, N.Y.: Syracuse University Press, 1963), 38–68. See also Salvatore, "Herbert Gutman's Narrative of the American Working Class," for a sharp criticism of the interpretations expounded in Gutman's essays on Paterson.

12. Herbert Gutman, "Labor in the Land of Lincoln: Coal Miners on the Prairie," in *Power and Culture,* 117–212.

13. Gutman borrowed the notion of culture as a resource and society as an arena from the work of Sidney Mintz and Eric Wolfe.

14. The resemblance between Gutman's description of industrial conflict and violence in U.S. history as most intense during the period of initial proletarianization and that of the dominant industrial relations school of the 1950s and 1960s, in which the major names were Clark Kerr, John Dunlop, Charles Myers, Walter Galenson, and Lloyd Ulman, is too close to ignore. See, for example, Clark Kerr, ed., *Labor and Management in Industrial Society* (Garden City, N.Y.: Doubleday, 1964).

15. Herbert Gutman, "The Reality of the Rags-to-Riches 'Myth': Paterson, New Jersey, Locomotive, Iron, and Machinery Manufacturers, 1830–1880," in *Work, Culture, and Society,* 211–33 (the quotation is on p. 232).

16. Ibid., 225.

17. For the global economy of silk and the creation of a labor market that encompassed much of Western Europe and the Americas, see Sione, "Industrial Work, Militancy, and Migrations of Northern Italian Textile Workers." For the reality of an international working class, see Donna Gabaccia, "An International Proletariat? Italian Labor Migration and Worker Internationalism, 1870–1914," paper read at the Fourteenth Annual North American Labor History Conference, Wayne State University, Detroit, Michigan, October 1992.

18. On these points, see Herbert Gutman, "A Note on Immigration History, 'Breakdown Models,' and the Rewriting of the History of Immigrant Working-Class Peoples," in Gutman, *Power and Culture,* 255–59.

19. Three decades ago, David Brody made just that observation about the immigrant laborers who filled the unskilled jobs in the steel industry. See Brody, *Steelworkers in America: The Nonunion Era* (1960; rpt., Urbana: University of Illinois Press, 1998), chap. 5. Cf. also Sione, "Industrial Work, Militancy, and Migrations of Northern Italian Textile Workers"; Gabaccia, "International Proletariat?"; and Rudolph J. Vecoli and Suzanne M. Sinke, eds., *A Century of European Migrations, 1830–1930* (Urbana: University of Illinois Press, 1991). In the latter, see especially Vecoli, "Introduction," 1–14; Frank Thistlethwaite, "Migrations from Europe Overseas in the Nineteenth and Twentieth Centuries," 17–57; and Dirk Hoerder, "International Labor Markets and Community Building by Migrant Workers in the Atlantic Economies," 78–107. Daniel T. Rodgers ventured a similar critique of Gutman's portrait of immigrant workers in 1977. See Rodgers, "Tradition, Modernity, and the American Industrial Worker: Reflections and Critique," *Journal of Interdisciplinary History* 7 (Spring 1977): 665–73.

20. Among other works, see the following: Josef J. Barton, *Peasants and Strangers: Italians, Rumanians, and Slovaks in an American City, 1890–1950* (Cambridge, Mass.: Harvard University Press, 1975); Vecoli and Sinke, *Century of European Migrations;* Donna Gabaccia, *Militants and Migrants: Rural Sicilians Become American Workers* (New Brunswick, N.J.: Rutgers University Press, 1988); Dirk Hoerder, *Labor Migration in the Atlantic Economies: The European and North American Working Classes during the Period of Industrialization* (Westport, Conn.: Greenwood Press, 1996); idem, *European Migrants: Global and Local Perspectives* (Boston: Northeastern University Press, 1996); and *People in Transit: German Migrations in Comparative Perspective, 1820–1930,* ed. Dirk Hoerder and Jörg Nagler (Cambridge: Cambridge University Press, 1995); Jan Lucassen, *Migrant Labour in Europe: The Drift to the North Sea* (London: Croom Helm, 1987); *Migration, Migration History, History: Old Paradigms and New Perspectives,* ed. Jan Lucassen and Leon Lucassen (Bern, Switzerland: Peter Lang, 1997); *Peasant Maids, City Women: From the European Countryside to Urban America,* ed. Christiane Harzig (Ithaca, N.Y.: Cornell University Press, 1997); and Patrizia Sione, "Patterns of International Migrations: Italian Silk Workers in New Jersey, USA," *Review: A Journal of the Fernand Braudel Center* 17 (Fall 1994): 555–76.

21. See the essays on artisans in France and Germany in *Working-Class Formation: Nineteenth-Century Patterns in Western Europe and the United States,* ed. Ira Katznelson and Aristide R. Zolberg (Princeton, N.J.: Princeton University Press, 1986). They include: William H. Sewell Jr., "Artisans, Factory Workers, and the Formation of the French Working Class, 1789–1848," 45–70; Michelle Perrot, "On the Formation of the French Working Class," 71–110; Alain Cottereau, "The Distinctiveness of Working-Class Cultures in France, 1848–1900," 111–54; and Jürgen Kocka, "Problems of Working-Class Formation in Germany: The Early Years, 1800–1875," 279–351.

22. Sanford Jacoby, *Modern Manors* (Princeton, N.J.: Princeton University Press, 1997).

23. See especially Robert Orsi, *The Madonna of 115th Street: Faith and Community in Italian Harlem, 1880–1950* (New Haven, Conn.: Yale University Press, 1985); idem, *Thank You, St. Jude: Women's Devotion to the Patron Saint of Hopeless Causes* (New Haven, Conn.: Yale University Press, 1996); John T. McGreevy, *Parish Boundaries: The Catholic Encounter with Race in the Twentieth-Century Urban North* (Chicago: University of Chicago Press, 1996).

24. Aristide Zolberg, "How Many Exceptionalisms?" in Katznelson and Zolberg, *Working-Class Formation,* 397–455.

SELECTED PUBLICATIONS

Books

When Workers Organize: New York City in the Progressive Era. Amherst: University of Massachusetts Press, 1968.

We Shall Be All: A History of the Industrial Workers of the World. Chicago: Quadrangle Books, 1969; reissued with a new preface, 1974; 2d ed., with a new bibliographic essay, Urbana: University of Illinois Press, 1988.

American Labor since the New Deal (ed.). Chicago: Quadrangle Books, 1971.

Industrialism and the American Worker, 1865–1920. New York: T. Y. Crowell, 1975; 2d ed., Arlington Heights, Ill.: Harlan Davidson, 1985; 3d ed., Wheeling, Ill.: Harlan Davidson, 1996.

John L. Lewis: A Biography (with Warren W. Van Tine) New York: Quadrangle/ New York Times Book Co., 1977.

The United States in the Twentieth Century (with Daniel Smith and Athan Theoharis). Englewood Cliffs, N.J.: Prentice-Hall, Inc. 1978.

Imperial Democracy: The United States since 1945 (with Athan Theoharis). Englewood Cliffs, N.J.: Prentice-Hall, 1983.

Labor in America. 4th ed., Arlington Heights, Ill.: Harlan Davidson, 1984; 5th ed., Arlington Heights, Ill.: Harlan Davidson, 1993; 6th ed., Arlington Heights, Ill.: Harland Davidson, 1999. (First through third editions prepared by F. R. Dulles.)

Workers and Technological Change (ed.). Beverly Hills, Calif.: Sage Publications, 1985.

John L. Lewis: A Biography (with Warren Van Tine). Abridged ed. Urbana: University of Illinois Press, 1986.

Labor Leaders in America (with Warren Van Tine). Urbana: University of Illinois Press, 1987.

"Big Bill" Haywood. Manchester, U.K.: University of Manchester Press, 1987; New York: St. Martin's Press, 1987.

The Great Depression and the New Deal (ed. with Stephen Burwood). 7 vols. New York: Garland Publishing, 1990.

The New Deal: Conflicting Interpretations and Shifting Perspectives (ed.). New York: Garland Publishing, 1992.

The State and Labor in Modern America. Chapel Hill: University of North Carolina Press, 1994.

Labor Unrest in the World Economy, 1870–1990 (ed. with G. Arrighi and B. Silver). Special issue of *Review* 18 (Winter 1995).

Articles and Book Chapters

"Organized Labor and the Immigrant in New York City, 1900–1918." *Labor History* 2 (Spring 1961): 182–201.

"Organized Labor in New York City and the First World War, 1914–1918." *New York History* 42 (October 1961): 380–400.

"The Leadville Strike of 1896–1897: A Reappraisal." *Mid-America* 48 (April 1966): 99–118.

"The Origins of Western Working-Class Radicalism, 1890–1905." *Labor History* 7 (Spring 1966): 131–54. Reprinted in several anthologies, including *The Labor History Reader*, ed. Daniel J. Leab (Urbana: University of Illinois Press, 1985), 230–53.

"James H. Hawley and the Origins of the Haywood Case, 1892–1899." *Pacific Northwest Quarterly* 58 (January 1967): 22–30.

"Success and Failure of Socialism in New York City, 1900–1918: A Case Study." *Labor History* 10 (Fall 1968): 361–75.

"The Radicalism of the Dispossessed: William D. Haywood and the IWW." In *Dissent: Explorations in the History of American Radicalism.* Ed. A. F. Young. DeKalb: Northern Illinois University Press, 1968. 177–213.

"Introduction." In *Industrial Pioneer.* New York: Greenwood Reprint, 1968.

"Daniel Webster and the Whig Theory of Economic Growth, 1828–1848." *New England Quarterly* 42 (December 1969): 551–72.

"The Radical Goad." *The Nation,* September 4, 1969, 218–21.

"Dreams Deferred, Promises Betrayed," *The Nation,* April 13, 1970, 438–40.

"The I.W.W.: An Exchange." *Labor History* 11 (Summer 1970): 364–72.

"Introduction." In *The Agitator/The Syndicalist.* New York: Greenwood Reprint, 1970.

"Introduction." In *The Industrial Union Bulletin.* New York: Greenwood Reprint, 1970.

"Introduction." In *Industrial Worker.* New York: Greenwood Reprint, 1970.

"American Trade Union Ideology: Radical Wing." In *Transactions of the Biennial Meeting, 1972.* Madison, Wis.: Conference Group for Social and Administrative History, 1972. 46–55.

"Italian Anarchism and the American Dream: A Comment." In *Proceedings of the 5th Annual Conference of the American-Italian Historical Association.* Boston, Mass.: American-Italian Historical Association, 1972. 52–55.

"Education and the Italian and Jewish Community Experiences," *Proceedings of the*

7th Annual American-Italian Historical Association. Baltimore, Md.: American-Italian Historical Association, 1974. 57–63.

"John L. Lewis." In *Heritage of '76.* Ed. Jay P. Dolan. Notre Dame, Ind.: University of Notre Dame Press, 1976. 111–18.

"Tom Mann and William D. Haywood: Culture, Personality, and Comparative History." In *Toward a New View of America: Essays in Honor of Arthur C. Cole.* Ed. Hans L. Trefousse. New York: Burt Franklin, 1977. 189–208.

"The 'New' Labor History: Achievements and Failures." *Reviews in American History* 5 (June 1977): 249–54.

"The Homestead Strike of 1892." In *Conflict in America: A History of Domestic Confrontations.* Comp. Allen Weinstein. Washington, D.C.: USIA, 1978, 133–48.

"Adam's Curse; or, The Drudgery of Work." *Reviews in American History* 6 (December 1978): 429–34.

"Industrialization and Urbanization in Ohio's Gilded Age." *Toward an Urban Ohio.* Ed. John R. Wunder. Columbus: Ohio Historical Society, 1978. 23–38.

"Not So 'Turbulent Years': Another Look at the American 1930s." *Amerikastudien* 24 (1979): 5–20.

"Labor Organizations." *Encyclopedia of American Economic History.* Ed. Glenn Porter. 3 vols. New York: Charles Scribner's Sons, 1980. 2:524–51.

"John L. Lewis and the United Mine Workers of America," *USA Today,* January 1980, 55–57.

"The Legacy of the New Deal." *Executive* 6 (Spring 1980): 8–10.

"Neither Upstairs nor Downstairs: Domestic Service in Middle-Class American Homes." *Reviews in American History* 8 (March 1980): 86–91

"John L. Lewis and American Isolationism." In *Three Faces of Midwestern Isolationism.* Ed. John N. Schacht. Iowa City: Center for the Study of the Recent History of the United States, 1981. 23–33.

"Hold the Fort: The Dynamics of Twentieth-Century American Working-Class History." *Reviews in American History* 9 (June 1981): 244–51.

"Film as History: History as Drama." *Labor History* 22 (Winter 1981): 136–40.

"Legal Theory and Workers' Rights: A Historian's Critique." *Industrial Relations Law Journal* 4 (1981): 496–502.

"Worker Movements in North America, 1873–1970: A Preliminary Analysis." In *Labor in the World Social Structure.* Ed. Immanuel Wallerstein. Beverly Hills, Calif.: Sage Publications, 1983. 22–43.

"Abortive Reform: The Wilson Administration and Organized Labor, 1913–1920." In *Work, Community, and Power: The Experience of Labor in Europe and America, 1900–1925.* Ed. James E. Cronin and Carmen Sirianni. Philadelphia: Temple University Press, 1983. 197–220.

"The Political Wilderness." *American Jewish History* 73 (December 1983): 157–62.

"Socialism." In *Encyclopedia of American Political History.* Ed. Jack P. Greene. New York: Charles Scribner's Sons, 1985. 1187–1201.

"Give Us That Old-Time Labor History: Philip S. Foner and the American Worker." *Labor History* 26 (1985): 118–37.

"The New Deal and Labor." In *The Roosevelt New Deal: A Program Assessment Fifty Years After.* Ed. Wilber J. Cohen. Austin: University of Texas Press, 1984, 73–82.

"Economic Crises and American Workers: The Changing Situation of the Labor Movement." *GEMDEV Cahiers No. 7: "The Present Downturn of the World Economy Compared to Previous Downturns."* Paris: GEMDEV, March 1986. Pt. 2, 61–98.

"Industrial Relations: Comparing the 1980s with the 1920s." In *Proceedings of the 38th Annual Industrial Relations Research Association Meeting.* New York: Industrial Relations Research Association, 1986. 227–36.

"Technological Change and American Worker Movements, 1870–1970." In *Technology, the Economy, and Society.* Ed. Joel Colton and Stuart Bruchey. New York: Columbia University Press, 1987. 162–85.

"The Extension of Solidarity Conflicts with the Spirit of Individualism." *Monthly Labor Review* 110 (August 1987): 36–37.

"Labor's Odd Couple: Philip Murray and John L. Lewis." In *Forging a Union of Steel: Philip Murray, SWOC, and the United Steelworkers.* Ed. Paul F. Clark, Peter Gottlieb, and Donald Kennedy. Ithaca, N.Y.: ILR Press, Cornell University, 1987. 30–44.

"Introduction." In special issue of *Labor History* 29 (Fall 1988): 411–15.

"A New Look at the Original Case: To What Extent Was the U.S. Fordist?" In *Cahier du GEMDEV No. 12: "Le Processus de Salarisation dans L'Economie Mondiale."* Paris: GEMDEV, 1989. 9–42.

"American Trade Union Leaders: A Historical Perspective. *"Mitteilungsblatt des Instituts zur Erforschung der europäischen Arbeiterbewegung (IGA)* [Essen] 9 (1989): 61–71.

"The Historical Transformation of Violence in the American City." In *Villes et Violence dans le monde anglophone.* Ed. Sophie Body-Gendrot and Jacques Carré. Clermont-Ferrand: University Blaise Pascal, 1989. 25–32.

"The Rise and Fall of Revolutionary Syndicalism in the United States." In *Revolutionary Syndicalism.* Ed. Wayne Thomas. London: Scolar Press, 1990. 203–20.

"Lost in a Fog: Labor Historians' Unrequited Search for a Synthesis." *Labor History* 32 (Spring 1991): 295–300.

"Some of Our Mothers and Grandmothers: The Making of the 'New' Jewish Woman." *Reviews in American History* 19 (September 1991): 385–90.

"Gli operai dell'industria statunitense e i partiti politici da Roosevelt a Reagan." In *Il partito politico americano e l'Europa.* Ed. Maurizio Vaudagna. Milan: Giancomo Feltrinelli Editore, 1991. 211–35.

"The Origins of the Labor Movement in the United States: Themes from the Nineteenth Century." *Pennsylvania History* 58 (October 1991): 269–77.

Review of *Law and the Shaping of the American Labor Movement* by William Forbath. *Industrial and Labor Relations Review* 45 (July 1992): 810–13.

"On Treacherous Terrain: Labor, Politics, and the State in the United States." Working Paper No. 3. Seattle: Center for Labor Studies, University of Washington, November 1993.

"Old Deal, New Deal, Raw Deal: The Evolution of the Liberal State in the Modern United States." *Labour/Le Travail* 32 (Fall 1993): 269–77.

"Starting Out in the Fifties: True Confessions of a Labor Historian." *Labor History* 34 (Fall 1993): 473–78.

"Labor Unrest in the United States, 1906–1990." In *Labor Unrest in the World Economy, 1870–1990.* Ed. Melvyn Dubofsky, G. Arrighi, and B. Silver. Special issue of *Review* 18 (Winter 1995): 125–36.

"Raising Less Corn and More Hell: Two Disciples of Mary Ellen Lease." *Reviews in American History* 23 (June 1995): 236–71.

"Jimmy Carter and the End of the Politics of Productivity." In *The Carter Presidency: Policy Choices in the Post–New Deal Era.* Ed. Gary M. Fink and Hugh Davis Graham. Lawrence: University Press of Kansas, 1998. 95–116.

"Syndikalismen: 'Hjarnarbetarnas' internaticnal." *Arbetarhistoria* 87–88 (Fall 1998): 36–43.

"The Federal Judiciary, Free Labor, and Equal Rights." In *The Pullman Strike and the Crisis of the 1890s: Essays on Labor and Politics.* Ed. Richard Schneirov, Shelton Stromquist, and Nick Salvatore. Urbana: University of Illinois Press, 1999. 159–78.

INDEX

Melvyn Dubofsky, Distinguished Professor of History and Sociology at Binghamton University, SUNY, held the John Adams Chair in American History at the University of Amsterdam, The Netherlands, during the spring of 2000. He is the author of numerous books and essays on U.S. labor and twentieth-century history, including a history of the IWW, biographies of John L. Lewis (co-written with Warren Van Tine) and "Big Bill" Haywood, and *The State and Labor in Modern America*.

The Working Class in American History

German Workers in Chicago: A Documentary History of Working-Class Culture
from 1850 to World War I   *Edited by Hartmut Keil and John B. Jentz*

On the Line: Essays in the History of Auto Work   *Edited by Nelson Lichtenstein and Stephen Meyer III*

Upheaval in the Quiet Zone: A History of Hospital Workers' Union, Local 1199
Leon Fink and Brian Greenberg

Labor's Flaming Youth: Telephone Operators and Worker Militancy, 1878–1923
Stephen H. Norwood

Another Civil War: Labor, Capital, and the State in the Anthracite Regions of
Pennsylvania, 1840–68   *Grace Palladino*

Coal, Class, and Color: Blacks in Southern West Virginia, 1915–32
Joe William Trotter Jr.

For Democracy, Workers, and God: Labor Song-Poems and Labor Protest,
1865–95   *Clark D. Halker*

Dishing It Out: Waitresses and Their Unions in the Twentieth Century
Dorothy Sue Cobble

The Spirit of 1848: German Immigrants, Labor Conflict, and the Coming of the
Civil War   *Bruce Levine*

Working Women of Collar City: Gender, Class, and Community in Troy, New York,
1864–86   *Carole Turbin*

Southern Labor and Black Civil Rights: Organizing Memphis Workers
Michael K. Honey

Radicals of the Worst Sort: Laboring Women in Lawrence, Massachusetts,
1860–1912   *Ardis Cameron*

Producers, Proletarians, and Politicians: Workers and Party Politics in Evansville
and New Albany, Indiana, 1850–87   *Lawrence M. Lipin*

The New Left and Labor in the 1960s   *Peter B. Levy*

The Making of Western Labor Radicalism: Denver's Organized Workers,
1878–1905   *David Brundage*

In Search of the Working Class: Essays in American Labor History and
Political Culture   *Leon Fink*

Lawyers against Labor: From Individual Rights to Corporate Liberalism
Daniel R. Ernst

"We Are All Leaders": The Alternative Unionism of the Early 1930s   *Edited by Staughton Lynd*

The Female Economy: The Millinery and Dressmaking Trades, 1860–1930
Wendy Gamber

"Negro and White, Unite and Fight!": A Social History of Industrial Unionism in
Meatpacking, 1930–90   *Roger Horowitz*

Power at Odds: The 1922 National Railroad Shopmen's Strike   *Colin J. Davis*

The Common Ground of Womanhood: Class, Gender, and Working Girls' Clubs,
1884–1928   *Priscilla Murolo*

Marching Together: Women of the Brotherhood of Sleeping Car Porters
Melinda Chateauvert

Down on the Killing Floor: Black and White Workers in Chicago's Packinghouses,
1904–54   *Rick Halpern*

Labor and Urban Politics: Class Conflict and the Origins of Modern Liberalism in
    Chicago, 1864–97   *Richard Schneirov*
All That Glitters: Class, Conflict, and Community in Cripple Creek
    Elizabeth Jameson
Waterfront Workers: New Perspectives on Race and Class   *Edited by*
    Calvin Winslow
Labor Histories: Class, Politics, and the Working-Class Experience   *Edited by*
    Eric Arnesen, Julie Greene, and Bruce Laurie
The Pullman Strike and the Crisis of the 1890s: Essays on Labor and Politics
    Edited by Richard Schneirov, Shelton Stromquist, and Nick Salvatore
AlabamaNorth: African-American Migrants, Community, and Working-Class
    Activism in Cleveland, 1914–45   *Kimberley L. Phillips*
Imagining Internationalism in American and British Labor, 1939–49
    Victor Silverman
William Z. Foster and the Tragedy of American Radicalism   *James R. Barrett*
Colliers across the Sea: A Comparative Study of Class Formation in Scotland and
    the American Midwest, 1830–1924   *John H. M. Laslett*
"Rights, Not Roses": Unions and the Rise of Working-Class Feminism, 1945–80
    Dennis A. Deslippe
Testing the New Deal: The General Textile Strike of 1934 in the American South
    Janet Irons
Hard Work: The Making of Labor History   *Melvyn Dubofsky*

Typeset in 10/13 Esprit
with Helvetica Neue Extended display
Designed by Paula Newcomb
Composed by Jim Proefrock
at the University of Illinois Press
Manufactured by Maple-Vail
Book Manufacturing Group

University of Illinois Press
1325 South Oak Street
Champaign, IL 61820-6903
www.press.uillinois.edu